W9-AUV-620

SOVIET ECONOMIC AID

The New Aid and Trade Policy in Underdeveloped Countries

SOME PUBLICATIONS OF THE

COUNCIL ON FOREIGN RELATIONS

FOREIGN AFFAIRS (quarterly), edited by Hamilton Fish Armstrong.

THE UNITED STATES IN WORLD AFFAIRS (annual). Volumes for 1931, 1932, and 1933, by Walter Lippmann and William O. Scroggs; for 1934-1935, 1936, 1937, 1938, 1939 and 1940, by Whitney H. Shepardson and William O. Scroggs; for 1945-1947, 1947-1948 and 1948-1949, by John C. Campbell; for 1949, 1950, 1951, 1952, 1953 and 1954, by Richard P. Stebbins; for 1955, by Hollis W. Barber; for 1956 and 1957, by Richard P. Stebbins.

DOCUMENTS ON AMERICAN FOREIGN RELATIONS (annual). Volume for 1952, edited by Clarence W. Baier and Richard P. Stebbins; for 1953 and 1954, edited by Peter V. Curl; for 1955, 1956 and 1957, edited by Paul E. Zinner.

POLITICAL HANDBOOK OF THE WORLD (annual), edited by Walter H. Mallory.

RAW MATERIALS: A Study of American Policy, by Percy W. Bidwell.

FOREIGN POLICY: THE NEXT PHASE, by Thomas K. Finletter.

NATO AND THE FUTURE OF EUROPE, by Ben T. Moore.

AFRICAN ECONOMIC DEVELOPMENT, by William A. Hance.

DEFENSE OF THE MIDDLE EAST: Problems of American Policy, by John C. Campbell.

INDIA AND AMERICA: A Study of Their Relations, by Phillips Talbot and S. L. Poplai.

JAPAN BETWEEN EAST AND WEST, by Hugh Borton, Jerome B. Cohen, William J. Jorden, Donald Keene, Paul F. Langer and C. Martin Wilbur.

NUCLEAR WEAPONS AND FOREIGN POLICY, by Henry A. Kissinger.

MOSCOW-PEKING AXIS: Strengths and Strains, by Howard L. Boorman, Alexander Eckstein, Philip E. Mosely and Benjamin Schwartz.

CLIMATE AND ECONOMIC DEVELOPMENT IN THE TROPICS, by Douglas H. K. Lee.

WHAT THE TARIFF MEANS TO AMERICAN INDUSTRIES, by Percy W. Bidwell.

UNITED STATES SHIPPING POLICY, by Wytze Gorter.

RUSSIA AND AMERICA: Dangers and Prospects, by Henry L. Roberts.

STERLING: Its Meaning in World Finance, by Judd Polk.

KOREA: A Study of U.S. Policy in the United Nations, by Leland M. Goodrich.

FOREIGN AFFAIRS BIBLIOGRAPHY, 1942-1952, by Henry L. Roberts.

AMERICAN AGENCIES INTERESTED IN INTERNATIONAL AFFAIRS, compiled by Ruth Savord and Donald Wasson.

JAPANESE AND AMERICANS: A Century of Cultural Relations, by Robert S. Schwantes.

THE FUTURE OF UNDERDEVELOPED COUNTRIES: Political Implications of Economic Development, by Eugene Staley.

THE UNDECLARED WAR, 1940-1941, by William L. Langer and S. Everett Gleason.

THE CHALLENGE TO ISOLATION, 1937-1940, by William L. Langer and S. Everett Gleason.

MIDDLE EAST DILEMMAS: The Background of United States Policy, by J. C. Hurewitz.

BRITAIN AND THE UNITED STATES: Problems in Cooperation, a joint report prepared by Henry L. Roberts and Paul A. Wilson.

TRADE AND PAYMENTS IN WESTERN EUROPE: A Study in Economic Cooperation, 1947-1951, by William Diebold, Jr.

PUBLIC OPINION AND FOREIGN POLICY, by Lester Markel and Others.

SURVEY OF AMERICAN FOREIGN RELATIONS (in four volumes, 1928-1931), prepared under the direction of Charles P. Howland.

Soviet Economic Aid

The New Aid and Trade Policy in Underdeveloped Countries

JOSEPH S. BERLINER

Published for the
COUNCIL ON FOREIGN RELATIONS
by
FREDERICK A. PRAEGER, INC.
New York

SOVIET ECONOMIC AID: THE NEW AID AND TRADE POLICY
IN UNDERDEVELOPED COUNTRIES

Printed in the United States of America

For information, address Council on Foreign Relations, 58 East 68th Street, New York 21

THIRD PRINTING

The Colonial Press Inc., Clinton, Mass.

Library of Congress catalog card number: LC 58-11206

Published in Great Britain and the British
Commonwealth, excluding Canada, by
London: Oxford University Press

PREFACE

It is said that a dog pursuing a moving object heads constantly toward the position occupied by the object an instant before. The pursuit of the study of Soviet foreign policy engenders a sympathetic kinship with the dog. On the night that this preface is being written the newspapers have announced that Soviet economic aid to Yugoslavia has been postponed for five years. A telephone call would bring the manuscript back from the publisher once more, and with a bit of effort we could once more head toward the position of our object on tomorrow's instant. But this canine approach to the pursuit of understanding could scarcely produce a book, particularly a topical book. I deem it wiser to call a halt to the chase, and to trust the reader's understanding that the things I have written about are moving rapidly and cannot be pinned down for leisurely examination.

Not only is the Soviet program of economic aid very much in flux, but its history covers the short span of only three or four years. This is indeed a brief period in which to search for trends and to distinguish the essential from the accidental. The justification for a book on this subject must rest therefore not on the tractability of the material but rather on its vital importance. The inauguration by the U.S.S.R. of a program of economic aid to the underdeveloped countries has given rise to a pervading uneasiness among all who are concerned with the future of those countries and with the position of the United States in world affairs. If we as a nation are to react with calm and wisdom, we must understand the nature of the Soviet policy. If the time is too short and events moving too rapidly to permit a definitive evaluation, it is nevertheless important to collect as much information as we can and to render as balanced a judgment as possible. (The State Department's report, *The Sino-Soviet Economic Offensive in the Less Developed Countries*, appeared too late to be used in this study, except for minor corrections at a few places.)

In writing this book I had the great pleasure and invaluable experience of working with a study group organized by the Council on Foreign Relations. I wish to thank the Council and its Director of Studies, Philip E. Mosely, for their support of this work. The members of the study group represented a wide range of expertise on the immediate subject of the study and on closely related areas. I am deeply in their debt for the generous contribution of their knowledge and opinions, and their candid criticism of my own views. Working with a study group of this kind is particularly valuable when the subject is such that the data are rather shadowy and the ramifications spread into many more areas than can be investigated within the compass of a small and timely book. I wish to express my gratitude to the members of the study group and particularly to the Chairman, Stacy May. The members of the group were:

Stacy May, Chairman

Robert Loring Allen
Frank Altschul
Robert Amory, Jr.
Henry C. Aubrey
Frederick C. Barghoorn
William H. Baumer
Abram Bergson
Herbert Block
William Diebold, Jr.
Alexander Eckstein
Solomon Fabricant
John N. Hazard
Hans Heymann, Jr.
Charles J. Hitch
Holland Hunter
Oliver J. Lissitzyn
Wayne S. Miller
Philip E. Mosely
Vernon Munroe, Jr.
G. Warren Nutter
Henry L. Roberts
Geroid T. Robinson
Harry Schwartz
John Scott
Willard L. Thorp
R. Gordon Wasson

Robert H. McNeal prepared digests of the group's discussions.

Beyond their contributions to the discussions of the study group, a number of the members were kind enough to read and criticize drafts of the manuscript. I wish to thank Henry Aubrey, Hans Heymann, Jr., Stacy May and Willard Thorp for the thoroughness with which they took my drafts apart and assisted in putting them back together in greatly improved form. Finally, from beginning to end I benefited from the excellent substantive and editorial judgment of William Diebold, Jr., the Council's Director of Economic Studies. Working with him was the finest of my experiences in the course of this association. I am grateful to Helena Stalson of the Council staff for her help in putting the manuscript in final form.

While many of the ideas put forth in the book were suggested by the people named above, nothing I have said should be construed as indicating their endorsement of my views. Sole responsibility for this study rests with me.

JOSEPH S. BERLINER

Syracuse University
May 28, 1958

CONTENTS

TABLES

CHARTS

SOVIET ECONOMIC AID

The New Aid and Trade Policy in Underdeveloped Countries

I

THE PROBLEM

IN THE heart of the Madhya Pradesh region of Central India a great steel mill is rising from the earth. Indian engineers are sharing offices with Soviet engineers who have come to assist in the construction. The machinery and equipment will be brought from the Soviet Union, financed by a generous Soviet credit to the Indian government. When construction is completed, the Soviet engineers will go home and the plant will belong to the Indian nation, to be run by Indians for the benefit of the Indian national economy.

Farther north, in Afghanistan, a new asphalt road stretches through the main street of the capital city of Kabul. The road, financed by Soviet credits, was built by Afghan laborers with Soviet machinery, under the supervision of Soviet civil engineers. To the west, in Cairo, an experimental nuclear reactor is under construction. The equipment and technical personnel are Soviet, and the Egyptian scientists who will staff the laboratory are studying nuclear physics in Moscow. To the south in Ceylon, Czech engineers are building and equipping sugar and cement plants, and to the east in Cambodia, equipment from Communist China will be delivered free to be installed in new textile mills, cement plants and plywood factories.

It requires no great stretch of memory to recall days when things were different. Only five years ago one could rarely find a citizen of a Communist country outside the Soviet Bloc unless he was attached to a diplomatic mission. It was unthinkable that students and workers of non-Communist countries would be invited in any appreciable number to study and train in Soviet universities and factories. In the space of a few years the Communist world has changed from a deliberately self-insulated community to one in which there is an active passage of goods and people both ways across its borders.

Increased Soviet activity in the underdeveloped countries is but one of many changes in Soviet policy in recent years. Within the U.S.S.R. itself the terror that prevailed in Stalin's day is much less in evidence. Within the community of Communist nations some of the reins that bound the national governments to the will of Moscow have been slackened. While the Soviet press still sometimes reaches peaks of anti-American hostility that rival the worst of Stalin's day, the pattern has often been interrupted by periods of relative calm. And while such events as the brutal suppression of the Hungarian uprising remind us that the Soviet leadership has in no sense abjured the use of force, the new regime has succeeded in reducing the extreme level of international tension that prevailed in Stalin's last years. Conciliatory advances have been made at various times in such matters as disarmament, flow of information and freedom of travel. Increased economic activity in the underdeveloped countries is part of a general increase in Soviet Bloc participation in international economic affairs.

The changes in Soviet policy since the death of Stalin have for the most part been welcomed in the West. But Soviet economic activity in the underdeveloped countries has evoked mixed feelings. The West, for a variety of reasons, is committed to the encouragement of economic development and rising living standards in these lands, and the Soviet contribution toward the attainment of this goal should therefore be greeted with warmth. On the other hand, in no portion of the world is the sense of competition between the West and the U.S.S.R. so keen as in these countries. In the nations of Asia, Africa, the Middle East and Latin America, many of which have only recently won their independence, an earnest search for the best path to rapid economic development is the constant preoccupation of thoughtful men. National leaders have set as their objective the elevation of their peoples from the poverty and economic backwardness that have characterized them for centuries. Few doubt that in time their political, economic, and military weight in the world will amount to sizable proportions. The West has hoped that by its friendly assistance in the process of economic development, the weight of those nations would be added to the forces of economic and political freedom. Now the appearance of the U.S.S.R. on the scene seems to threaten to pull them in the opposite direction, toward economic regimentation, political dictatorship and eventual Soviet dominance over their policies.

In addition to a political interest in the future of the underdeveloped countries, the West has an economic stake. Many industrial raw materials that are vital to the welfare of the West, such as tin, rubber, oil, and now uranium ore, are imported from those countries. They are also the source of important foodstuffs such as coffee, tea, tropical fruits, cocoa. With the foreign exchange earned from the sale of these products, the underdeveloped countries purchase manufactured commodities from Western countries and thus stimulate employment in the export industries of the latter. The growing importance of the Soviet Bloc in the foreign trade of the underdeveloped countries has given rise to uneasy feelings about the future of commercial intercourse between the advanced and the underdeveloped nations of the free world.

Soviet economic activity in the underdeveloped countries has added a major new factor to be taken account of in the formulation of a foreign economic policy for the United States. If that policy is to be effective, it will have to rest on answers to a number of important questions about the Soviet aid program. This book suggests answers to some of those questions.

The new Soviet economic policy toward the underdeveloped countries represents an abrupt shift from the policy of the past. Before we can begin to gauge its significance, we must strive to understand the reasons for the change. Chapter II explores the political background out of which the new policy evolved, and considers the question of what the U.S.S.R. may hope to gain from its new intercourse with the underdeveloped countries. This is treacherous ground on which to tread. Obviously we cannot be sure what is in the minds of the Soviet leaders, but to interpret the aid program we must try to form the best possible judgment of its real objectives. At the least we must guard against the tendency to consider every foreign policy objective of the U.S.S.R. as *ipso facto* an objective of the aid program too, and to ascribe every Soviet diplomatic victory in the underdeveloped countries to the success of the aid program. There are some objectives of Soviet policy that the aid program does *not* appear to be designed to achieve, and some Soviet diplomatic successes in underdeveloped countries could well have occurred even if there were no economic aid program.

What is the nature of this program of economic aid which has come to play so prominent a part in Soviet foreign policy? What do Soviet officials mean by "economic aid" and how large is their program of aid to the underdeveloped countries? How does its size compare with Western aid, and with Soviet aid to the other Communist countries? What are the relative contributions of the U.S.S.R. and the other Soviet Bloc countries to the over-all Soviet Bloc aid program? Which countries are the chief recipients of Soviet aid? And how does the volume of aid committed in agreements compare with the volume of aid thus far actually delivered? Chapters III and IV provide some answers to these questions.

The term "economic aid" commonly includes both grants for which no repayment is expected and long-term credits. The Soviet program, however, consists almost exclusively of credits. Properly speaking, we should perhaps refer to it as the "Soviet credit program," in order to distinguish its character from that of the United States aid program with its large proportion of grants. But at this point in history, with public attention fixed on the issue of "Soviet economic aid to underdeveloped countries," such terminological rigidity would be more like pedantry than purity. As used in this study, therefore, the term "Soviet aid" refers primarily to the long-term credits. Soviet publicists, however, extend the term "aid" even further, to include their normal commercial exports of machinery and industrial products to the underdeveloped countries in exchange for raw materials. Only confusion could come from adopting this usage and classifying trade under the rubric of aid. Nevertheless, in a consideration of the economic and political impact of the U.S.S.R. on the underdeveloped countries, account must be taken of the expansion of trade. Chapter V raises with respect to commercial trade the same questions discussed in the preceding chapters with respect to aid.

It should be stated at the outset that only by a most charitable interpretation can our information be said to be based on "facts" and "statistics." The U.S.S.R. does not publish a detailed summary of its economic aid activities; there is no equivalent to the United States Department of Commerce publication, *Foreign Grants and Credits by the United States Government*, or to the annual reports of the International Bank for Reconstruction and Development. For lack of such systematic data, analysis must be based on bits of information gathered from a wide variety of sources in countries throughout the world. A good deal of judgment must be used in evaluating conflicting information, and in many cases we must be content with "orders of magnitude," an unsatisfactory basis of analysis but the only one available.

After the discussion of the magnitude of the Soviet aid and trade programs, the argument proceeds in Chapter VI to an evaluation of the ability of the Soviet economy to support a program of economic aid. It is sometimes argued that in view of the historical development of the Soviet economy, the program of aid and trade, far from being a drain on economic resources, may actually be a source of economic gain. This important proposition is appraised in Chapter VII.

The eagerness with which a number of non-Communist

countries have accepted Soviet offers of aid and trade is the source of some puzzlement in the West. Is it some incredible naïveté or some propensity for committing national suicide that has moved those nations to invite the subversive minions of Moscow to their lands? Those who think in these terms fail to understand that the U.S.S.R. possesses a number of potent advantages which help explain the substantial degree of success that the new economic policy has enjoyed thus far.

If the visage of the U.S.S.R. bears the blemish of revolution and subversion to many, certain of its other features have a considerable appeal to the peoples of the underdeveloped countries. The Soviet Union comes as an anticapitalist nation to parts of the world where the merchant has long been an object of contempt; it comes as a part-Asian nation to the colored peoples, and as the historic antagonist of Western imperialism to the nations which were most lately the objects of that imperialism. To peoples whose great aspiration is economic development, it comes as a highly pertinent model of how such development can be achieved. The very novelty of the fact that the Soviet Union is providing aid helps give its program a warm reception. The terms under which the Russians offer their aid are well designed to encourage acceptance. And finally, the totalitarian character of the Soviet state provides the government with certain advantages in conducting an aid program, although there are certain disadvantages as well of which we must take account. These and related questions are discussed in Chapter VIII.

If Soviet aid is given with something other than purely philanthropic purposes in mind, the final question is what the Soviet leaders may be expected to earn for their pains. A suitor cannot reckon the success of his wooing by the number of gifts his beloved has consented to accept; however honorable his intentions, he has an ulterior purpose in mind. Is economic aid an effective lever for achieving the objectives underlying the Soviet aid program? Chapter IX is devoted to a discussion of this concluding question.

The Soviet economic aid program is intimately related

to numerous other aspects of Soviet policies. The present study has deliberately avoided pursuing those other aspects beyond their immediate relevance to economic aid. Military aid, for example, is a subject for special study; it has been treated here only to the extent that it bears directly upon the economic aid program. The U.S.S.R. is the focus of interest; the role of the other Communist countries is depicted statistically but its implications are not pursued.[1] And Soviet foreign policy in general is treated only as a background within which to delineate the place of the economic aid program. It is our hope that what the study loses by narrowing the field of view, it gains by sharpening the focus.

[1] The term "Soviet aid program" will be used in statements applying to the U.S.S.R. alone, as well as to statements applying to the whole Soviet Bloc. Where the argument demands a distinction between the U.S.S.R. and the other Bloc countries, the distinction will be made explicit.

II

THE POLITICS OF ECONOMIC AID

"THE FOREIGN trade policy of the U.S.S.R.," says the *Great Soviet Encyclopedia*, "is part of the over-all foreign policy of the U.S.S.R." And, indeed, the evolution of the Soviet economic aid and trade program coincides in many ways with the evolution of Soviet foreign policy toward the underdeveloped countries. Before World War II, the outside world presented itself to the Soviet leaders in a fairly simple way. The U.S.S.R. was a solitary Communist bastion surrounded by a more or less uniformly hostile capitalist world. The task of Soviet foreign policy was to play upon the "contradictions" that Bolshevik theory found in the capitalist world. At least three contradictions existed. First, there was the traditional class conflict within each capitalist country. Second, there was the potential conflict among the capitalist countries for world markets. And third, there was the growing conflict between the colonial powers and their colonies. At various times and places, Soviet foreign policy sought to achieve its ends by influencing the course of events in all three types of conflict when they appeared to be reaching explosive levels.

The world that emerged from World War II was considerably more complicated. For one thing, the U.S.S.R. was no longer the solitary home of communism, but was now the center of a number of Communist countries in Eastern Europe, and later in Asia. Several years passed before the policy toward those countries fully evolved, and the new policy required the use of methods that were different from the traditional prewar methods of foreign policy. For one thing, the economic requirements of the Soviet Bloc countries demanded a considerable expansion of the foreign economic relations of the U.S.S.R. The old drive for autarky thus underwent modification to the extent of accepting the need for a sizable volume of trade with foreign countries—Communist allies, to be sure, but nonetheless foreign. Official pronouncements on the advantages of economic isolation came to encompass the Communist Bloc as a unit.[1] The Soviet leaders became used to a moderate degree of interdependence between the U.S.S.R. and other countries. This involved a weakening of the traditional idea of national autarky without leading to anything like willing dependence on imports for supplies of major importance.

Moreover, the Soviet Union quickly learned to respect the economic advantages that can be derived from economic intercourse with other countries. The huge war booty from Poland, Czechoslovakia, Rumania and Hungary, the dismantling of industrial plants in East Germany and Manchuria, and the eventual reparations payments from the former enemy countries provided a much needed boost for the war-torn Soviet economy of the late forties. But apart from this, the growth of regular trade with the European Bloc countries enabled the Soviet Union to enjoy economic advantages that would have been sorely missed in the absence of that trade. The gains from foreign trade were magnified in this case by the fact that the U.S.S.R. was able to call the tune as far as the terms and prices were concerned. But even discounting this factor, Soviet economic planners must have been impressed with the ease with which deficiencies could be met by importing Polish coal, Rumanian oil, Hungarian bauxite, Chinese oil-seeds, and German and Czech machinery.

Perhaps most important for the present discussion is the fact that in their transactions with the Bloc countries the

[1] The best known of these pronouncements are Stalin's remarks in his pamphlet, *Economic Problems of Socialism in the U.S.S.R.* (New York: International, 1952), published a year before his death. Stalin looked forward to the day when the Communist camp of nations would be in "no need of imports from capitalist countries." See pp. 26-27.

Russians found themselves for the first time in the business of exporting capital goods and technical assistance.[2] Only two decades earlier the U.S.S.R. itself had been a large-scale importer of capital goods and technical assistance. A considerable number of Soviet industrial enterprises owe their existence to the equipment and technical services extended by such United States corporations as Ford, Du Pont, General Electric, RCA, and a host of others.[3] World War II found the U.S.S.R. once more a heavy recipient of economic as well as military aid under Lend-Lease, followed by postwar credits that extended Lend-Lease deliveries, and by the UNRRA program, under which the U.S.S.R. was a recipient of aid contributed by the United States and other Western countries.

As a recent beneficiary of economic aid, the U.S.S.R. may have a fuller appreciation than Western governments of its importance to the leaders of underdeveloped countries. Dealings with the Bloc countries, in which the U.S.S.R. exported capital goods and technical assistance to Bulgaria, Rumania and China, may have accustomed the Soviet planners to a type of economic activity that had been unthinkable a decade earlier. For many years, the theme of Soviet economic planning was that machines are scarce things, to be carefully husbanded and produced even at great sacrifice. It requires a considerable adjustment in a traditional way of thinking to look upon machines as something that can be exchanged for other things or to realize that machines are now abundant enough to be worth exporting for the sake of imports of other kinds of "goods," whether economic or political. Economic relations with the Bloc countries paved the way psychologically for the new program of aid to the non-Communist underdeveloped countries.

The Communist Bloc was an important new element in the political world of the postwar years. A second major factor was the rapid progress to independence of most of

[2] In the early thirties, the Soviet Union once helped Turkey construct a textile factory, but this was an isolated event and did not develop into a large-scale program.

[3] Robert Paul Browder, *The Origins of Soviet-American Diplomacy* (Princeton: Princeton University Press, 1953), pp. 29-31.

the former colonial lands of Asia and the Middle East. The independence movement required a revision of traditional Soviet foreign policy toward those countries. In the past, the basis of Soviet policy in those areas was anticolonialism. Under this banner the U.S.S.R. was able to support both the Communist and the "bourgeois nationalist" movements. But with the colonial powers gone from the scene, the immediate common goal of the two movements vanished and the antagonism of their ultimate goals could no longer be submerged. The former allies in a common cause were now competitors striving for opposite goals. The end of the old colonialism thus confronted the architects of Soviet foreign policy with a choice. They could choose the direct path toward their ultimate objective, the communization of the former colonial countries, by throwing their entire support to the domestic Communist parties. Or they could, if Soviet foreign policy required it, support the new nationalist governments in the kind of tactical shift that Soviet diplomacy has often adopted in the past.

If we forgo the advantage of hindsight, it is not difficult to see which policy promised the richer harvest in the immediate postwar years. The Communists saw themselves engaged in a struggle for world domination with the weakened forces of capitalism and imperialism, as the Cominform declaration of October 1947 made clear. The strength of the newly independent governments was still untested, and there was no way of knowing how firmly they held the unfamiliar reins of government. The Communist parties in some of these countries were strong, and some were armed and experienced in warfare against the Japanese. The Western democracies had rapidly disarmed after the war, and there was reason to doubt that they could or would react with vigor to Communist expansion in distant areas of the world. As the world appeared to Moscow in the early postwar years, no more favorable circumstances could be imagined for a direct move forward to the ultimate goal of Communist domination of Asia.

From the founding of the Cominform to some time in 1951, Soviet policy gave vigorous support to the domestic

Communist parties of the new countries in their open bid to wrest power from the nationalist governments. These parties adopted policies of extreme militancy and violence and civil war. The Soviet press reflected Moscow's policy in its treatment of the nationalist leaders. When the Soviet foreign policy objective had been the dislodging of the colonial powers, the nationalists were glorified as progressive leaders of oppressed peoples. Now that the objective was Communist control, the nationalist leaders were depicted as traitors to their people and lackeys of Western imperialism.[4]

The policy of force reached its climax at different times in different countries. Between 1950 and 1953, signs of hesitancy in Soviet policy could be discerned, some of it connected with world-wide reactions to the Korean war. The Communist parties in India and Indonesia discontinued their tactics of extreme violence, although the Soviet line toward the nationalist governments continued to be one of hostility. Though Stalin's speech of October 1952 established the doctrine of separate and possibly peaceful "paths to socialism," it was not until the dictator's death, in 1953, that the policy of violence was decisively and dramatically returned to the status of inactive reserve. In its place emerged the new policy we know under such labels as the "new look" and "peaceful coexistence."

In the light of this chronology, how can we explain the sharp shift in policy? It would seem that the tactic of force had run the full course of its fruitfulness. Turkey and Iran had soon shown themselves capable of resisting Soviet direct demands on their sovereignty and territories.[5] In Korea, Indochina and Malaya, the Western powers were both able and willing to match force with force. In India, Burma and Indonesia, the nationalist governments proved stable enough to maintain their power against attempts at

[4] See G. F. Hudson, "Soviet Policy in Asia," *Soviet Survey*, no. 16/17 (June-July 1957), pp. 1-2.

[5] Robert Loring Allen, *Middle Eastern Economic Relations with the Soviet Union, Eastern Europe, and Mainland China* (Charlottesville: University of Virginia Press, 1958), p. 10.

subversion. This is not to say that the policy of force had borne no fruit. The biggest plum of all, China, had been plucked for communism. Nor was there any way of knowing whether the West would react with armed might until something like Korea was tried. The agreement in Indochina in 1954 reflected the juncture of the two policies: the Communists had gained the North but were willing to reach a settlement instead of continuing to fight for the whole country. The policy of force made sense when the will of the West to fight was in doubt and the stability of the new nationalist governments was untested. When the doubts were removed, the old policy had little left to recommend it.

The policy of force was presented in Soviet propaganda as a continuation of communism's traditional struggle against colonialism. This neat trick was accomplished by depicting the nationalist leaders as tools of the imperialist powers. Stalin's successors seem to have come to the realization that the slogan of anticolonialism had lost its old meaning when the new nations became independent. The politics of the 1950's could not be conducted successfully with the methods of the 1930's. In the past, anticolonialism meant the support of indigenous popular movements against the European governments of the colonial lands. Nobody likes to lose a good issue, and perhaps inertia carried the Russians along in trying to fight the old fight that nobody cared about very much any more. New conflicts arising among the recently established governments were generating antagonisms far stronger than the memories of the old colonialism: the Indian-Pakistani conflict, for example, and the Arab-Israeli issue. Such conflicts often lead to a demand for arms, a situation brimming with exploitable possibilities. But emphasis on the anachronistic policy of treating the nationalist leaders as imperialist tools would have prevented the U.S.S.R. from reaping the rich diplomatic harvests sprouting from these seeds of conflict. Meanwhile, the men around Stalin, while faithfully carrying out his policies, were watching the progress of Western diplomacy in seeking the political, and sometimes military, cooperation of the former colonial lands and strengthening alliances with the new technique of economic aid.

It is therefore not surprising that, with Stalin out of the way, the new leaders were quick to tear off the fetters that had kept Soviet policy from making headway in the new countries. Nehru was no longer an imperialist lackey, but a glorious leader of a free people; and the U.S.S.R. was now free to support Indian claims against Pakistan in Kashmir and against Portuguese authority in Goa.[6] Nasser, who had been castigated as a fascist usurper when he first rose to power, became the champion of a downtrodden people; and the ground was laid for supporting Egypt in its conflict with Israel and with Britain and France.[7] The U.S.S.R. could welcome the Bandung conference as the friend of the nationalist governments represented there, and as the supporter of their aspirations against the alleged aims of the imperialist West.

THE ROLE OF ECONOMIC AID

With the barriers to political rapprochement with the new nations swept away, Soviet policy was freed from the shackles that had prevented the establishment of cordial political relations in the past. To be most effective, a new policy had to be attuned to the dominant aspirations of the underdeveloped countries. What they want above all are the maintenance of their newly won independence, a rapid rate of economic development, and a world of peace within which their new nations can grow and prosper. No single policy could be better calculated to appeal to all three aspirations than the policy of economic aid. And, indeed, the form of the Soviet economic aid program is intelligently fashioned to appeal to the underdeveloped countries on all three counts. By its nature, a program of economic aid appeals to aspirations for economic development. To underscore Soviet respect for the sovereignty of the recipient

[6] Hudson, cited, p. 1.

[7] Walter Laqueur, "Soviet Prospects in the Middle East," *Problems of Communism*, v. 6 (July-August 1957), p. 20.

countries, Soviet aid is offered with insistent protestations that there are "no strings attached." The Soviet leaders ostentatiously refrain from substituting their own judgment for that of the recipients as to what projects are best suited to the needs of the developing countries. Couched in the context of a broad policy of "peaceful coexistence," the economic aid program is designed to obliterate the image of the U.S.S.R. as the remote, military power spreading the power of communism by war and revolution, and to substitute the image of a benevolent, industrial people who desire only to live and trade in peace.

The new policy was launched at a time when the Soviet economy was best prepared to undertake it. Not until about 1948 did Soviet industry recover from the devastation of the war and regain prewar levels of production. Soon afterward the support of the Communist forces in the Korean war placed an additional burden on the economy. However attractive a policy of foreign economic aid might have looked to Soviet political strategists before 1953, it would certainly have pressed hard on an economy ill-prepared for additional burdens. But by 1953 an increased economic capability made it possible to seek the political gains of a foreign aid program.

Advocacy of economic aid and trade was not an entirely new adjunct to Soviet foreign policy. In the early United Nations deliberations on aid to underdeveloped countries, the U.S.S.R. had heartily supported the principle of a UN program of technical assistance. Indeed, the Soviet delegates insisted that "any technical assistance should be given with the participation of the United Nations as the body best fitted to safeguard objectivity." [8] But when the first United Nations technical assistance program came into being in 1948, the Russians refused to participate, arguing that the program was really a tool of Western imperialists designed to undermine the sovereignty of the underdeveloped countries. The warm reception the rest of the world gave to

[8] Alvin Z. Rubinstein, "Soviet Policy toward Underdeveloped Areas in the Economic and Social Council," *International Organization*, v. 9, no. 2 (May 1955), p. 236.

President Truman's announcement of a "bold new program" in 1949 must have convinced the Russians that they could no longer afford to pursue the purely negative policy of the past. Thereafter, denunciations of the Point Four program were accompanied by counteroffers of large-scale Soviet aid to those countries that resisted the overtures of the American imperialists. At the meetings of the Economic and Social Council and the Economic Commission for Asia and the Far East, Soviet delegates spoke of the willingness of the U.S.S.R. to aid in economic development by providing technical assistance and industrial machinery and equipment to all underdeveloped countries on terms of sovereign equality instead of imperialist domination. But Soviet words were not matched by deeds, the generous offers rarely materialized and, as the American delegate frequently reminded the United Nations, the U.S.S.R. did not contribute "one red ruble" to the United Nations technical assistance program.

What changed in 1953 was not Soviet espousal of the principle of economic aid, but the willingness to do something about it. In a speech at the United Nations in July 1953, criticizing Western aid and private investment in underdeveloped countries, the Soviet delegate announced that the U.S.S.R. would contribute four million rubles to the technical assistance program. There followed an earnest drive by Soviet trade delegations in the underdeveloped countries to enter into agreements for an expansion of trade. Economic development loans were offered and negotiated in ways that made it increasingly clear that the U.S.S.R. was no longer merely talking about aid as in the past, but was now prepared to do business. The importance of the new program in Soviet policy was such that it could no longer be entrusted to underlings. No less a person than the former Minister of Foreign Trade, M. A. Menshikov, was appointed to the crucial position of Ambassador to India. Even the heads of state and party, Bulganin and Khrushchev, played the part of traveling salesmen for the new aid and trade program during their good-will tour of Asian capitals in 1955. In Moscow the administration of the aid program was at one time entrusted to two former heads of the U.S.S.R. State Planning Commission, M. G. Pervukhin and M. Z. Saburov.

ECONOMIC AID AND SOVIET OBJECTIVES

The economic aid program appears, then, to be a prominent component of a broader tactical shift in foreign policy designed to extend Soviet influence in the underdeveloped countries. There are at least two significant aspects to the recent growth of Soviet influence and power. One is the increasing ability to deflect the policies of the underdeveloped countries in directions favorable to Soviet objectives. The second is the weakening of the influence of the West, and of the United States in particular. Just how the U.S.S.R. will make use of these new circumstances will vary according to the country and the local conditions. Perhaps the Soviet leaders are not much clearer in their own minds about the precise results to be hoped for from the aid program than the Western governments are. But this much is clear: before 1953 the policy of economic isolation had deprived the Russians of direct participation in the shaping of the economic development of the underdeveloped countries. Now at least they have dealt themselves into the game and are there to play a hand according to the way the cards fall.

The Soviet leaders may have felt that they had little choice but to get into the aid business, if they wanted to exercise continuing influence on the course of events in the underdeveloped countries. Their policy may involve a good measure of playing by ear, moving where there seem opportunities to move, watching and participating quietly in other places. Moreover, the aid program is still relatively new, and its history is too short to afford a rich store of experiences in which we might find patterns. Obviously the situation will differ from country to country. Many countries have as yet received very small quantities of aid, and among those that have received the largest amounts, such as Egypt and Syria, the situation is complicated by special military and political problems. In one country,

Soviet influence may affect the relative strength of domestic political forces, while in another only the foreign policy of the recipient may be involved. In short, there is a wide range of possibilities and experience is too brief to tell us very much as yet.

Although we cannot be precise about just how Soviet influence will manifest itself in specific circumstances, it is not difficult to point to a variety of broad objectives which the aid program could help the Soviet Union to achieve. A major Soviet objective in Asia and the Middle East is to destroy the system of military and political alliances forged by the West, such as the Baghdad Pact and the Southeast Asia Treaty Organization (SEATO). Within the member countries of these organizations are powerful groups opposing their governments' policies of alliance with the West, and supporting either neutralist or pro-Soviet policies. In the past such groups had to run the risk that, although the United States gave economic aid to uncommitted countries, rupture of an alliance might well lead to the loss of at least some aid. Now they can argue that the U.S.S.R. would fill the gap. At the same time, the U.S.S.R. can increase indirect pressure on some governments through the influence of the countries, outside the alliances, that have accepted aid. In these ways, the Soviet Union may hope to detach some of the pro-Western countries from their pacts with the West.

Similarly, the Soviet aid program increases the attractiveness of neutralism for the uncommitted countries. The availability of Soviet aid increases the independence of the neutral countries and strengthens their bargaining power with the West.

The aid program puts the U.S.S.R. in a better position to exacerbate tensions that may arise between the Western democracies and the countries of Asia and the Middle East. The most important example is the Suez crisis. What promises, if any, the U.S.S.R. made to Egypt with respect to the High Aswan Dam are not clear. But the very existence of the Soviet aid program made it seem plausible that the U.S.S.R. should offer to finance part of the project. Though Soviet military aid and political support were probably more significant, the possibility of getting Soviet economic aid undoubtedly encouraged Egypt to take as strong a stand as it did. When similar instances arise in the future, the U.S.S.R. will be in a better position to score diplomatic gains than it would if it had no aid program.

In various ways, the Soviet economic aid program may raise new problems for the Western governments in carrying out their aid programs. For example, United States aid agencies and the International Bank for Reconstruction and Development insist on a detailed analysis of the economic usefulness of projects they are asked to finance. The Soviet Union, on the other hand, represents itself as willing to finance any project that the recipient considers desirable, and will suggest or evaluate projects only if specifically asked to do so. When the government of Pakistan was bitterly split on the question of whether the nation could afford a new steel mill, United States foreign aid officials supported those who argued against undertaking the project at that time. The Russians stepped into the controversy with a grand offer to build and finance a steel mill for the Pakistani people.[9] Whatever judgment the Soviet officials may have had of the economic merits of the case, their action created new problems for the United States and affected the balance of forces inside Pakistan. The contrast between Soviet and Western approaches to aid may increase the resentment in the recipient countries of what appears to them to be unwarranted and high-handed interference by Western agencies. The latter may come under greater pressure to extend aid in the form of "impact" projects that attract public attention while contributing little to the economic development of the countries. Relaxation of standards may result in the financing of costly, unworthy projects that may in the long run kindle resentment rather than appreciation. This problem, of course, confronts Soviet as well as Western aid.

[9] *The New York Times*, January 31, 1958.

The Soviet Union can also use trade to take quick advantage of Western errors or difficulties.[10] A well-known instance is the Burmese rice crisis. In 1954, Burma, finding itself faced with mounting difficulties in selling its rice surplus, felt that American rice exports were the cause of some of its problems but could get no satisfaction from the United States government. When the U.S.S.R. and other Bloc countries stepped in with offers to buy a large portion of Burma's rice, they were looked upon as welcome friends in a time of crisis.[11] In another case, when a conflict between Iceland and Great Britain broke out over fishing rights, the Russians helped Iceland by purchasing its mounting surplus of fish. No doubt the Soviet Union could score such political victories by intelligent action regardless of the character of its foreign economic policy, but increased activity in trade and aid probably makes it easier to seize these opportunities by keeping the administrative machinery well oiled.

Mounting political tensions have increased the demand for arms by a number of underdeveloped countries. The economic aid program may well have increased the disposition of recipient countries to accept Soviet military aid. Military aid strengthens the influence of the donor upon the recipient, through the medium of training personnel and military advisers, and through a continuing need for spare parts and munitions. It may also improve the strategic position of the U.S.S.R. in the event of war. Egypt, Syria and Afghanistan are the best-known cases of countries that have received military aid from the U.S.S.R., but Soviet efforts have gone further afield. Following a $50-million trade agreement with Argentina, for example, the U.S.S.R. offered to sell a number of Soviet fighter and bomber planes

[10] Council for Economic and Industry Research, Inc., *Foreign Assistance Activities of the Communist Bloc and Their Implications for the United States*, in *Foreign Aid Program*, Senate Doc. no. 52, 85th Cong., 1st sess. (Washington: GPO, 1957), pp. 649-650.

[11] A somewhat similar situation arose in 1952. The United States would not pay more than the world price (which was falling) for Ceylon's rubber, so the Ceylonese bartered about half their rubber for five years at favorable prices to Communist China which delivered rice in return.

at prices believed to be lower than production costs.[12] The objective apparently was to switch the Argentine air force away from the British Hawker Hunter. An effort was also made to sell Soviet warplanes to India, but the offer was not accepted.[13] There are other links between military and economic aid. Payment for military supplies may substantially expand a country's economic ties with the U.S.S.R. and lead it to seek credit in other fields as well. If the military equipment is obsolete by Soviet standards, this may be a cheaper venture for the U.S.S.R. than provision of civilian industrial products.

SOVIET AID AND COMMUNIST REVOLUTION

The reasons for the Soviet aid and trade program listed thus far have one common property: they all relate to ways in which the U.S.S.R. might hope to influence the foreign policy of the underdeveloped countries. What of the domestic policies of the recipient countries? Can the aid program plausibly be construed as a device for influencing the course of events within the recipient countries?

Many people have pointed out that the underdeveloped countries face a choice of two roads to economic development, the democratic and the totalitarian. India is the prime example of the former, China of the latter. If the Indian way should fail, or if China should forge dramatically ahead, the cause of communism would be greatly strengthened throughout the underdeveloped regions of the world. It would seem, then, that the U.S.S.R.'s interests would be served by the failure of economic development in India and in the other non-Communist lands. Does not the aid program conflict with Soviet interests in this respect?

It may well be true that economic development is not a prime objective of the Soviet leaders. This view would help explain the indiscriminate character of Soviet aid projects. The huge sports stadium in Rangoon and the paving of the main street of Kabul are hardly projects

[12] Council for Economic and Industry Research, Inc., *Foreign Assistance Activities of the Communist Bloc . . .*, cited, p. 715.

[13] *The New York Times*, February 4, 1957.

calculated primarily to promote economic development. Military aid to Egypt and Syria will tie up the foreign exchange-producing exports of those countries for many years and thus hinder economic development. The objective of Soviet aid in such cases appears rather to be political. To be sure, most Soviet economic aid has not taken the form of "impact" projects—which attract attention without contributing greatly to economic development—but consists of useful installations. But this too may be attributed not so much to Soviet desire to promote economic development as to the recipient governments' understanding of where their own interests lie and the Soviet willingness to oblige. Thus the question still stands: even if the Soviet government has no particular wish to promote the economic progress of non-Communist countries, does not its aid program nevertheless foster that end?

One can find statements in Soviet sources that, through mutual assistance and cooperation, Asian countries can foster economic development "irrespective of their political and social structure," [14] and that the Soviet leaders "appreciate the striving of the Indian people to build up an independent economy and we feel sure they will overcome the formidable difficulties facing them," particularly in view of expanded economic ties with the U.S.S.R.[15] However, it is doubtful that the Soviet leaders really believe that rapid economic progress is possible under non-Communist governments. Before economic advancement can be achieved, the underdeveloped countries must throw off the yokes of imperialism and feudalism, the first by terminating foreign control over the nation's industry, the second by breaking up the landed estates and distributing the land to the peasants.[16] Only when peasants are given the land is their initiative stimulated and their productivity increased. On the face of it, this sounds like advocacy of the kind of land reform often recommended by Western liberals. But, in fact, the Russians have in mind something quite different

[14] *New Times*, no. 21, May 21, 1955, p. 14.
[15] Same, no. 22, May 28, 1955, p. 13.
[16] Same, no. 47, November 19, 1952, pp. 1-3.

from private landholding. The country held up as the prime example of land distribution to landless peasants is Communist China.[17] And China remains the model offered to the Asian peoples as the sole path to economic development, "for only its solution will enable these countries to put an end to the poverty and semi-starvation" of the past.[18]

Thus, while the Soviet leaders concede the possibility of some economic amelioration in the non-Communist underdeveloped countries, they have not abandoned their view that the Communist solution must eventually be adopted. Nor do they believe that Soviet economic aid will reverse this expected course of history. Soviet analysts have stressed the view that economic development is primarily a national problem and depends on the changes the underdeveloped countries are willing to make in their economic and social organization. Foreign credits are not the chief means to economic development, but are at best a supplement to the efforts of the people themselves.[19] The Soviet aid program can be expected to further economic growth in the non-Communist underdeveloped countries, but only those countries that follow the program of China can expect to realize the full potential of their economic capabilities.

Looked at from a Soviet point of view,[20] such economic development as does occur under non-Communist conditions may hasten rather than defer the advent of communism. World War II forced the colonial powers to encourage the growth of certain forms of industry in their colonies, to produce manufactured goods that could no longer be imported from the metropolitan centers and to produce goods needed by the metropolitan centers for war

[17] Same, no. 16, April 15, 1953, p. 14.

[18] Same, no. 21, May 21, 1955, p. 14.

[19] L. Fituni, "Ob ekonomicheskoi pomoshchi slaborazvitym stranam" (Economic Aid to Underdeveloped Countries), *Voprosy ekonomiki*, no. 11 (1953), p. 92.

[20] V. Vasil'eva, "Ekonomicheskoe razvitie kolonii v gody vtoroi mirovoi voiny" (Colonial Economic Development during World War II), *Mirovoe khoziaistvo i mirovaia politika*, no. 6 (1947), pp. 55-64.

purposes. The rise of industry fostered the growth of a working-class proletariat, which has traditionally been the stronghold of the Communist movement. In the Soviet analysis, the growth of the proletariat has been one of the important factors leading to the rise of revolutionary ferment in the underdeveloped countries after the war. Further economic development, which to the U.S.S.R. is virtually synonymous with industrialization, will lead to the further strengthening of the proletariat and the revolutionary movement. On this count, too, the Russians feel that history is on their side. If industrialization fails in the underdeveloped countries, the people will turn to the methods of the U.S.S.R. and China. If industrialization proceeds, the rising proletarian movement will lead to the eventual establishment of communism. Therefore, the program of economic aid does not conflict with the long-run expectations and objectives of Soviet policy.

Perhaps here is the solution of the paradox that some observers have noted in the simultaneous efforts of the United States and the U.S.S.R. to extend economic aid to the same countries. The United States is committed to the view that the sponsorship of economic growth will help them develop and strengthen democratic traditions and processes, and thus support the position of the non-Communist nations in world affairs. The U.S.S.R. hopes for and expects the eventual triumph of communism in those same countries, and presumably believes that support of economic development is one means to that end. Since the contradictory ends are not likely to be achieved by the same means, must not either the United States or the U.S.S.R. be fatally wrong in its policies?

One of the basic categories in the Bolshevik, or the Marxist-Leninist, world-view is the sharp distinction between tactics and strategy. Soviet policy has historically demonstrated a remarkable ability to adapt tactics to changes in political conditions, while maintaining the same long-run strategy and goals. The most relevant illustration is the policy of alternately supporting or attacking bourgeois-liberal and democratic-socialist parties in non-Communist countries, depending on the constellation of political forces at the time. A similar alternation has occurred in the sharp denunciation of the governments of the newly independent countries between 1947-1953, and the strong support given them since that period. Thus, the present policy of economic aid to underdeveloped countries can be plausibly interpreted as a tactical move consistent with Bolshevik ideology. One need not assume that the Soviet leaders have abandoned their belief in the eventual victory of communism. The friendship and support of the governments of the underdeveloped countries are needed to strengthen the Soviet position in world affairs at this point in history. Such support may be best obtained by furthering the dominant aspiration of those governments—economic development.

Nor does Soviet aid necessarily entail a postponement in history's time schedule of Communist revolution in those countries. The Soviet leaders undoubtedly appreciate the relatively small contribution a foreign aid program can make to the enormous task of economic development. They take the risk that the Western view is right, that the economic progress their aid helps to achieve will weaken the appeal of communism. There are compensating factors, however. The good will engendered by Soviet aid has undoubtedly changed the Asian and Middle Eastern image of the U.S.S.R. Viewed as a greathearted friend and benefactor, the U.S.S.R. is in a much more favorable position to preach the virtues of its own path to industrialization. And as a model of economic growth, the U.S.S.R. has often seemed a much more pertinent example to the underdeveloped countries than have the older, Western democracies. The presence of many Soviet citizens living among the underdeveloped peoples, and of technicians and students from the underdeveloped countries visiting or studying in the U.S.S.R., may increase ideological sympathies for the U.S.S.R. in those countries. The domestic Communist parties, though pledged to a role of peaceful propagation of communism because of the new foreign policy of the U.S.S.R., may be expected to enhance their own prestige along with that of the U.S.S.R. Thus, even if we assume that the primary objective of the Soviet aid program is to influence the foreign policies of the underdeveloped countries, there are also favorable influences to be expected on the course of domestic political developments in those countries.

Indeed, if the pace of economic development should fail to match the aspirations of the increasing populations of the underdeveloped countries, and if social and political unrest should therefore grow, the Soviet Union would still be in a favorable position to exploit that unrest. The bankruptcy of the non-Communist course could be underscored by arguing that, even with the abundant assistance of the U.S.S.R., the non-Communist governments were unable to solve the problems of economic development. The Communist course would appear as an untried alternative. The appeal of communism would be stronger than it would be if the U.S.S.R. had remained in a position of economic isolation.

ESPIONAGE AND CONSPIRACY

Some observers have anticipated that the Soviet technical assistance program would be used as a mask for concealing espionage and conspiratorial activities. This expectation conforms so nicely to the simple cloak-and-dagger image many people have of the U.S.S.R. that it may distort their understanding of the broader significance of the aid program. It is of course true that the multiplication of contacts and the increased involvement of the U.S.S.R. in the economies of underdeveloped countries enlarge the opportunities for espionage and subversion. It does not follow that these opportunities will always be exploited. We can expect the Soviet Union to be careful not to jeopardize the other important benefits it expects from the aid program.

Soviet practice in these matters is likely to differ widely according to circumstances. At one extreme, where the political situation is highly fluid and pro-Soviet forces are in positions of strength, the Soviet Union may well make a bid for all-out control. There appears to have been an effort at a great extension of Soviet influence in Syria in the summer of 1957, in connection with the military and economic aid program announced at that time. Where the situation is such that military and economic aid could shift the balance from a neutralist to a strongly pro-Soviet government, one can expect the Russians to use their aid program for that purpose.

In a country such as India, on the other hand, the U.S.S.R. confronts a government that has dealt harshly with conspiratorial Communist activities, but which nevertheless faces the threat of Communist victories in open elections in various sections of the country. While there is no immediate prospect of an overthrow of the government by pro-Soviet forces, the government is highly sensitive to the domestic Communist danger. An espionage or conspiratorial scandal involving technical assistance personnel might well be ruinous to the goals the Russians hope to attain through their economic aid program. And, indeed, their representatives have been extremely correct in this respect in India.

The case of Egypt is particularly interesting. Egypt is the largest recipient of Soviet arms and one of the large recipients of Soviet economic aid. Yet the Communist party is firmly outlawed, and newspapers periodically report that local Communists have been thrown into prison for one reason or another. The Soviet government is reported to be somewhat less than pleased at the union of Syria and Egypt because of the fate of the Syrian Communist party which was outlawed when the country fell under Egyptian authority. With respect to propaganda gains from its loan to Egypt, the Soviet Union does not have its accustomed advantage of a controlled press at home competing against a free press abroad; the controlled Egyptian press had little to say about the loan negotiations, and the Russians have been reported to be distressed at the apathetic reception their generosity has encountered in Egypt.[21] Whatever gains the U.S.S.R. may hope for from

[21] *The New York Times,* December 18, 1957.

its military and economic aid to Egypt, it has not yet been shown that immediate subversion is one of them. In the longer run, however, the increase of Soviet influence in such fields as education may strengthen the domestic Communist movement and help create a generation vulnerable to the appeals of Marxism.

Even on the assumption that Soviet policy will usually subordinate conspiracy to other purposes, one must make allowance for miscalculation or bungling. This may have happened in Burma, with which the U.S.S.R. had established extremely cordial relations following an exchange of state visits between Khrushchev and Bulganin and Premier U Nu in 1955. In 1956, U Nu resigned his premiership, remarking at the time that the policy of neutralism was made difficult by the activities of the Soviet and Chinese embassies in Rangoon.[22] One may also reasonably anticipate conflicts of interest among the separate Soviet bureaucracies involved in diplomatic, economic, military and espionage activities; such mistakes in policy are sometimes too easily interpreted as evidence of changes in policy.

Where opportunities for important political victories present themselves, the Soviet Union may be expected to act upon them. Perhaps the aid program will pave the way for such opportunities. A tradition of correct behavior by Soviet representatives, once established, may cause some countries to let down their guard against possibilities of subversion. Soviet technical personnel abroad will certainly gather the usual kind of economic intelligence that all governmental missions are expected to gather. Those forms of espionage and intelligence work that the Russians employed before the inauguration of the aid program will undoubtedly continue to function, probably independently of the economic missions. But as a general proposition it would be misleading to think of the aid program as an important part of the espionage and conspiratorial network of the U.S.S.R. If we are correct in believing that a major objective of the aid program is to influence the foreign policies

[22] Same, June 5, 1956.

of the recipient countries, we must assume that the Soviet Union will be very cautious about jeopardizing its basic objectives by such activities.

III

THE CHARACTER AND SIZE OF THE AID PROGRAM

WHAT THEN is the nature of the aid program with which the Soviet leaders hope to establish their power and influence in the affairs of the underdeveloped countries? As it has developed thus far, it is a many-pronged instrument composed of a variety of elements. Its central feature is the construction of industrial installations financed by the U.S.S.R. In addition, a wide variety of technical assistance projects have been carried out in such fields as mining and prospecting. These projects are undertaken, for the most part, by direct agreement with the recipient countries and, to a small extent, by Soviet contributions to the United Nations technical assistance program. Military aid is not properly a part of the economic aid program, but it does have important economic and political implications, and in a reckoning of the size of the economic aid program it will be instructive to examine the size of military aid.

ECONOMIC DEVELOPMENT LOANS

The most highly publicized feature of the Soviet program[1] of economic aid to underdeveloped countries is the series of capital construction agreements. Under these agreements, the U.S.S.R. undertakes to provide the equipment and engineering services for the construction of a wide variety of installations such as factories, grain eleva-

[1] Although, as this chapter makes clear, the other Bloc countries play an important part in the aid and trade program, it will frequently be convenient to speak of it as "the Soviet program."

tors and power plants. The Soviet government also agrees to finance the construction under medium- or long-term credits. The recipient country usually provides the labor and the locally produced materials. The Soviet Union agrees to train the engineering and skilled-labor personnel of the recipient country to operate the plant and, on completion of the construction, to turn the plant over to the recipient country for operation.

The most celebrated example of this kind of transaction is the steel mill now under construction at Bhilai, in India.[2] The plans were drawn up by a team of Soviet engineers, and provide for a steel mill with a capacity of a million tons of ingots. It will be capable of producing about 750,000 tons of rails, structural steel, sleeper bars, and billets, and, in addition, 300,000 tons of salable pig iron. The plans provide for the eventual expansion of the plant to a capacity of 2,500,000 tons of ingots. In the construction of the mill, as much use as possible is to be made of materials and equipment available in India, particularly metallurgical, engineering and other industrial products. Materials and equipment not available in India are provided by the U.S.S.R. Indian personnel are used wherever possible in the course of the construction, not only to economize on the use of Soviet technicians, but also for training purposes. Under the technical assistance provisions, Soviet engineers assist in supervising construction; about 700 Indian skilled workers, engineers and technicians are being trained in the Soviet Union; and 4,500 unskilled workers and 500 engineers are receiving training in India by Soviet specialists.

The total cost of the plant, the town that will surround it, and the mines to be constructed has been estimated at about $231 million.[3] The U.S.S.R. is to supply equipment, materials and technical assistance for the plant amounting to about $132 million. In addition, India paid about $5 million

[2] U. S. Senate, Subcommittee on Technical Assistance Programs, *Soviet Technical Assistance*, Staff Study no. 7, 84th Cong., 2d sess. (Washington: GPO, 1956), pp. 16-19.

[3] *The New York Times*, September 6, 1956.

for the preparation of the project report. Payment for the Soviet contribution is financed under a credit to be repaid in twelve equal annual installments, with an interest charge of 2½ per cent on the unpaid balance. The annual installments are to be paid in rupees, to be used by the U.S.S.R. for the purchase of commodities in India.

The Indian steel mill agreement is the prototype of similar agreements entered into with a number of underdeveloped countries. Appendix Tables A and B list all credit agreements believed to have been signed as of December 31, 1957. The projects are of many types: hydroelectric plants, oil storage facilities, airports, an asphalt factory, a nuclear physics laboratory, chemical and food plants, railroads, engineering and mechanical workshops, petroleum refineries, and so forth. Some of the agreements cover individual projects, such as the Indian steel mill. Other agreements are umbrella contracts providing for a line of credit to be used for a number of specific projects, the details of which are to be worked out later. For example, the $100-million credit to Indonesia is to be used for the construction of projects in coal mining, iron and steel, building materials, electric power and other industries. Not all of the loans, it should be noted, are for capital construction purposes. Some cover commodity purchases, usually of industrial commodities, and some cover purely technical assistance. It is not always possible, however, to separate the various types of loans. The tables should therefore be regarded as a catalogue of all economic development loans: for capital construction, commodity purchases and technical assistance.

In passing from a general description of the aid program to a discussion of specific economic data, one is bedeviled by difficulties. For one thing, neither the recipient nor the donor governments publish complete statistical information on their credit agreements. The large agreements are usually announced publicly at the time of signing, but there is no regular accounting of their fulfillment. Smaller credit agreements are often not announced officially, and their existence is known through a chance newspaper article or radio broadcast, or a speech by an official of the recipient nation. Unfortunately, information of the latter kind is not entirely satisfactory. Sometimes the existence of an agreement is reported, but the size of the credit is not made known. Sometimes it is not perfectly clear whether the report concerns an agreement actually concluded or simply an offer made. Sometimes a construction project is reported, but it is not known whether a credit is involved.

TABLE 1

Estimated Value of Soviet Bloc Nonmilitary Credit Agreements Signed with Underdeveloped Countries, 1953 to 1957

Lender	*Million U. S. Dollars*	*Per Cent*
U.S.S.R.	1,227	78
Other Bloc	354	22
Czechoslovakia	*176*	*11*
East Germany	*103*	*6*
China[a]	*58*	*4*
Hungary	7	
Poland	7	*1*
Rumania	*3*	
Total	1,581	100

Recipient	*Million U. S. Dollars*	*Per Cent Incl. Yugoslavia*	*Per Cent Excl. Yugoslavia*
Yugoslavia	444	28	—
India	362	23	32
Egypt[a]	213	14	19
Syria	184	12	17
Afghanistan	115	7	10
Indonesia	113	7	10
Ceylon[a]	26		
Cambodia[a]	22		
Burma	22		
Turkey	22		
Argentina	21	9	12
Paraguay	15		
Nepal[a]	13		
Sudan	5		
Lebanon	2		
Yemen	2		
Total	1,581	100	100

[a] Including Chinese grants of $22 million to Cambodia, $13 million to Nepal, $16 million to Ceylon and $5 million to Egypt. These are the only instances of grants. All the rest are credits.

Source: Appendix Tables A and B.

Agencies of the United States government have gathered information on Soviet Bloc credit agreements by a systematic scanning of hundreds of foreign newspapers, journals and monitored radio broadcasts. Government reports are the principal source of the data presented in Appendix Tables A and B. In order to compute a total, however, a number of guesses and assumptions have had to be made. For instance, certain of the smaller credit agreements are of unknown value; on the basis of whatever descriptive material was available, values were assigned to them here. Another vexing problem involved the choice of an exchange rate at which to convert ruble values to dollars. In presenting data of this kind, the writer is under obligation to be his own severest critic. It is hoped that the explanation and cautions presented in detail in Appendix A will discharge that obligation.

These caveats will undoubtedly prove distressing to persons who prefer to deal with "hard facts" and with figures that can be taken at face value. Such readers are advised that there is more of this to come. The subject of this study cannot honestly be presented in other than speculative terms, and while statistical information is useful for gaining some sort of perspective, it is well that such information be shown in its true light.

Table 1 presents the results of the effort to establish the approximate total value of Soviet Bloc credit agreements signed between 1953 and 1957. The total is about $1.6 billion, subject to an unknown margin of error.[4]

GEOGRAPHICAL DISTRIBUTION OF BLOC AID

In the distribution of the credits, the most striking feature is the high degree of concentration. Among the lenders, the U.S.S.R. alone accounts for about three-quarters of all

[4] As for the probable direction of error in this estimate, one can think of some reasons why the figure may be too large, and others why it may be too small. Some items may have been erroneously included as credit agreements actually signed because of deliberate or accidental errors in the source. But this is not likely to have happened in more than a few instances and least of all in the large and highly publicized agreements that account for the greatest part of the total. It is more reasonable to expect that the tabulation has omitted some items, for the data were gathered by a dragnet-like operation, in which one knows what he has but not whether he has everything. It is doubtful that any substantial number of secret agreements has been signed; in general the Bloc countries would have no interest in understating the volume of aid. Thus the most likely sources of error operate in opposite directions.

credits extended. The three largest lenders together have contributed about 95 per cent of the total. In fact, the predominant role of the U.S.S.R. is even greater than is indicated by these figures, for in certain instances the East European countries have acted as "brokers" for credits actually extended by the U.S.S.R. to non-Communist countries. That is, some of the credits extended by East European countries to non-Communist countries (and therefore included in Table 1) are the counterpart of credits extended by the U.S.S.R. to Eastern Europe (and therefore not included in Table 1). In any case, while Soviet Bloc aid is not exactly a one-country show, the paramount role of the U.S.S.R. as the chief source of credits is clear.

On the recipient side, the treatment of Yugoslavia poses certain problems of exposition. As a Communist country, formerly a member of the Soviet Bloc, Yugoslavia plays a different role from that of the non-Communist underdeveloped countries in the political calculations of the U.S.S.R. The influence of Yugoslavia on the politics of such Communist countries as Poland, Bulgaria and Hungary and the economic relations of Yugoslavia with the West are problems with which the U.S.S.R. would have to cope, even in the absence of an aid program for the non-Communist underdeveloped countries. Thus, in considering the impact of that program on the non-Communist world, we should properly treat Soviet aid to Yugoslavia in a separate category. On the other hand, in the cost of the entire aid program to the U.S.S.R. the credits to Yugoslavia must be taken into account. For the sake of comprehensiveness, we have included Yugoslavia in the total picture in the following discussion, but wherever this factor obscures a relevant point of difference between Yugoslavia and the other recipients, we have sought to note the difference in the text.

The distribution of Bloc aid among recipients also shows a high degree of concentration, though less than on the donor side. Yugoslavia and India each account for about a quarter of the total of Bloc aid. Egypt and Syria together account for another quarter. Thus, four countries account for about three-quarters of all Bloc aid. The eight other countries account for the remaining quarter. If we exclude Yugoslavia, roughly the same degree of concentration holds. The four leading recipients (India, Egypt, Syria and Afghanistan) have received about three-quarters of all the aid, and the first five (including Indonesia) have received almost 90 per cent.

If we digress for a moment from our main task of reckoning the total volume and distribution of Bloc credits, it is instructive to glance at the significance of the credits for the recipient countries. A full exploration of this question would require a detailed consideration of the economic system and development plans of each recipient, a task that ought certainly to be undertaken but which is beyond the scope of this study. It is of some interest, however, to compare the size of the credits with the economic "size" of the recipient countries. Table 2 presents some crude estimates of the national incomes of the countries that have received Bloc credits. Syria, before the formation of the United Arab Republic, stands out as the most dramatic case of the impact of Bloc credits on an economic system; the total volume of credits contracted for equals 40 to 50 per cent of one year's national income (at the 1955 level). To be sure, the credits will be drawn upon over a series of years, but taken as a whole they amount to a larger percentage of one year's national income in Syria than in any other country. In this sense the Syrian economy has gained the most from the Soviet aid program, and, by the same token, the possibility of the loss of Soviet aid would carry the most serious consequences for Syria. If any country's economy can be said to have become "dependent" for its economic progress on the Soviet aid program, it was that of Syria before it joined Egypt in the United Arab Republic.

In Afghanistan, the ratio of total Soviet credits to one year's national income at the 1955 level is about half that of Syria, and in Egypt and Yugoslavia it is about half again.[5] India, the largest single recipient of Bloc credits after Yugoslavia, shows the smallest ratio of any of the large

[5] For the United Arab Republic (Egypt, Syria, Yemen) the figure would be about 13 per cent.

recipients. Since the $360 million of Bloc credits to India will be spread out over a number of years, in any year Bloc aid will amount to significantly less than one per cent of the national income. By comparison, the United States food loan to India in 1956 amounting to $360 million, most of which was delivered within a single year, had a greater quantitative impact on the Indian economy than the entire Soviet Bloc credit program.

Table 2 thus underscores what may be the obvious fact that the smaller the country, the more it has to gain (or lose) from the Soviet aid program. There is, indeed, almost a perfect inverse relationship between the national incomes of the recipients and the ratio of credits to national income. Consider the six principal recipients, who account for over 90 per cent of the total of Bloc credits extended. In the two with the largest national incomes, India and Indonesia, the credits are the smallest percentages of national income (2 per cent and 5 per cent). In the two with the smallest national incomes, Afghanistan and Syria, the credits are the largest percentages of national income (23 per cent and 46 per cent).

Of the many speculations in which one might engage on the basis of these observations, perhaps the most significant is that we ought not to expect the U.S.S.R. to employ the same techniques or even pursue the same objectives in all the recipient countries. In Syria and Afghanistan the sheer weight of economic aid in the domestic economies of the recipients may be sufficient for the Soviet Bloc to acquire a considerable measure of influence. It would be fearfully expensive for the Soviet Bloc to strive for a similar position in India and Indonesia. It remains to be seen whether the gains that can be enjoyed from a volume of aid that is relatively small will be judged to be worth the cost. In absolute terms, Soviet credits to India are substantially larger than those to Afghanistan and Syria combined. If "relative weight" turned out to be a decisive factor in judging the success of the economic aid program, the Soviet Union might find it desirable to withdraw from India and concentrate its credits on smaller countries. A

TABLE 2

Total Volume of Bloc Credit Commitments as Related to the 1955 National Income and Population of Recipient Countries

Recipient	*Credits 1953-1957* (*million U.S. dollars*)	*Estimated National Income 1955*	*Credits as a Percentage of National Income* (*per cent*)	*Population 1955* (*million*)	*Credits Per* (*dollars per person*)
Yugoslavia	444	3,900[a]	11	17.6	25.20
India	362	20,800[a]	2	381.7	.95
Egypt	213	2,500[a]	9	22.9	9.30
Syria	184	400	46	4.1	45.00
Afghanistan	115	500	23	12.0	9.60
Indonesia	113	21,100[b]	5	81.9	1.40
Ceylon	26	1,100	2	8.6	3.00
Cambodia	22	n.a.	n.a.	4.4	5.00
Burma	22	900	2	19.4	1.10
Turkey	22	5,100[a]	*	24.1	.90
Argentina	21	13,600[a]	*	19.1	1.10
Paraguay	15	600[a]	3	1.6	9.40
Nepal	13	n.a.	n.a.	8.4[a]	1.50
Sudan	5	n.a.	n.a.	n.a.	n.a.
Lebanon	2	500[a]	*	1.4	1.40
Yemen	2	200	1	4.5	.40

* Signifies less than 1 per cent.

a 1954.

b 1952.

Sources: Population—United Nations, Statistical Office, *Demographic Yearbook, 1956* (New York: Author, 1956), pp. 136-150.

National Income—United Nations, Statistical Office, *Statistical Yearbook 1956* (New York: Author, 1956), pp. 480-482. National income estimates in local currencies were converted to dollars at the prevailing exchange rates given in the same source, pp. 470-471. For Afghanistan, Syria and Yemen, the source contained no national income estimates, and they were therefore calculated by the following procedure: Per capita national income estimates for 1953 are presented in Charles P. Kindleberger, *Economic Development* (New York: McGraw-Hill, 1958), p. 6; the ratios of per capita national incomes were then calculated for Afghanistan and India, Syria and Egypt, and Yemen and Egypt; by applying these ratios to the population and national income estimates obtained from the United Nations sources cited above, the national incomes of Afghanistan, Syria and Yemen were estimated.

pound of meat that would scarcely tempt the appetite of the lion may prove excellent bait for a number of foxes.

Size alone is not decisive. Indeed, a good portion of the success of the Soviet program is due not to its size, but to a variety of psychological and other factors, which will be considered in subsequent chapters. But these other factors are more or less operative in all the underdeveloped countries to which the Russians have directed their attention, and in this sense "other things are equal." Where the psychological impact of the aid program is reinforced by a relatively large impact on the recipient's economy, the U.S.S.R. may reap a richer harvest than where the aid program depends primarily on its psychological impact.

THE LOANS OVER A PERIOD OF YEARS

The granting of the $1.6 billion in Soviet Bloc credits has been strung out over a number of years, as Table 3 shows. The program began in earnest after Stalin's death in 1953, but it was not until 1955 that any sizable volume of credit agreements was signed; over half the total for that year is accounted for by one project, the Indian steel mill. The momentum attained by the Soviet drive is reflected in the great increase in 1956. About 60 per cent of all credits extended during the period under review were granted in that year. But of the $960 million extended about $700 million consisted of large loans to four countries: Yugoslavia, India, Indonesia and Afghanistan. (See Appendix Table A.)

TABLE 3

Bloc Credit Agreements Signed, by Year
(millions of U. S. dollars)

	1953	*1954*	*1955*	*1956*	*1957*
U.S.S.R.	5	10	137	713	362
Other Bloc	1	5	52	247	49
Total	6	15	189	960	411

Source: Appendix Tables A and B.

When we look at the total for 1957, however, we note a sharp fall in the volume of new loans extended. Of the $411 million in credits extended in that year, $345 million is accounted for by only two loans, to Egypt and Syria (and the Egyptian loan had not been made final by the end of the year). It is clear that the great momentum of the aid program in 1956 did not carry over into 1957. We shall have occasion later to comment on this slowdown.

The *use* of the credits is spread over a longer period. The United States government distinguishes among "allotments," "obligations" and "expenditures" in statistical reports on its aid program.[6] An "allotment" is a sum declared to be available to a recipient country during a specified period. When a concrete project is presented and approved, a portion of the allotment is then "obligated" for that project. As the project goes into operation, the obligated funds are gradually disbursed, and are then classified as "expenditures." The Bloc credit agreements under discussion are a combination of allotments and obligations. For instance, the $175-million loan to Egypt has been agreed to by both parties, and has thus been allotted, but there is no information on what portion has been obligated for concrete projects; nor can we know how long it will take before the full amount is obligated, or even whether it will be fully obligated. The Indian steel mill is an example of a credit that has been fully obligated. In the case of the $110-million credit granted to Yugoslavia in 1956, we do not know what portion of the allotment has been obligated.

Allotment and obligation are only two of the steps in the aid process. For the credits are not utilized as soon as they are obligated. It takes time to plan projects, time for the equipment to be built in the U.S.S.R., time for the structure to be erected so that the equipment can be installed. The Indian steel mill, for instance, is scheduled for completion in 1959, five years after the conclusion of the agreement. The rolling-mill equipment will not be shipped until several years after construction has begun. To be sure, it is the

[6] See the quarterly *Operations Reports* of the International Cooperation Administration.

total size of an aid agreement that makes headlines and determines the political impact of the loan. Even Western commentators fall into the error of comparing the volume of Soviet aid *agreements* signed with United States aid actually *delivered*[7] in the course of a single year. While the total volume of aid agreements provides a guide to their political impact, as a measure of the economic impact of Soviet aid it is less interesting than the actual annual expenditures under the agreements.

Unfortunately, data on expenditures to date are not available, and future expenditures are obviously not known. The point is important enough, however, to warrant some estimate of the rate of expenditures, however rough. The question may be posed in the following form: Suppose all known allotments are obligated, and all obligations eventually expended in full; what would be a reasonable time schedule of the rate of expenditures?

To provide some rough orientation on this question, I have estimated for each known credit agreement the proportion of the principal amount that might be utilized each year. The estimates are based on such bits of information as are available on the anticipated dates of completion of various projects, on a comparison between projects for which such information is available and those for which it is not, and on the experience of the International Bank for Reconstruction and Development in the rate at which funds are disbursed under it loans. The details of the estimates are presented in Appendix B. The estimates obviously contain a large degree of arbitrariness, but the broad outlines presented in Table 4 should be fairly reliable.

The table shows that by the end of 1955, when a total of about $200 million in loans had been contracted for,

[7] Data on U. S. foreign aid refer to the utilization of the grants and credits, not to the amounts agreed upon in aid negotiations. The grants and credits are in terms of goods delivered or shipped, services rendered, or cash disbursed to the account of a foreign government or other foreign entity. For convenience I shall use the word "deliveries" to cover all U. S. aid which has been utilized, whether these deliveries are actually received in the form of goods and services or only as a transfer of funds to a foreign account. The same term will be applied to estimated utilization of Soviet Bloc credits.

actual deliveries had probably amounted to something less than $50 million. This was the period of the Bulganin-Khrushchev political tour of South Asia, during which the Soviet leaders endeavored to persuade the underdeveloped countries of the great benefits the U.S.S.R. was prepared

TABLE 4

Estimated Annual Rate of Utilization of Bloc Credits
(millions of U. S. dollars)

Lender	*1954*	*1955*	*1956*	*1957*	*Remainder (To be Utilized Sometime After January 1, 1958)*
U.S.S.R.	5-10	8-12	45- 65	100-120	900-1,100
Other Bloc	0- 5	20-30	55- 75	60- 80	175- 215
Total	5-15	28-42	100-140	160-200	1,075-1,315

Source: Appendix Tables E and F.

to bestow upon them. By the end of 1956, the cost to the Bloc in funds actually expended was about $150 million, less than 15 per cent of the total of credit agreements signed as of that date. One year later, at the end of 1957, in the neighborhood of $350 million had actually been spent, amounting to 20 to 25 per cent of the value of credit agreements signed as of that date.[8] Thus, of the total amount of credits agreed upon as of the end of 1957, less than one-quarter was probably used by that date; deliveries representing the remaining three-quarters may be spread out over a number of years. The Bloc as a whole has not yet had to

[8] The increase in the percentage, as compared with 1956, is due to the sharp fall in the volume of new loans extended in 1957. A State Department study estimates that as of November 30, 1957, probably only 10 to 15 per cent had actually been expended. (*The New York Times*, January 4, 1958.) Since the details of the Department's estimates have not been published, we cannot attempt to reconcile its procedures with ours. The substantial difference between the two estimates reflects the difficulty of making reliable quantitative statements about the Soviet aid program, but for the broad purpose of gauging orders of magnitude, the two estimates are reasonably consistent.

pay the largest part of the price of the economic aid program.

In a comparison of actual deliveries by the U.S.S.R. and by the other countries of the Soviet Bloc, the U.S.S.R. appears to have delivered less than its allies up to the end of 1956. By the end of 1957, the U.S.S.R. had forged slightly ahead. Our estimates are too rough to warrant very much confidence in the precise relationships, but they suggest that the U.S.S.R. and the other Bloc countries have delivered about equal amounts of aid, although U.S.S.R. credit commitments far overshadow in volume the commitments by other Bloc countries. The difference in performance reflects the fact that most of the U.S.S.R. credit agreements take the form of large lines of credit to finance projects to be specified in the future, whereas the other Bloc countries concentrate, for the most part, on specific projects.

In no sense should the long time lags between agreement and delivery be construed as reflecting on the Soviet Union's ability or willingness to honor its agreements. Such lags are normal. However, their existence suggests several important points. First, the Western public's attention has focused on the size of the agreements and not on the actual deliveries, which may have resulted in a somewhat exaggerated impression of what the Soviet Union has actually done thus far. Second, the U.S.S.R. can secure the political advantages of agreeing to provide aid without having to "pay up" for several years. Third, and perhaps most important, the Soviet economy has not yet had time to feel the full impact of the credit program. From 1958 on the burden of the capital goods exports committed under past agreements will begin to mount to significant proportions. The test of Soviet ability to support the aid program is yet to come.

TECHNICAL ASSISTANCE

Soviet Bloc credits for construction of industrial installations are but one part of the economic program, though perhaps the most important part. Another aspect is the provision of technical assistance, as distinct from the supplying of capital goods. The range of these activities is indicated by the following examples:[9]

Czechoslovakia provided technical aid in the construction of a meat-processing plant and sugar refinery in Afghanistan.

Sixteen Soviet experts conducted a survey of possible industrial and agricultural investment projects in Cambodia.

Egyptian scientists and students are studying nuclear physics in Moscow.

Numerous Indian missions have travelled in the U.S.S.R. studying the Soviet glass industry, oil refineries, fertilizer plants, railways, broadcasting, dairy farming and animal husbandry. Soviet technical experts have made studies in India of possibilities for a pharmaceutical industry, glass and electric-power plants, and heavy machinery manufacturing.

Hungarian experts advised on the construction of hydroelectric and diesel stations in Indonesia.

The U.S.S.R. assisted in modernization of spinning looms and mills in Lebanon.

Czechoslovakia provided technical aid in the establishment of a flour mill in Paraguay.

Polish engineers assisted in construction of an enamelware factory in Egypt.

East German experts conducted a survey of water resources, and assisted in the construction of waterworks and water systems in the Sudan.

Czechoslovakian technicians assisted in the construction of an international airport in Damascus and in the construction of an oil refinery in Syria.

Czechoslovakia provided technical assistance in the construction of a cement factory in Yemen.

A Yugoslav delegation of chemical experts went to study in the U.S.S.R.

Very little is known of the details of these activities.

[9] Council for Economic and Industry Research, Inc., *Foreign Assistance Activities of the Communist Bloc and Their Implications for the United States*, in *Foreign Aid Program*, Senate Doc. no. 52, 85th Cong., 1st sess. (Washington: GPO, 1957), Appendix C.

Presumably the cost is usually charged to a Bloc loan, although sometimes a grant may be involved. In some instances, technical assistance missions operate in conjunction with a construction project, as in the case cited above of Czechoslovakian assistance in building a Yemeni cement factory. Yemen seems to have borne the cost of building the factory without benefit of a credit, and we might guess that the equipment was purchased from Czechoslovakia under a regular commercial trade arrangement. In other cases, technical assistance is provided along with a construction agreement; Egyptian technical personnel studying nuclear physics in Moscow are to staff the nuclear physics reactor constructed under a credit agreement. Sometimes, a technical assistance mission is the preliminary to a credit agreement; the credit for the development of a diamond mining industry in India followed a favorable report by a Soviet mission of diamond experts.

In addition to the bilateral technical assistance described above, the Bloc also participates in the activities of the multilateral United Nations technical assistance programs. In the years 1953-1957, Soviet pledges amounted to 22.8 million rubles ($5.7 million)[10] and the pledges from other countries of Eastern Europe brought the Bloc total up to about $6.5 million. For various reasons, the United Nations has had difficulty using the East European currencies, so that by the end of 1956 only about 32 per cent of the Bloc pledges had actually been spent.[11]

Information on the number and activities of the Bloc technical assistance personnel at work under the bilateral agreements is sparse and sporadic, coming as it does in bits and pieces from various places in the world. The State Department estimates that during the first six months of 1957 more than 2,000 Bloc technicians worked for a month or longer in nineteen underdeveloped countries. Eighty per cent of them worked in four countries, Egypt, Syria,

[10] Dollar equivalents are shown at the official rate. This is not a reliable indication of the real value of the ruble. See pp. 195-197.

[11] Robert Loring Allen, " United Nations Technical Assistance: Soviet and East European Participation," *International Organization*, v. 11, no. 4, (Autumn 1957), pp. 620, 627.

Afghanistan and India. About a third were involved in military assistance, particularly in Egypt and Syria. Most of the others have been attached to construction projects or involved in advisory work or prospecting. Relatively few agricultural specialists have been employed.[12]

No data at all are available on the amount spent on the bilateral technical assistance projects. Yet it is worth trying to gauge the size of those expenditures, if only to determine whether we are talking of orders of magnitude of $1 million or $100 million. About forty technical assistance missions of various kinds have been identified.[13] About half of them are Soviet missions, the other half sponsored by other Bloc countries. Since there are many small technical assistance missions, there is a greater likelihood that some have escaped public attention than in the case of credit agreements. To avoid underestimating Soviet aid, let us assume that there are twice as many missions as have been reported, that all eighty are bilateral and that all are fully financed by Bloc credits. These missions would vary greatly in size and length of service abroad. To put the cost of each mission at $100,000 would be guessing on the high side. At that rate, the eighty missions would cost $8 million. Perhaps $5 to $10 million is a reasonable order of magnitude. Thus, the Bloc may have spent on bilateral technical assistance roughly about the same amount as it contributed to the United Nations technical assistance programs.

GIFTS

Grants, which play an important part in the aid the United States gives to underdeveloped countries, are of minor importance in the Soviet program. Instead "gifts" are used ceremonially, or for propagandist purposes, to demonstrate Soviet good will and accomplishments, rather than as major contributions to economic development.

To demonstrate its desire for friendship with the peoples

[12] *The New York Times*, January 4, 1958.

[13] *Foreign Assistance Activities of the Communist Bloc and Their Implications for the United States*, cited, Appendix C.

of the underdeveloped countries, the Soviet government makes a practice of giving expensive gifts to the leaders of governments or to the nations at large. During their tour of South Asia in late 1955, Bulganin and Khrushchev gave the government of Afghanistan 15 buses and the equipment for a 100-bed hospital. To India, they presented a number of farm machines, valued at 5 million rupees (about $1 million), for equipping a 40,000-acre mechanized farm.[14] Burma and India each received a Soviet twin-engined IL-14 transport plane, with technicians for maintenance and operation.[15] A curious instance of ceremonial gift exchange occurred in the joint communiqué issued at the end of the visit to Burma. The Soviet government offered to construct and equip a technological institute in Rangoon as a gift to the people of Burma. Burma in turn offered to present an equivalent gift of rice and other Burmese goods to the people of the U.S.S.R. On the conclusion of Premier U Nu's return visit to Moscow, the ceremony was repeated. The U.S.S.R. gave a hospital, a sports center, a hotel and an exhibition hall. In return Burma gave more rice.

The total value of these gifts is probably not large. Thirteen such gifts are on record, including the Burmese gift exchanges. Of these, nine were given by the U.S.S.R., the rest by other Bloc countries.[16] The total is hardly likely to exceed $10-$20 million in value. But the significance of the gifts is obviously not to be found in their monetary value. They are part of a public relations campaign designed to persuade the leaders and peoples of the underdeveloped countries of Soviet good wishes and intentions. The gifts probably received more publicity than any $20 million worth of United States "grants" in the form of wheat or technical assistance. A grant is, after all, something a richer nation gives a poorer. A gift is something a friend gives a friend.

[14] *Soviet Technical Assistance,* cited, p. 23.

[15] *Foreign Assistance Activities of the Communist Bloc and Their Implications for the United States,* cited, pp. 718, 738.

[16] Same, Appendix C.

MILITARY ASSISTANCE

Although the focus of our study is the economic assistance provided by the Soviet Bloc, a word should be added about military assistance. The amounts of military aid are particularly difficult to estimate because greater secrecy surrounds some of these activities and because it is questionable what value should properly be assigned to military supplies, both new and obsolete. For our purposes, this latter difficulty can be largely removed. Most Soviet military aid is on a loan basis, and where the negotiated amount of a loan can be ascertained it presumably has at least the meaning that the recipient feels the benefits to be worth that amount. However, it is hard to establish the figures with any precision. Dispatches appearing in the press from various places in the world give widely differing estimates of Soviet military aid deliveries, and the private citizen has little basis for evaluating them. The figures published by the United States Department of State are among the more conservative; they indicate that about $400 million worth of military loans have been extended to Egypt, Syria, Afghanistan and Yemen. Egypt received $250 million, Syria a minimum of $100 million and Afghanistan and Yemen $25 million each.[17] The loans and arms have been provided by both the U.S.S.R. and Czechoslovakia. The Egyptian military loan agreement provides for repayment in cotton shipments over a period of seven to ten years.[18] The Afghan loan provides for repayment in Afghan goods over a period of eight years.[19] The Syrian loan is reported to be repayable in ten annual installments, at a low rate of interest.[20]

If we add the arms loans to economic development credits, Egypt becomes the largest single debtor of the Soviet Bloc, slightly surpassing Yugoslavia. Syria, whose national income and population are so small that the eco-

[17] *The New York Times*, January 15, 1958.

[18] *Foreign Assistance Activities of the Communist Bloc and Their Implications for the United States*, cited, p. 724.

[19] *The New York Times*, September 5, 1956.

[20] Same, August 11, 1957.

nomic credits alone make it the largest debtor on a per capita basis, becomes an even heavier debtor, relatively (see Table 2). The United Arab Republic of Egypt, Syria and Yemen has received a total of about $775 million in arms and economic loans. This is about two-thirds as much aid as all the other underdeveloped countries received from the Soviet Bloc. If we exclude Yugoslavia, the federated Arab state has received about as much aid as all the other non-Communist underdeveloped countries combined.

If the arms loans are to be repaid primarily by exports from the recipient countries directly to the Bloc, they will require a considerable expansion in the volume of trade. If we assume that the loans will be repaid in ten annual installments, Egypt's obligation will amount to $25 million per year, or about one-third of its total exports to the U.S.S.R. and Czechoslovakia in 1956 ($75.7 million). Syria's annual installment of $10 million is about 40 per cent greater than its total exports to the U.S.S.R. and Czechoslovakia in 1956 ($7.0 million).

If exports to the Bloc are generated by the diversion of exports that otherwise would have gone to the non-Bloc world, trade with the latter will show an appreciable decrease; Egypt's annual installment on the arms loan is equal to about 10 per cent of its total 1956 exports to the non-Bloc world, and Syria's is nearly 8 per cent.[21] Thus, while repayment of the arms loan will absorb cotton exports which might otherwise raise surplus-disposal problems, it does tie up resources needed to pay for regular commercial imports and to repay economic development credits. This

[21] International Cooperation Administration, *East-West Trade Developments, 1956-1957*, Tenth Report to Congress under the Mutual Defense Assistance Control Act of 1951 (Washington: GPO, 1958), p. 53. Egyptian exports of cotton to the U.S.S.R. came to 105.6 million pounds in the crop year 1956-1957 (compared to 32.3 million in 1954-1955 and 26.2 million in 1955-1956). National Bank of Egypt, *Economic Bulletin*, v. 10, no. 4 (1957), p. 413. The Communist countries' share in Egypt's cotton exports rose from 30 per cent in 1954-55 to 60 per cent in January 1958. *The London Times*, February 12, 1958. Total Egyptian exports to the U.S.S.R. in 1957 came to about $90 million (at the official exchange rate). *The London Times*, March 26, 1958. Thus between a quarter and a third of Egyptian exports to the U.S.S.R. in that year went to pay off the arms debt (according to our estimate of the rate of repayment).

mortgaging of foreign exchange earnings was one of the factors that led the United States, Britain and the World Bank to withdraw their proposals for financing the Aswan Dam. But from the Soviet point of view military aid has two special advantages: it helps increase the volume of trade with the recipient countries, and it helps get rid of obsolete matériel under the most favorable political and economic circumstances.

SOVIET ECONOMIC ASSISTANCE TO BLOC COUNTRIES

The first Soviet venture into the field of economic aid was in its relations with other countries of the Communist Bloc. This is too complicated a subject, even statistically, to be examined here in any detail. A rough indication of the magnitudes involved, however, is relevant to this study, for two reasons. First, in examining in a later chapter the capacity of the Soviet economy to extend aid, we shall want to know something about the amount of aid that has been given in the past. Second, there is reason to suppose that the Bloc countries may regard the underdeveloped countries as competitors for Soviet aid.

In his report to the Twentieth Party Congress on February 14, 1956, Khrushchev stated that the U.S.S.R. had granted a total of 21 billion rubles in long-term economic credits to the "peoples" democracies." [22] At the official rate of exchange, this amounts to the substantial sum of $5,250 million. Unfortunately, Khrushchev did not give the details of his figure, leaving to others the task of verifying the total. The most diligent efforts of the staff of the U.S. Department of Commerce, however, have succeeded in uncovering published records of credits amounting to only $1,772 million as of February 1956—and that only by including several short-term credits. A large part of the

[22] *Pravda*, February 15, 1956, p. 2. On July 14, 1957 *Pravda* reported that in the whole postwar period the U.S.S.R. had extended a total of 28 billion rubles in credits to the Bloc. This figure exceeds that quoted by Khrushchev in February 1956 by 7 billion rubles, or $1,750 million at the official rate, for credits after February 1956. The difference is roughly equal to that shown in Table 5.

discrepancy between Khrushchev's figure and the Department of Commerce tally (shown in Table 5) may be due to the inclusion in Khrushchev's total of the satellite debts to the U.S.S.R. incurred by the liquidation of some of the "joint companies" in late 1954. China alone would account for $1.4 billion of those debts, and Hungary $700 million. The meaning of Khrushchev's figure is thus too obscure to permit of further consideration. On the other hand, the Department of Commerce figure may well have omitted some Soviet credits actually extended but not made public —though it is doubtful that the Soviet Union would wish to conceal the fact of having given economic aid to its allies. With these considerations in view, we might judge the volume of Soviet aid to the Bloc between 1946 and 1955 to have amounted to about $2 billion or about $200 million a year. This is a gross figure, i.e., it does not take account of the considerable Soviet benefits extracted from the Bloc countries in such forms as war booty, reparations payments, profits of "joint companies," and Soviet-dictated prices in commercial trade, or the repayment of the credits.

Compared to the estimated credits to the Bloc, Soviet credit agreements with non-Communist countries in 1953 and 1954, shown in Table 3, were of insignificant size. But in 1955 the volume of Soviet credit agreements with non-Communist countries was approaching the average annual volume of credits to Bloc countries. And in 1956, new Soviet credit agreements with non-Communist countries were over four times as great as the average annual credits to other Bloc countries in the preceding decade. The picture is modified somewhat if we look, not at credit agreements signed, but at the rate of utilization of credits by non-Communist countries, as shown in Table 4. In 1955 and 1956, Soviet deliveries under credits to non-Communist countries were still well below the average annual deliveries to the other Bloc countries. But if the average annual rate of new credit to Bloc countries remained the same in 1957 as in the preceding decade, then in 1956 the Russians would have been extending as much aid to the non-Communist

TABLE 5

Soviet Credits and Cancelled Debts to Bloc Countries, 1946–1957

Country	*Date of Agreement*	*Amount (Million U. S. Dollars)*	*Brief Description*
I. Credits (before February 1956):			
Poland	Mar. 5, 1947	28.0	Short-term loan in gold and convertible currency.
Poland	Jan. 26, 1948	450.0	Credit to cover Soviet equipment.
Czechoslovakia	Dec. 1948	28.0	Short-term credit in gold and free exchange.
North Korea	Mar. 1949	40.0	Short-term credit for Soviet raw materials.
Albania	Apr. 1949		Unspecified credit for Soviet equipment.
Poland	June 1949	100.0	Credit to cover Soviet industrial equipment.
China	Feb. 14, 1950	300.0	Credit to cover Soviet industrial equipment (interest rate, 1 per cent).
East Germany	July 1953	121.0	Short-term credit for excess Soviet exports.
North Korea	Sept. 1953	250.0	Only known major grant; for postwar reconstruction.
Outer Mongolia	1945-55	225.0	Total credits for industrial development.
China	Oct. 12, 1954	130.0	Long-term credit for industrial equipment.
Vietnam		100.0	Credit for economic development.
Total of recorded items		1,772.0	
II. Credits (February 1956-May 1957):			
Bulgaria	Feb. 3, 1956	92.5	Credit for agricultural and industrial equipment from U.S.S.R.
China	Apr. 7, 1956	625.0	Credit to equip 55 Chinese plants.
Poland	Sept. 24, 1956	25.0	Partly in free exchange; partly in raw materials.

Hungary	Oct. 4, 1956	25.0	Free exchange, 40 per cent; raw materials, 60 per cent.
Poland, pt. I	Nov. 18, 1956	175.0	Credit for industrial equipment.
Poland, pt. II	Nov. 18, 1956	100.0	Credit for wheat (1.4 million tons).
Rumania	Dec. 3, 1956	67.5	Credit to cover Soviet machinery and grain.
East Germany	Jan. 7, 1957	85.0	Loan in free exchange to buy in world market.
East Germany	Jan. 7, 1957	20.0	Credit for Soviet equipment.
Bulgaria	Jan. 12, 1957	50.0	Credit to pay for Soviet wheat.
Czechoslovakia	Jan. 29, 1957		Credit to cover expansion of uranium mines.
Hungary, I	Mar. 28, 1957	187.5	Economic aid and payment assistance.
Hungary, II	Mar. 28, 1957	31.25	
Albania	Apr. 17, 1957	7.75	Credit to cover excess exports.
Outer Mongolia	May 15, 1957	50.0	Credit for future Soviet deliveries of equipment, materials and service.
Total of recorded items		1,541.5	
III. Cancelled Debts (post-1956):			
East Germany	July 1956	350.0	Reduced German share in occupation costs from $700 million to $350 million.
Poland	Nov. 18, 1956	525.0	Cancelled Polish debt in payment for full price on coal, 1946-1953.
Rumania	Dec. 3, 1956	700.0	Cancelled Rumanian debt for Soviet share in "joint companies."
Hungary	Mar. 28, 1957	90.0	Cancelled Hungarian debt in "joint companies."
Albania	Apr. 17, 1957	105.5	Cancelled debt for 14 industrial plants ($87 million) and for other goods ($18.5 million).
Total of cancelled debts		1,770.5	

Source: European Division, Department of Commerce, August 26, 1957; cited in *Congressional Record*, 85th Cong., 1st sess. (August 27, 1957), p. 14617. (Daily edition.)

underdeveloped countries as to their own Communist allies.

If it were a matter of a fixed-size Soviet pie to be divided between Communist and non-Communist countries, the former would have real cause to be concerned. In fact, however, the absolute amount of Soviet aid to the other Bloc countries has grown rapidly since 1955. In 1956 Poland and Hungary forced a loosening of the grip in which the U.S.S.R. had previously held its Communist allies. At least one consequence of the eruption was that the U.S.S.R. found it expedient to bail Eastern Europe out of an economic crisis, and to introduce a measure of persuasion and genuine negotiation into its relations with the Bloc. In 1956 and 1957 a series of new credit agreements were made with Communist countries, and in a number of cases oustanding debts were cancelled. Table 5 summarizes the agreements signed in that period. During the seventeen months following the Twentieth Party Congress, the Soviet Union extended $1,542 million in new credits to various countries of the Bloc, or roughly the same amount as that extended to the non-Communist underdeveloped countries. In addition, the U.S.S.R. cancelled a volume of debts amounting to $1,770 million. Many of these debts consisted of Soviet holdings in the "joint companies" acquired by seizure of former enemy assets in the Bloc countries. While the cancellation of these debts is not economic aid in the same sense as new credits, it does relieve the Bloc countries of a substantial volume of obligations to the U.S.S.R.

As part of their contribution to the Soviet aid program to underdeveloped countries, the other Bloc nations have extended about $350 million in credits. This amounts to about one-fifth of the gross direct credits they have received from the U.S.S.R. since February 1956; this sum of $350 million should therefore be deducted from the gross figure in order to arrive at the net direct aid of the Soviet Union to the Bloc. The other Bloc countries have also played a major role in the expansion of Bloc trade with underdeveloped countries, but this trade has probably been of commercial advantage to them. It is clear that the net increase in Soviet aid to its Bloc is substantial, and may be expected to dull the edge of any disgruntlement that Soviet extension of credits to non-Communist countries may have caused.

The principal reason for the increase in Soviet largesse to the Bloc countries is undoubtedly the turbulent events in Poland and Hungary in 1956. In the absence of this stimulus, it is doubtful that the U.S.S.R. would have undertaken so large an increase in aid to its allies merely to mollify their discontent over the aid program to non-Bloc countries. But the weakening of Soviet ability to dictate arbitrary terms to the Communist Bloc is now a fact and will continue to play a role in Soviet economic relations. In the future, if the aid program to non-Bloc countries should grow, it will be increasingly difficult to avoid a simultaneous increase in aid to Communist countries. Therefore, in considering the burden on the U.S.S.R. of the aid program to non-Bloc countries, one should properly take account of the secondary burden of increasing aid within the Soviet Bloc itself.

IV

SOVIET AID AND WESTERN AID

By the end of 1957 the Soviet Bloc had entered into aid agreements with the underdeveloped countries amounting to somewhat more than a billion and a half dollars. How big is a billion and a half dollars? The most relevant comparison is with the aid flowing to the underdeveloped countries in various forms from the wealthier countries of the free world. This includes United States government nonmilitary aid, contributions to the United Nations technical assistance programs, private investment, the lending program of the International Bank for Reconstruction and Development and aid extended by other countries of the free world.

The $60-odd billion in foreign aid that the United States government provided to the rest of the world between June 1945 and June 1957 can be subdivided in a number of ways. According to the periods, countries, and types of aid considered, one can find a number of answers to the question, "How large is Soviet aid compared to American aid?" It is not altogether obvious which basis of comparison is most enlightening or appropriate. Clearly one should exclude from the American account military aid, the European Recovery Program, assistance to Japan, and various other items. This still leaves a number of possible combinations, several of which are examined here.

We begin with United States nonmilitary aid to the sixteen countries that have received economic aid from the Soviet Bloc. The data presented in Table 6 for Soviet Bloc aid and American aid are dissimilar in two principal respects:

TABLE 6

Economic Aid by the Soviet Bloc and the United States Government to Sixteen Countries (millions of U. S. dollars)

	Soviet Bloc Credits 1953-1957[a]		*U. S. Government Aid Deliveries 1945-1957[a]*		
	Credit Agreements Signed	*Estimated Deliveries*	*Credits*	*Grants*	*Total*
Recipient	*A*	*B*	*C*	*D*	*E*
Yugoslavia	444	92	55	780	835
India	362	89	225	273	498
Egypt	213	17	24	64	88
Syria	184	6	*b*	1	1
Afghanistan	115	29	39	8	47
Indonesia	113	23	158	128	286
Ceylon	26	6	*b*	6	6
Cambodia	22	18	n.a.	83	83
Burma	22	7	5	21	26
Turkey	22	3	169	413	582
Argentina	21	21	102	*b*	102
Paraguay	15	15	4	11	15
Nepal	13	8	n.a.	6	6
Sudan	5	4	n.a.	*b*	*b*
Lebanon	2	2	*b*	22	22
Yemen	2	2	n.a.	n.a.	n.a
Totals	1,581	342	781	1,816	2,597

a Bloc data are for calendar years; U. S. data are for fiscal years ending June 30.

b Less than $500,000.

"n.a." signifies not available in the source. Actual figures are either zero or else so small that the countries are included in a residual category such as "Other and Unspecified South Asia."

Note: The U. S. figures show the actual disbursement of aid under credit and grant agreements, with no deduction made for repayment of credits during the period covered. Grants subsequently converted into credits appear under "grants" and not under "credits." In the terminology of the official U. S. aid reports, the two categories shown here are "new credits" and "gross grants."

Source: Appendix Tables E and F; and U. S. Department of Commerce, Office of Business Economics, *Foreign Grants and Credits by the United States Government*, June 1957 Quarter (Washington: Author, 1957), Tables 2, 3 and 6.

although both sets of figures cover the full period since the inception of the respective aid programs, the United States has been in the business for a much longer period; and the first column of figures (column A) consists of credit *agreements* signed by the Soviet Bloc, whereas all the United States data refer to the actual use of aid funds during the period covered. These figures are reported by the U. S. government; those for the use of Soviet Bloc aid (column B) are my estimates. (As in Chapter III, the *use* of aid will be referred to as "deliveries.") In spite of these differences, comparisons are of interest. By the end of 1957, the Bloc countries had signed credit agreements totaling $1.6 billion; estimated deliveries of aid amounted to about $340 million. With the exception of Chinese grants of about $56 million, all Bloc aid has taken the form of credits. Credits extended by the United States and used by the sixteen countries during the entire life of the postwar American aid program (up to the middle of 1957) amounted to something more than $780 million.[1] This is about half the total volume of Bloc agreements, and about double the volume of estimated Bloc deliveries.

The discussion of credits virtually exhausts the Bloc aid program but leaves the larger part of United States aid still unexplored. Column D of Table 6 shows that, in addition to credits, the United States has given more than $1.8 billion in nonrepayable grants to the sixteen countries. The total of United States grants and credits is about $2.6 billion, or more than seven times as much as Bloc aid actually delivered.

In a country-by-country comparison of Bloc and United States aid to the six largest signers of Bloc aid agreements, all but Syria had received more from the United States by mid-1957 than they had received from the Bloc by the end of the year. Yugoslavia, India and Indonesia had received from six to twelve times as much from the United States, and Egypt five times as much. Even Afghanistan had received half again as much from the United States as from the Bloc. Among the other countries, Turkey, Argentina,

[1] See note to Table 6 for a definition of these figures.

Burma, Cambodia and Lebanon received substantially more aid from the United States than from the Soviet Bloc; for Ceylon and Paraguay the figures are roughly equal; Nepal, Yemen and the Sudan may well have received more aid from the Soviet Bloc, although the American data are incomplete; and Syria has had far more aid from the Bloc. If we look not at deliveries but at agreements signed (column A), it is interesting to note that the two chief signers of Bloc aid agreements, Yugoslavia and India, had actually received from the United States more than the total of credits available from the Bloc. The same is true of Indonesia and some of the smaller countries, but not of Egypt, Syria and Afghanistan.

Thus, while the Bloc aid program has been in existence less than one-half as long as the United States program, it has provided its recipients by the end of 1957 with less than one-seventh the amount of aid they had received from the United States in the postwar period. If the comparison were widened to include all underdeveloped countries, the relative American contribution would be many times larger. The impact of the Soviet program, however, cannot be gauged solely by these relative magnitudes. For one thing, the size of Bloc deliveries as estimated in column B is rarely brought to public attention; most public discussion of the Soviet program concentrates on the Bloc's commitments, shown in column A, a practice which exaggerates its actual performance. For another, American aid has been spread over a longer period, a fact which calls for other comparisons.

Table 6, however, is a piece of economic history and covers a number of years in which there was no Soviet aid program. By contrast Table 7 compares the performance of the two aid programs in 1956 and 1957, with the Soviet program well under way. Here we find a rather different picture. While in 1956 estimated delivery of Bloc aid to the sixteen countries was still only about one-third of United States aid, in 1957 it amounted to nearly two-thirds of United States aid. The relative increase in Soviet aid was due in part to an absolute increase in estimated Soviet

TABLE 7

Soviet Bloc and United States Government Economic Aid Delivered to Recipients of Bloc Aid, 1956 and 1957 (millions of U. S. dollars)

	1956[a]				1957[a]			
	Soviet Bloc Credits	U.S. Grants and Credits			Soviet Bloc Credits	U.S. Grants and Credits		
Recipient		Total	Grants	Credits		Total	Grants	Credits
Yugoslavia	46	43	43	0	46	45	45	0
India	22	103	81	22	58	64	54	10
Egypt	6	29	29	0	10	13	7	6
Syria	1	*b*	*b*	n.a.	5	*b*	*b*	n.a.
Afghanistan	10	8	2	6	12	13	4	9
Indonesia	5	15	7	8	16	13	9	4
Ceylon	0	*b*	*b*	n.a.	6	6	6	n.a.
Cambodia	10	28	28	0	8	41	41	0
Burma	1	*b*	*b*	0	6	*b*	*b*	0
Turkey	1	112	87	25	1	98	82	16
Argentina	5	0	0	0	5	*b*	*b*	0
Paraguay	8	2	2	n.a.	0	2	2	n.a.
Nepal	3	1	1	n.a.	5	2	2	n.a.
Sudan	1	*b*	*b*	n.a.	3	n.a.	0	n.a.
Lebanon	1	4	4	n.a.	1	5	5	n.a.
Yemen	1	n.a.	n.a.	n.a.	1	n.a.	n.a.	n.a.
Totals	121	345	284	61	183	302	257	45

a Bloc data are for calendar years; U. S. data are for fiscal years ending June 30 of indicated year.

b Less than $500,000.

"n.a." signifies not available in source. Actual figures are either zero or else so small that the countries are included in a residual category such as "Other and Unspecified South Asia."

Note: For definition of terms used in this table, see note to Table 6, p. 57.

Sources: Appendix Tables E and F; and U. S. Department of Commerce, Office of Business Economics, *Foreign Grants and Credits by the United States Government*, June 1957 Quarter (Washington: Author, 1957), Tables 2 and 3.

deliveries, but nearly as much to the decline in American deliveries. In any case, Table 7 shows the momentum attained by the Soviet aid drive by 1957. In view of the large backlog of deliveries yet to be made under existing agreements, the rate may well rise in the next few years. However, if the rate at which new credit agreements are signed does not rise above the sharply decreased level of 1957, the rate of delivery will eventually begin to fall again.

In 1956 and 1957 estimated Bloc aid to the six principal receiving countries was 70 per cent of that of the United States. In India and Egypt, Bloc aid was much smaller than United States aid in 1956 but in 1957 it approached it in both. (U. S. aid to Egypt was virtually suspended after the Suez crisis.) Aid to Yugoslavia and Afghanistan from both sources was roughly equal both years. In Indonesia, Soviet Bloc deliveries may have drawn ahead of those from the United States in 1957, but the reader is reminded that these figures cannot be used with precision because those for Soviet deliveries are estimates and the comparison is between calendar and fiscal years.[2]

There is another category of United States aid for which there is no Soviet equivalent: assistance in the form of sales of agricultural commodities for local currencies.[3] Most of the local currencies obtained from such sales are later used to provide long-term loans or grants to the recipient countries, at which time they enter the statistics of government long-term credits and grants, as in Table 7. But between the time of receipt of the local currency in payment for the agricultural exports and the time the local currency is used for loans or grants, the United States has in effect granted a short-term loan to the recipient. The significant volume to which such short-term assistance had mounted in 1957 is shown in Table 8. Eleven of the sixteen countries that have accepted Bloc aid participated in this United States program in the 1957 fiscal year. They received from the United States $461 million in agricultural commodities, an amount equal to the sum of all Soviet Bloc and United States long-term aid in that year. Of the local currencies it received from these transactions, the United States used $44 million to extend long-term credits or grants or to cover various local administrative costs of United

[2] The estimates of deliveries of Soviet Bloc aid probably have a greater margin of error for individual countries than for aid as a whole.

[3] Under the Mutual Security Act of 1954 (Public Law 83-665) and the Agricultural Trade Development and Assistance Act (Public Law 83-480).

States personnel abroad. The balance of $417 million consists of short-term assistance, most of which will be used eventually for long-term aid. Among the eleven countries, the three largest recipients of short-term assistance, India, Yugoslavia and Indonesia (which together received $335 million of the total of $417 million), are also among the six largest recipients of Soviet Bloc aid.

One of the most significant facts shown by Tables 6, 7 and 8 is the relatively large role of nonrepayable grants in the United States aid program. In fiscal 1956 and 1957 between 80 and 90 per cent of all United States aid to the sixteen countries took this form. Soviet aid, in contrast, consisted almost exclusively of loans that will have to be repaid with interest. For rather curious reasons, to be dis-

TABLE 8

United States Government Short-Term Assistance from Sale of Agricultural Commodities, Fiscal 1957 (millions of dollars)

	Currency Claims Acquired Through Sales of Agricultural Commodities	*Use of Foreign Assets for Extending Long-Term Credits or Grants, or for U. S. Government Administrative Expenses*	*Net Short-Term Assistance*
Yugoslavia	110.1	20.1	90.0
India	175.9	4.5	171.4
Egypt	2.6	2.1	0.5
Afghanistan	3.9	0	3.9
Indonesia	74.1	0.5	73.6
Ceylon	0.9	0	0.9
Cambodia	0.9	2.1	-1.2
Burma	20.2	0.4	19.8
Turkey	64.4	11.6	52.8
Argentina	5.5	3.1	2.4
Paraguay	2.9	0	2.9
Totals	461.4	44.4	417.0

Source: U. S. Department of Commerce, Office of Business Economics, *Foreign Grants and Credits by the United States Government*, June 1957 Quarter (Washington: Author, 1957), Table 10.

cussed in Chapter VIII, the heavy reliance on grants, which would appear to be an act of generosity, may have hurt rather than helped the United States in its relations with underdeveloped countries, and partly for this reason the tendency of late has been to increase the share of loans in the United States program. But as of 1957 the ultimate impact of the United States aid program on the recipient countries was quite different from that of the Soviet Bloc because of the contrast in reliance on credits and grants. What the underdeveloped countries have received from the Soviet Bloc they have to pay for with interest. Most of what they have received from the United States government has been received as a gift. Since loans are repaid primarily with exports, a dollar of Soviet aid places a greater strain on the future foreign exchange-earning capacity of the recipient countries than does a dollar of United States aid. On the other hand, Soviet loans are used primarily for the construction of industrial installations, some of which may eventually increase the foreign exchange-earning capacity of the nation, either by the increased production of exportable commodities, or by increased domestic production of commodities that substitute for imports. In the United States program, installations of this kind are also usually financed by loans. Grant aid consists of agricultural and raw materials shipments, technical assistance, and some machinery products such as vehicles and agricultural equipment.

This aid is shown in Table 9, which presents the commodity distribution of deliveries under United States grants to Yugoslavia and India during the fiscal year 1956. About 80 per cent of the grant aid to Yugoslavia consisted of foodstuffs and raw materials of agricultural origin; and of the industrial commodities, machinery products consisted of a very minor proportion. In contrast, Soviet credits to Yugoslavia are to be used principally for the construction of nitrogen plants, power plants, an aluminum plant, etc. (A part of the Soviet credits, however, is to be used for raw materials imports from the U.S.S.R.) In the case of India, about 80 per cent of United States grants was used for the purchase of industrial commodities, and about 55 per cent of the total consisted of machinery products. But of the latter, the largest proportion consisted of railroad equipment and motor vehicles and engines, much less of industrial machinery to be installed in factories. Soviet credits to India, on the other hand, are to be used primarily for the construction of such projects as the steel mill, petroleum extraction and refining installations, fertilizer plants, etc.

The difference between Soviet and United States aid is not in fact as sharp as the preceding paragraph might suggest. Some Soviet credits to Yugoslavia have financed raw materials imports from the U.S.S.R.; and, apart from the grants mentioned above, United States credits to India are used for industrial and public works projects. Moreover the form in which aid is imported does not measure its contribution to economic development; United States aid in the form of wheat frees India to import machinery from other countries. The full comparison must also take account of the larger total volume of United States aid, as well as the preponderance of free grants rather than repayable credits. But whatever the economic merits of the two aid programs, the Soviet program may well enjoy a psychological advantage that is out of proportion to its economic contribution. The factories and engineering structures that dominate the Soviet program are long-lasting and imposing monuments; whereas the foodstuffs and raw materials in the United States program disappear in the production process and lose their identity. The factories continue to produce tangible goods, whereas the benefits of improved health and agricultural technique are not as readily apparent to the eye.

The discussion thus far has been confined to a comparison of Soviet Bloc and United States government aid to the sixteen countries that have accepted Soviet aid. For a different perspective on the relative size of the Bloc program, it may be compared with total United States government economic aid to all underdeveloped countries, as presented in Table 10. In twelve years the United States government

TABLE 9

Commodity Distribution of United States Government Grants[a] to Yugoslavia and India, Fiscal 1956 (thousands of U. S. dollars)

Commodity	*Yugoslavia*		*India*	
Food, Feed and Fertilizer	16,499		15,362	
Bread Grains		15,143		12,047
Fats and Oils		1,357		—
Fertilizer				3,315
Fuel (coal)	5,138		—	
Raw Materials and Semi-finished Products	12,959		17,715	
Cotton		8,083		264
Iron and Steel Products		65		13,000
Chemicals		173		4,343
Wool, unmfd.		4,116		—
Machinery and Vehicles	189		41,155	
Machinery & Equipment		189		8,943
Motor Vehicles & Engines		—		3,099
Railroad Equipment				29,028
Miscellaneous	—		1,371	
Commodity Total	34,786		75,603	
Food & Agricultural Commodities		28,699		15,626
Industrial Commodities		6,086		59,976

a Includes both "project" and "non-project" expenditures for India; all expenditures for Yugoslavia were "non-project."

Source: International Cooperation Administration, *Operations Report*, Data as of June 30, 1956 (Washington: Author, 1956), pp. 42-50.

extended a total of $12.8 billion, about eight times the amount of aid pledged by the Soviet Bloc in the four years since the inception of its aid program. Of the United States total, $3.2 billion consisted of credits, about twice the volume of Soviet credits pledged since 1953. Three-quarters of the United States aid consisted of grants, for which there is no Bloc counterpart except for a number of small items. In fiscal 1957 alone, the United States delivered to the underdeveloped countries about $1.6 billion in aid, or just about the total pledged thus far by the Soviet Bloc. Under credit arrangements the United States delivered in 1957 $286 million compared to the $160-$200 estimated for the Bloc (Table 4); in addition the United States delivered $1.3 billion in nonrepayable grants.

While it is important to note that, on the global basis discussed above, United States aid is considerably greater than Soviet Bloc aid, this fact is not decisive. Equally significant is the distribution of aid among the recipient nations, particularly among the so-called "uncommitted" nations. United States aid to the American republics, for instance, has little immediate bearing on the success of the Soviet aid program, which is concentrated elsewhere. A large proportion of United States government economic aid takes the form of "defense support" to countries that receive United States military assistance. "Defense support" consists of economic aid designed to "provide the supplemental economic resources required if the participating countries are to carry out adequate defense efforts and sustain minimum economic growth." [4] In fiscal 1956, of a total of $763 million expended for economic aid in the Far East, $724 million consisted of "defense support," principally in Korea, Taiwan and Vietnam. Of the $449 million expended in the Near East, Africa and South Asia, $287 million consisted of "defense support," principally in Turkey and Pakistan.[5] Economic aid to the American republics and "defense support" are vital adjuncts to United States foreign policy. But while they contribute to the global preponderance of United States aid over Soviet, one must not lose sight of the fact that a large proportion of that aid goes to nations already "committed" in some sense to the West. If total United States aid is larger, it is also spread over a great many more countries, and therefore the impact of Soviet aid in those countries where it is concentrated may be substantial.

In addition to bilateral governmental economic programs,

[4] International Cooperation Administration, *Operations Report,* Data as of June 30, 1956 (Washington: Author, 1956), p. 5.

[5] Same, pp. 29-30.

TABLE 10

United States Government Economic Aid: Grants and Credits to Underdeveloped Countries since Inception of Foreign Aid Program and in 1957 (millions of U. S. dollars)

Recipient	*Since End of World War II (July 1, 1945-June 30, 1957)*			*1957 (July 1, 1956-June 30, 1957)*		
	Total	*Grants*	*Credits*	*Total*	*Grants*	*Credits*
Yugoslavia	835	780	55	45	45	0
Near East and Africa[a]	3,404	2,668	736	343	275	68
South Asia	915	584	331	145	120	25
Other Asia and Pacific[b]	5,706	5,083	623	847	807	40
American Republics	1,945	460	1,485	248	95	153
Totals	12,805	9,575	3,230	1,628	1,342	286

a Including Greece and Turkey and excluding Union of South Africa.
b Excluding Japan.
Source: U. S. Department of Commerce, Office of Business Economics, *Foreign Grants and Credits by the United States Government*, June 1957 Quarter (Washington: Author, 1957), Table 2.

the United States and the U.S.S.R. have engaged in other forms of aid. It was noted earlier that the Soviet Bloc countries have pledged about $6.5 million to the United Nations expanded program of technical assistance in the years since 1953 when they began participating. Of the total, the U.S.S.R. contributed about $5.7 million. During the same five years (1953-1957) the United States government pledged $72 million. In 1957 the Soviet Bloc pledged $1.4 million, the United States $15.5 million.[6] These figures do not include contributions to other regular technical as-

[6] Stuart Rice Associates, Inc., *Foreign Aid Activities of Other Free Nations*, in *Foreign Aid Program*, Senate Doc. no. 52, 85th Cong., 1st sess. (Washington: GPO, 1957), pp. 1155-1156; Robert Loring Allen, "United Nations Technical Assistance: Soviet and East European Participation," *International Organization*, v. 11, no. 4 (Autumn 1957), p. 620; International Cooperation Administration, *Operations Report*, Data as of June 30, 1956, cited, p. 7.

sistance activities, such as those of the Food and Agriculture Organization, the World Health Organization and the UN Children's Fund. In these, too, the United States share is substantially larger than that of the Soviet Bloc.

In looking to a totalitarian nation for economic aid, an underdeveloped country can deal only with the government of that nation. In looking to nations with private market-type economies, it can deal with two potential sources of aid: the government, and private citizens and institutions. Therefore, in considering the contribution of the United States toward the economic development of foreign countries, we must take account of private foreign investment.[7] To be sure, private investment differs in many ways from government aid—not least in the attitudes of many underdeveloped countries toward it—but it clearly plays a very important part in the process of economic development. Table 11 summarizes the results of a special Department of Commerce study on long-term investment in underdeveloped countries in 1956.[8] This shows that net foreign investment amounted to about $1.3 billion, of which direct

[7] Lack of data prevents the inclusion of the substantial contributions made in recent years by American educational and religious organizations, in addition to the work of foundations, such as the Ford and Rockefeller Foundations, in the underdeveloped countries.

[8] Net foreign investment is defined here as the sum of net capital outflow to United States-owned companies abroad, plus undistributed earnings of those companies, plus net portfolio investment in foreign securities. There is room for argument about this or any other measure of private investment, especially if one is concerned with its contribution to economic development. For instance, "net portfolio investment" does not necessarily register a flow of new capital since the securities may have been bought from owners in third countries or the issues may have been outstanding for a long time. However, portfolio investment is a small proportion of the total. A larger difference would appear if one measured gross investment (ignoring the return flow of interest, dividends, etc.) on the ground that it is the new spending that contributes to economic growth. Furthermore, it has been argued recently that the concept of net foreign private investment understates the full amount of capital expenditures in foreign countries by United States firms abroad. In particular, it fails to take account of outlays on plant and equipment, increases in inventories, and exploration and development expenses, part of which are charged against income and therefore not reflected in earnings. See Samuel Pizer and Frederick Cutler, "The Role of U. S. Investment in the Latin American Economy," *Survey of Current Business*, U. S. Department of Commerce, v. 37 (January

TABLE 11

United States Long-Term Net Private Capital Investments in Underdeveloped Countries, 1956 (millions of dollars)

	Latin American Republics	*West European Dependencies*	*Other Underdeveloped Countries*	*Total*
Direct Investments				
Net Capital Outflow	612	35	160[a]	807
Undistributed Subsidiary Earnings	212	45	76[a]	333
Total	824	80	236	1,140
Portfolio Investments[b]	67	—	61[c]	128
Grand Total	891	80	297	1,268

a Obtained by eliminating Australia, Japan, New Zealand and the Union of South Africa from row labeled "other countries, total," on p. 25 of source.

b Change between 1955 and 1956 in the sum of the rows labeled "foreign dollar bonds," "other foreign securities" and "other," on p. 23 of source.

c Includes certain countries not normally considered underdeveloped, such as those named in footnote a.

Source: Samuel Pizer and Frederick Cutler, "Record Growth of Foreign Investments," *Survey of Current Business* (U. S. Department of Commerce), v. 37 (August 1957), pp. 23, 25.

investment in United States-owned companies abroad accounted for about 90 per cent. Thus, investment in underdeveloped countries by private United States persons and companies in 1956 alone was equal to about 80 per cent of the total volume of all credit agreements signed by Soviet Bloc governments since the inception of their aid

1957), pp. 6-15; and Emilio G. Collado and Jack F. Bennett, "Private Investment and Economic Development," *Foreign Affairs*, v. 35, no. 4 (July 1957), pp. 631-645.

program. However, 75 per cent of United States private investment went to Latin America and European dependencies, leaving only 25 per cent for areas of the world where the Soviet aid program is concentrated.

Turning from the United States contributions to economic development to those made by the rest of the world, we must assign a major role to the International Bank for Reconstruction and Development. No Soviet Bloc countries are members of the Bank or have provided any of the capital with which it operates. The funds that the Bank lends come principally from the capital subscriptions of member governments and the sale of the Bank's own bonds on the capital markets of the world. Thus the International Bank serves as an institution for channeling private and governmental funds from the wealthier non-Communist countries of the world to the underdeveloped countries. Like Soviet Bloc loans, the International Bank's loans are used for the purchase of machinery and for capital construction projects that become the property of the governments or citizens of the recipient countries. In receiving a Soviet loan, the recipient must ordinarily purchase the equipment and technical construction services from the U.S.S.R.; in receiving an International Bank loan, the recipient is free to choose the country and contractor that will supply the equipment and undertake the construction.

Table 12 summarizes the International Bank's lending activity in the underdeveloped countries from its establishment through fiscal year 1957. The volume of loans extended (but not necessarily fully utilized by June 30, 1957) is just about equal to the volume of loan agreements entered into by the Soviet Bloc. In fiscal 1957 $184 million of new loans were extended to underdeveloped countries, about 75 per cent of which went to countries outside the Western Hemisphere. Thus the Bank's lending activity is greatest in the same areas of the world in which the Soviet aid program is concentrated (but not necessarily in the same countries). Actual disbursements on loans in 1957 amounted to $332 million, of which about $200 million went to underdeveloped countries.[9] This is the same order of magnitude as the estimated utilization of Soviet Bloc credits in 1957 (Table 4). Thus in volume, character, and broad geographical distribution, the aid extended by the International Bank is roughly equivalent to that of the Soviet Bloc.

The final major sources of economic aid to underdeveloped countries are the other economically developed countries of the world. Through bilateral grants and loans, through international agencies such as the United Nations technical assistance programs, and through regional organizations such as the Colombo Plan and the South Pacific

TABLE 12

Loans to Underdeveloped Countries by the International Bank for Reconstruction and Development, 1947-1957 and 1957
(millions of U. S. dollars)

Recipients	*1947-1957*[a]	*1957*[a]
Africa[b]	231.4	19.8
Asia and Middle East[c]	559.5	113.8
Yugoslavia	60.7	0
American Republics	678.4	50.1
Total	1,530.0	183.7

a Fiscal years, ending on June 30 of years indicated
b Excluding the Union of South Africa.
c Excluding Japan and including Turkey.
Source: International Bank for Reconstruction and Development, *Twelfth Annual Report, 1956-1957* (Washington: Author, 1957), pp. 27-45.

Commission, the developed nations have contributed economic and technical aid to the underdeveloped countries. A detailed study prepared under the direction of the United States Senate Special Committee to Study the Foreign Aid

[9] International Bank for Reconstruction and Development, *Twelfth Annual Report, 1956-1957* (Washington: Author, 1957), p. 11. The proportion of total disbursements to underdeveloped countries was assumed to equal the ratio of loans to underdeveloped countries ($1,530 million as in Table 12) to total development loans ($2,528 million as in source, p. 16).

TABLE 13

Soviet Bloc and Free World Economic Aid to Underdeveloped Countries, 1957[a]

(millions of U. S. dollars)

Soviet Bloc			*Free World*		
Estimated Soviet Bloc aid disbursed to sixteen recipient countries.[b]		160–200	U. S. government aid disbursed to sixteen countries that are receiving Soviet Bloc aid.[d]		292
1. Credits[c]	140–180		1. Credits	35	
2. Grants[c]	20		2. Grants	257	
Soviet Bloc contributions to UN technical assistance program.		1.4	U. S. government aid disbursed to all other underdeveloped countries.[e]		1,336
			1. Credits	251	
			2. Grants	1,085	
			U. S. government short-term assistance under P. L. 480.[f]		417
			U. S. contribution to UN technical assistance program.[g]		15.5
			U. S. private net investment.[h]		1,268
			International Bank for Reconstruction and Development, disbursements on loans.[i]		200
			Governmental aid by other free world countries.[j]		750
			Private net investment from other countries.[k]		510-610
Total, rounded		160–200	Total, rounded		4,800–4,900

NOTES AND SOURCES:

a Soviet Bloc data are for the calendar year 1957. Free world data are for the fiscal year 1957 (July 1, 1956-June 30, 1957) except U. S. contribution to UN program (calendar 1957), U. S. private investment (calendar 1956), governmental aid by other free world (estimated calendar 1957), and private net investment by other countries (estimated calendar 1957).

b Table 4.

c Grants consist of deliveries under the Chinese grants to Cambodia, Nepal, Ceylon and Egypt (Appendix Table F) plus $2-$3 million annual expenditures under the bilateral technical assistance projects (estimated in the text at about $5-$10 million over several years). These two items are estimated in the table at roughly $20 million. Credits constitute the balance.

d Table 7.

e Data in Table 10, minus data in Table 7.

f Table 8.

g United Nations, *Annual Report of the Technical Assistance Board for 1956,* Economic and Social Council, *Official Records: Twenty-fourth Session,* Supplement no. 5 (New York: Author, May 1957), p. 86.

h Investments in 1957 are assumed to have been the same as in 1956, as shown in Table 11.

i International Bank for Reconstruction and Development, *Twelfth Annual Report, 1956-1957* (Washington: Author, 1957).

j The 1952-1955 annual average of $800 million is assumed to have been maintained in 1957.

k The 1955 volume of investment of $510-$610 million is assumed to have been maintained in 1957.

Program estimated that in the four-year period, 1952-1955, governmental economic and technical assistance provided through these channels amounted to $2.9 billion or about $750 million per year.[10] Estimates of private investment in underdeveloped countries are extremely difficult to make and subject to a margin of error of as much as 50 per cent. Most studies, however, place net foreign private investment by Western Europe in the underdeveloped countries at $500-$600 million in 1955; and by Canada at about $10 million.[11]

This completes the recital of the main sources of economic aid to underdeveloped countries. The discussion cries for a summary tabulation, which is presented with misgivings. Summaries are frequently perilous; too many essential qualifications are lost track of and what results is too often only a sharply focused distortion. The tabulation in Table 13 does indeed show that Soviet Bloc aid is a mere trickle compared with the flow of economic aid of various kinds from the free world to the underdeveloped countries. Even if some of our roughest estimates are in error by 100 per cent or more, this conclusion would not be greatly altered. The data are a sharp reminder of the

[10] *Foreign Aid Activities of Other Free Nations,* cited, p. 1070. The figure excludes subscriptions to the capital of the International Bank for Reconstruction and Development, which has already been treated separately.

[11] Same, p. 1071.

strength of the economic bonds that tie the economies of the underdeveloped to the Western nations. Many of these economic relationships, some with deep historic roots, have so blended in with the normal day-to-day economic activity of the nations that they no longer attract attention. The fate of the familiar, however important its contribution, is that it tends to be taken for granted. It is understandable that the surpassing importance of free world economic aid is sometimes lost sight of in the glare of the new and highly publicized Soviet aid program. The data further show that talk of Soviet aid supplanting Western aid on a broad scale is nonsense. It is amply clear that on a global basis the Soviet Bloc has a long way to go before its aid amounts to a substantial proportion of Western aid, and one can hardly consider seriously the possibility that Soviet Bloc economic aid might approach the total volume of Western aid in the foreseeable future.

These are important statements and must be made. But there are equally important elements of comparison that do not emerge from an examination of Table 13. The geographical distribution is missing, and we have noted that Soviet aid is heavily concentrated in a few countries. If there is no possibility of Soviet aid rivaling Western on a worldwide basis, there remains the possibility that it may equal or surpass Western aid in individual countries and regions. It may already have done so in a few cases. The table deals with the single year 1957. It fails to reflect the fact that Soviet Bloc aid is growing at a more rapid annual rate than American aid. Our estimates in Table 4 suggest that in 1957 Soviet Bloc aid was about 60 per cent greater than in 1956, and may well rise sharply again in 1958. Perhaps most important is the fact that by directing attention to quantitative comparisons, the table diverts attention from other vital differences. A dollar's worth of one kind of aid does not at all have the same economic, political or psychological impact as a dollar's worth of another kind of aid. A petroleum refinery in India built and operated by a United States firm has a very different impact from an identical refinery built by the U.S.S.R. and owned and operated by

Indians. A million-dollar gift of wheat is soon consumed; a million-dollar factory is a long-standing monument. A United States grant presented over the malediction of an articulate, isolationist Congressman enjoys a different reception from a Soviet gift presented with the unanimous approval of the Soviet press and officialdom. The story of Table 13 must be read with these differences in mind.

V

THE EXPANSION OF COMMERCIAL TRADE

All the underdeveloped countries are familiar with the products of Western technology. The cars in their streets, the trains on their railroads, the machinery on their farms and the ships in their harbors are visible evidence of the know-how of the West. The Soviet Union enters the business of exporting technology with a reputation for technological progress, but the people of the underdeveloped countries have little direct acquaintance with its products. To remedy the deficiency, the U.S.S.R. has undertaken an intense advertising campaign, consisting primarily of lavish participation in trade fairs.

Since 1953 the U.S.S.R. and various Bloc countries have lost few opportunities to exhibit in trade fairs held in underdeveloped countries. The Soviet pavilion is often the most elaborate of any country, and is well stocked with a display of industrial wares designed to impress the population of the underdeveloped countries with Soviet industrial prowess. The noneconomic facet of these exhibitions is revealed in the fact that the Bloc countries usually insist on displaying their commodities in their own pavilions, rather than placing each product alongside similar ones from other countries, as is the normal practice. Bloc exhibitions include noncommercial attractions such as displays showing their achievements at home, television cameras in operation, working models of great industrial installations in the U.S.S.R. Pamphlets are distributed and speeches made, explaining Soviet foreign policy, and urging the importance of peaceful coexistence, the removal of Western trade embargoes, etc.[1] The Russians withdrew from participation in the International Trade Fair in Bangkok in 1954 because the Thai authorities would not permit them to bring along a circus and a ballet corps.[2] Among the other Bloc countries, Czechoslovakia has been a most conspicuous exhibitor. At the Djakarta Fair in 1955, the Czech exhibit was reported to have been almost three times the size of the United States display.[3]

It is an axiom of Soviet Marxist philosophy that there is no such thing as a purely economic act. Every economic act has political implications. The political aspects of the trade fair program are fairly clear. Soviet published accounts of their exhibitions often report the attendance in the millions. Large numbers of simple people in the underdeveloped countries, and many not so simple, visit the spectacular Soviet Bloc pavilions and are impressed with the complex industrial commodities that the Communist world is able to produce. Nations that produce such wares are to be respected; one would be ill-advised to incur their enmity by joining the other camp of the world. One should take advantage of their expressed willingness to help the underdeveloped countries since the displays leave no doubt of their ability to contribute substantially to economic improvement.

The purpose of trade fairs is to provide a central location where potential customers can meet with potential sellers from other countries and examine their goods. When Bloc countries began to exhibit in trade fairs about 1951, there was some question about the amount of trade they really wished to engage in. There were cases in which Bloc exhibitors were unable or reluctant to supply information on prices, delivery schedules, spare parts and other terms.

[1] International Cooperation Administration, *Survey of East-West Trade in 1955*, Eighth Report to Congress on Operations under the Mutual Defense Assistance Control Act of 1951 (Washington: Author, 1956), p. 17.

[2] U. S. Senate, Subcommittee on Technical Assistance Programs, *Soviet Technical Assistance*, 84th Cong., 2d sess., Staff Study no. 7 (Washington: GPO, 1956), p. 39.

[3] *Survey of East-West Trade in 1955*, cited, p. 20.

It seemed that they were not prepared to accept orders for the commodities they exhibited.[4] Around 1955, however, the situation changed. A number of large orders were taken at trade fairs and discussions were held concerning future negotiations. The expansion of trade had become an active part of the new policy of increased economic relations with underdeveloped countries.

Soviet pronouncements represent the offers of increased trade as an integral part of the policy of assisting in the promotion of economic development. Since the resources for economic growth must come primarily from within the underdeveloped countries themselves, the advanced countries can merely assist the process in various ways, one of which is the sale of machinery and capital goods in exchange for raw materials. Thus ordinary commercial trade is put under the heading of "aid" to economic development. The leading capitalist countries, runs the Soviet argument, wish to keep the poorer countries of the world in a state of underdevelopment, to serve as "raw material appendages" to their own economies, and as markets for their consumer goods surpluses. They do not wish to sell capital goods with which the underdeveloped countries might establish their own factories and industrialize their economies. The Soviet Bloc members, on the other hand, having only peaceful objectives, wish sincerely to help the underdeveloped countries industrialize and therefore stand willing to sell capital equipment and machinery in return for raw materials.

We may dismiss as propaganda the U.S.S.R.'s insistence on including commercial trade as part of its "economic aid" to underdeveloped countries. But we cannot dismiss the fact that its efforts to promote commercial trade are prosecuted just as vigorously as its efforts to promote its credit program. What, we might ask, has the one to do with the other? Are they two separable components of Soviet economic policy, so that one could conceivably be pursued in the absence of the other, or does one depend for its effectiveness upon the other? Since the credit program gives

[4] Same, p. 17.

rise first to Soviet exports and then to Soviet imports purchased with the currencies received in repayment of the loans, the two components cannot be entirely separated. Moreover, aid and trade are more closely related in the Soviet than in the United States programs, for the Soviet Union does not face the same problems of absorbing imports as does the United States. But these considerations alone do not explain why the Soviet policymakers place so much stress on the expansion of trade. Presumably they expect that expanded trade has a contribution of its own to make toward the attainment of their objectives.

Trade helps destroy the old image of the U.S.S.R. as the isolated and withdrawn agent of revolution, and reinforces the new image of the peaceful and benevolent supporter of the aspirations of the underdeveloped countries. The credit program alone would scarcely be convincing testimony of the change in Soviet policy if the U.S.S.R. continued to remain self-insulated from the commercial intercourse of nations. Moreover, the existence of substantial trade makes it easier for the Soviet Union to be on the spot when there are political gains to be exploited, as in the Icelandic fish or the Burmese rice situations. It is perhaps too much to expect that any but a few countries could be made so dependent upon Soviet trade as to be vulnerable to pressure on major political issues. Still, even lesser dependence provides a degree of influence, so long as the trade is substantial. The inertia of established trade relations may well make a country reluctant to hunt for new markets or sources of supply. When there is a world market for a product, as in the case of some raw materials, the exporter may not be in great danger of becoming dependent on a single buyer. But if demand is slack, the loss of an established customer can be serious; some of the principal trade overtures the Soviet Union has made have been to countries with raw materials surpluses on their hands. Where industrial commodities are involved, particularly machinery products with their long-term demand for replacement parts, a change of supplier can also involve great disturbance. Or when an exporter's industry has been geared to the import market of a particular nation, the loss of that market could cause considerable distress. In these and other ways, the expansion of trade moves in the same direction as the provision of aid to expand Soviet influence in the underdeveloped countries. Just as in the case of aid, however (see pp. 166, 167, 178 ff), one cannot estimate in advance how much influence might be obtained in this fashion, much less how it may be used.

The promise of expanded commercial trade with non-Communist countries stands in sharp contrast to Soviet economic policy of the last few decades. Trade with the capitalist world has traditionally been viewed as a potential danger to the U.S.S.R. The dependence upon other countries implied in trade might make the U.S.S.R. subject to outside pressures which could undermine its sovereignty. Reliance on imports might weaken the nation's ability to defend itself in war. Pursuing these notions of autarky, the Soviet government reduced its trade with the world to negligible proportions in the years preceding World War II.

In the postwar years, the Russians permitted a departure from the traditional policy of autarky only in their greatly expanded trade with the other countries within the Communist Bloc—which still fell short of creating a serious dependence on imports. In 1950, 81 per cent of all Soviet foreign trade was conducted with countries within its own political orbit.[5] But the policy of autarky continued to prevail with respect to the rest of the world, and indeed was imposed on the other countries of the Bloc as well. The measure of autarky is sharply reflected in world trade statistics. As shown in Table 14, Russian imports in 1950 accounted for 2.3 per cent of total world imports. Imports from the non-Communist world, however, amounted to less than one per cent of world imports. Since that time total Soviet imports have grown somewhat faster than world imports, reaching a level of 3.4 per cent in 1956.

[5] V. Zolotarev, "Torgovye sviazi Sovetskogo Soiuza s sotsialisticheskimi stranami" (U.S.S.R. Trade Relations with Socialist Countries), *Vneshniaia torgovlia*, no. 11 (1957), p. 46.

But Soviet imports from countries outside its own Bloc have still not reached one per cent of total world imports. Thus the policy of trade expansion with underdeveloped countries began from an extremely small base of foreign trade.

SOVIET BLOC TRADE WITH UNDERDEVELOPED COUNTRIES

Soviet foreign trade is conducted under agreements in which the signatory governments say they will strive for stipulated levels of imports and exports. The agreements usually specify the commodities to be exchanged and often involve special barter and payments arrangements. The policy of expanding trade began with the signing of a considerable number of such agreements; the success of the policy is sometimes measured by the number of agreements signed and the amount of trade they provide for. This is misleading, however. The trade agreements merely signify intentions, and there is no assurance that the trade will actually reach the specified level.

Soviet trade agreements have been aptly dubbed "hunting licenses." They provide a formal framework within which Soviet purchasing missions may strive to sell to or buy from private companies or the government of the partner country. But the volume of trade that materializes depends on whether the commodities offered or desired meet the requirements of the trading partner, and whether satisfactory terms, such as price and delivery, can be arrived at. In numerous cases, actual trade has fallen far short of the volume stipulated in the highly publicized trade agreements. A well-known illustration is the series of barter agreements Burma had signed with a number of Bloc countries, calling for the export of up to 750,000 tons of rice annually. The agreements were announced with great fanfare and created a wide impression of a great expansion in Burmese trade with the Bloc. As it turned out, Burma signed contracts with Bloc countries in 1956 for the delivery of less than 500,000 tons of rice, and in fact shipped less than 300,000 tons. In 1957 both the amounts agreed upon and the deliveries were considerably reduced. Several reasons are given

TABLE 14

Soviet Imports in Relation to World Imports, 1950, 1955 and 1956

	1950	*1955*	*1956*
	(million current U.S. dollars)		
Total world imports	62,900	96,800	106,700
Soviet imports from East European Bloc	1,136	2,399	2,692
Soviet imports from non-Bloc countries	320	662	921
	(percentage of world imports)		
Soviet imports from East European Bloc	1.8	2.5	2.5
Soviet imports from non-Bloc countries	.5	.7	.9
Total Soviet imports	2.3	3.2	3.4

Source: United Nations, Economic Commission for Europe, *Economic Survey of Europe in 1957* (Geneva: Author, 1958), Chapter VI, p. 2.

for the cooling of Burma's originally keen interest in barter trade. By tying up its chief foreign exchange-earning export in long-term barter agreements, Burma lost potential cash customers at a time when world rice prices had begun to rise. Moreover, it was unable to find a sufficient volume of Soviet goods of acceptable quality and at reasonable prices to equal the value of the rice already shipped. As a result, Burma became an unwilling creditor to the Bloc by an amount estimated at $11 million toward the end of 1956. Only China exported more to Burma than it imported under the barter agreement.[6]

This is not an isolated instance. Indonesia is reported to have soured on its barter trade agreement with Bloc countries to the extent that the Soviet Union offered to pay in sterling.[7] Argentina, the first Latin American country to sign a large trade agreement with the U.S.S.R., was reported in 1957 to have accumulated $50 million in Bloc currencies.

[6] *The New York Times*, January 6, 1957.
[7] Same, August 21, 1956.

Faced now with an acute shortage of convertible foreign exchange, it has offered to resell the $50 million at a 40 per cent discount, in return for hard currencies or for United States coal.[8]

As these examples show, the number of trade agreements signed by the U.S.S.R., and the amount of trade mentioned when the agreements are negotiated, may be very misleading. The impressions they create may be important politically and psychologically, but, to appraise the economic significance of the Soviet program, one must look at the volume of trade that actually takes place. This is not as easy as it should be. Complete data on the trade of the Soviet Bloc with the underdeveloped countries are available at the time of writing only for the period through 1956. The Soviet government does not publish comprehensive trade statistics by countries so the analysis must be based on the statistics published by countries that trade with the U.S.S.R. These have been compiled by the U. S. Department of Commerce[9] and are set out in some detail in Appendix C for 23 underdeveloped countries. These 23 include all that have developed any appreciable amount of trade with Bloc countries except for Afghanistan, which unfortunately does not publish foreign trade statistics. The original sources are the governments of the countries involved and we must bear in mind that some of the underdeveloped countries lack the trained personnel, the resources or the traditions of statistical accuracy of the older countries of Europe and North America. One must also take account of the possibility that the countries involved may have political reasons for disguising the actual magnitude of their trade with the Soviet Bloc, perhaps for fear of offending pro-Western elements at home or jeopardizing their political and economic relations with the West. In addition,

[8] Same, August 27, 1957. For a statistical treatment and discussion of trade agreements and actual trade with Middle Eastern countries, see Robert Loring Allen, *Middle Eastern Economic Relations with the Soviet Union, Eastern Europe, and Mainland China* (Charlottesville: University of Virginia Press, 1958), Chapter 3.

[9] And converted from local currencies to U. S. dollars at the rates of exchange registered with the International Monetary Fund.

many of the barter transactions may remain unreported.[10]

On the basis of these figures, Chart 1 summarizes Soviet Bloc trade with the 23 underdeveloped countries over the past decade. Between 1948 and 1953 the value of Soviet trade with these countries fell by two-thirds and that of the European satellites fell by almost a half. The sharp fall was the combined result of the implementation of Stalin's autarkic views and of the tightened strategic trade controls introduced by the United States and its allies since 1951.[11] The year 1953 was the low point, and is therefore the base from which it is useful to measure the subsequent effect of the policy of expanded trade. By 1955 the trade of the U.S.S.R. and the European Bloc with the underdeveloped countries was more than two and a half times the 1953 levels. Soviet trade, however, had not yet regained the 1948 level, whereas the trade of the other European Bloc countries was well above the 1948 levels. This relationship would not be materially changed if account were taken of the rise in world prices that occurred between 1948 and 1955; in real terms, Soviet trade would be even further behind the 1948 level, and the advance of the European Bloc countries somewhat less than indicated.

In 1956 both Soviet and other European Bloc imports from the underdeveloped countries remained at about the same level as 1955. Exports from the European satellites fell off slightly, reflecting the turbulent events in Hungary and Poland in the second half of the year. Only U.S.S.R. exports advanced sharply, to almost double the 1955 value, reflecting perhaps the increasing size of the Soviet credit program.[12] The trade of Communist China with the under-

[10] Allen, *Middle Eastern Economic Relations . . .*, cited, p. 17.

[11] Oleg Hoeffding, "Recent Trends in Soviet Foreign Trade," *The Annals of the American Academy of Political and Social Science*, v. 303 (January 1956), pp. 75, 83.

[12] A Soviet source reports that in 1956 total trade turnover (exports plus imports) with the countries of Southeast Asia and the Near East was 47 per cent greater than in 1955. The data in our Chart 1 show an increase of about 40 per cent for the 23 underdeveloped countries. If we allow for the fact that the coverage is different for the two sets of data, the results are fairly consistent with each other. See V. Azov and D. Fokin, "Razvitie vneshnei torgovli SSSR v 1956 godu" (Development of Soviet Foreign Trade in 1956), *Vneshniaia torgovlia*, no. 11 (1957), p. 36.

CHART I

SOVIET BLOC TRADE WITH TWENTY-THREE UNDERDEVELOPED COUNTRIES, 1948, 1953, 1955, 1956

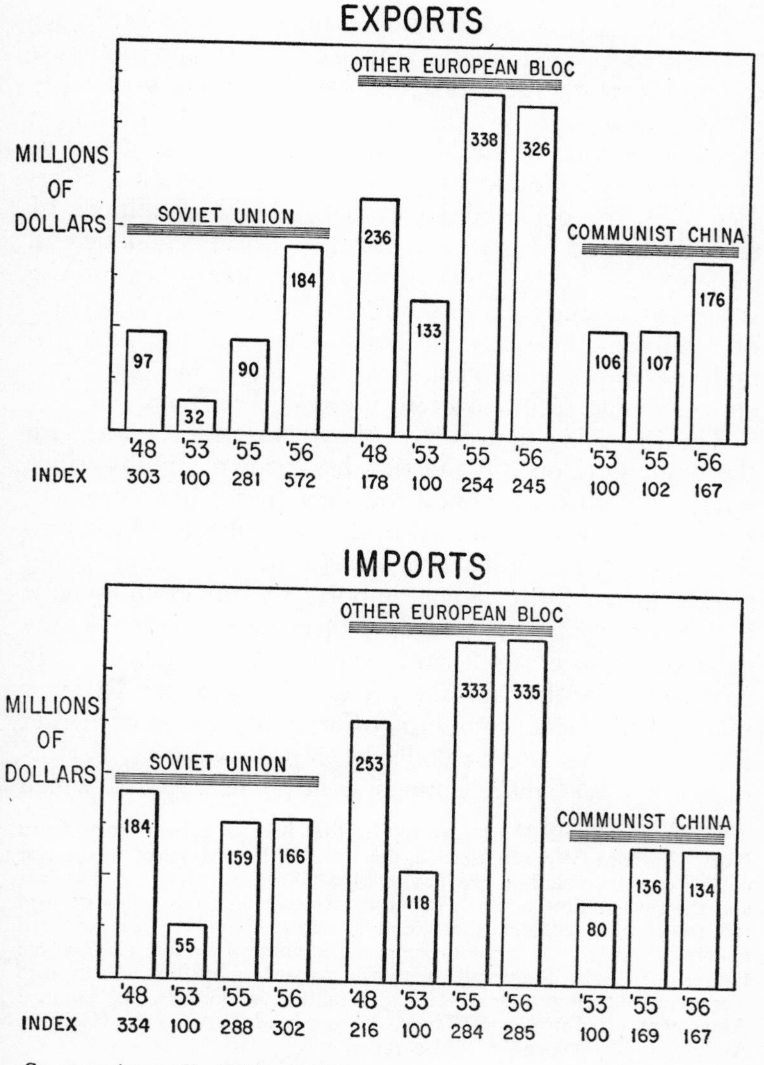

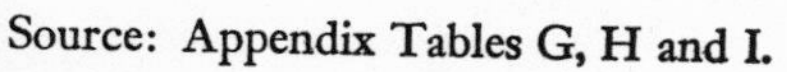
Source: Appendix Tables G, H and I.

developed countries has been least affected by the new Soviet policy. Imports remained stable in 1956, while exports advanced considerably. Preliminary and incomplete data for 1957 indicate that Bloc trade with the underdeveloped countries has continued to increase, but it is impossible to indicate the extent at this writing.[13]

To illuminate fully the importance of trade with the Soviet Bloc for the underdeveloped countries, and to discuss the prospects for the future, one would have to go far beyond the simple review of changes in the total trade presented here. One would have to look, country by country, into resources, production, complementarity with the Soviet Bloc, the commodities exchanged, the conditions of trade and terms of payment, and into world economic and trade trends. An endeavor of this magnitude is beyond the scope of this study. Here the aim is only to trace the course of total trade between the Soviet Bloc and the principal underdeveloped countries, since the aim of the policy we are examining seems to be to increase that trade.

The foregoing figures have shown that Bloc trade with the underdeveloped countries has grown rapidly since 1953, when the new policy was introduced. In this respect the policy has been successful. But we must avoid the predilection of the impulsive statistician for extrapolating trends. In the case of Soviet imports, the threefold increase between 1953 and 1956 has done little more than recoup the ground lost after 1948, and even that has not been fully achieved. The data do not yet establish that the Russians will redeem their promise of offering a great new market for the exports of the underdeveloped countries. Performance has been more impressive in Soviet exports, which

[13] From the first half of 1953 to the first half of 1956, exports from North America, Western Europe, the British Isles and Japan to the rest of the world (excluding the Soviet Bloc) increased about 30 per cent and the reverse flow of trade about 11 per cent. For the whole of 1956 this trade came to about $22 billion in exports from the industrialized countries and $20.7 billion moving in the opposite direction. Comparable figures for Soviet Bloc trade with the underdeveloped world in 1956 were $1.0 billion in exports and $911 million in imports. See General Agreement on Tariffs and Trade, *International Trade 1956* (Geneva: Author, 1957), Appendix Tables 1 and 2.

have surpassed the 1948 level in current prices. In real terms, Soviet exports in 1956 may have been about half again as great as in 1948. The data prove nothing about future trade, but they do indicate that as of 1957 the program has been far from spectacular.

In the discussion of the credit program, it was found that the U.S.S.R. accounted for the bulk of the credits extended by the Bloc. The relationship is reversed in the case of commercial trade. The trade of the U.S.S.R. with the underdeveloped countries is scarcely greater than that of China. It is about half that of the other European Bloc nations. To the extent that trade is a vital element in the Soviet aid program, the U.S.S.R. is heavily dependent on her allies for its success. The predominance of the other Bloc countries has certain advantages for the U.S.S.R. because they seem to be better traders than the Russians. The Chinese derive considerable advantage from the commercial experience and contacts of overseas Chinese who often serve as trade representatives of the Peiping government. Many of the East European countries have a longer and richer foreign trading tradition, and therefore operate more effectively than the Russians. The gusto with which the Bloc countries have supported the trade aspect of the Soviet aid program suggests that increased trade is very much to their liking. At the least, it reduces the degree of their dependence on trade with the U.S.S.R. and with each other. As the economies of Bloc countries become adapted to increased trade with underdeveloped countries, it may well become more difficult to halt that trade if Moscow should wish to do so in the future.

THE RELATIVE IMPORTANCE TO THE BLOC OF TRADE WITH THE UNDERDEVELOPED AND THE ADVANCED COUNTRIES

The U.S.S.R. represents its desire to trade as evidence of its good intentions and of its wish for "peaceful coexistence." It has aimed, therefore, to expand trade, not only with the underdeveloped countries, but with the rest of the non-Communist world as well. Is the increase in trade with the underdeveloped countries merely a by-product of the general policy of trade expansion, or have the underdeveloped countries been singled out for special emphasis?

Table 15 traces the changing role of trade with the underdeveloped countries as a proportion of total Bloc trade with the rest of the world. Between 1948 and 1953, Bloc exports to and imports from the 23 underdeveloped countries fell sharply as a percentage of their total exports and imports. For the U.S.S.R. this fall was sharper than for the East European countries. By 1955, the underdeveloped countries had regained their 1948 share in the extra-Bloc trade of the Bloc as a whole,[14] although the U.S.S.R.

TABLE 15

Soviet Bloc Trade with the Underdeveloped Countries as a Percentage of Trade with the Whole Non-Bloc World, 1948, 1953-1957

	Exports					Imports				
	1948	*1953*	*1955*	*1956*	*1957*	*1948*	*1953*	*1955*	*1956*	*1957*
	Per cent					*Per cent*				
U.S.S.R.	20	8	15	23	22	35	13	26	21	37
Other European Bloc Countries	22	16	26	22	22	28	17	29	25	26
China	—	24	22	28	27	—	28	43	31	36

Source: 1948 and 1953-1956 from Appendix Tables G, H, I; 1957 based on preliminary and incomplete data for January-June, in U. S. Bureau of Foreign Commerce, "Exports and Imports of Free World Countries to Soviet Bloc, January-June 1957" (mimeographed).

[14] Communist China is included in the 1955 figures but not in those for 1948. Chinese trade is complicated by the role of Hong Kong. China's exports to Hong Kong are about equal to its exports to all the underdeveloped countries. In view of the diligence with which the mainland Chinese government has been courting the favor of the Overseas Chinese communities, it is reasonable to assume that most of China's mounting exports of consumer goods to South Asia are exported through Overseas Chinese merchants, rather than through Hong Kong. The Hong Kong trade, in that case, would consist primarily of exports to other portions of the world. China's imports from Hong Kong have been falling rapidly since 1953, signifying, perhaps, that the Chinese are buying larger proportions of their imports directly from the producing countries. The omission of Hong Kong from the list of underdeveloped countries probably does not affect our results substantially.

continued to lag behind the rest. The most interesting observation is that, in 1956 and the first half of 1957, the underdeveloped countries showed no significant relative increase in the exports and imports of the Bloc over the 1955 level. The absolute volume of underdeveloped country trade with the Bloc rose as Bloc trade with the free world rose, but there has been no redirection of Bloc trade toward the underdeveloped countries. The data suggest that at best the new Soviet policy has succeeded in raising the proportion of trade with underdeveloped countries to the 1948 level.

How important is trade with underdeveloped countries to the economies of the Bloc countries? Table 15 shows that this trade is 20-30 per cent of Bloc trade with the whole non-Bloc world. But it must be remembered that Bloc trade with the non-Bloc world is small compared with trade among the Bloc countries themselves. For example, in 1955 and 1956 U.S.S.R. trade with the non-Bloc world amounted to 20 per cent and 24 per cent of its total trade.[15] In those years U.S.S.R. trade with the underdeveloped countries accounted for 15 per cent to 26 per cent of its trade with the whole non-Bloc world (Table 15). Thus, trade with the underdeveloped countries accounted for 3-6 per cent of total Soviet foreign trade. (The proportions would be greater for the other Bloc countries.) That this proportion is extremely small may be seen by comparison with United States foreign trade. If we define the underdeveloped countries as all the countries of Africa (excluding the Union of South Africa), Asia and Oceania (excluding Japan, Australia and New Guinea), and Latin America, the United States sold 31 per cent of all its exports to those countries in 1956, and bought 45 per cent of all its imports from them. If we omit all of Latin America from the definition of underdeveloped countries, the figures would still be 12 per cent and 16 per cent for United States exports and imports.[16] It is clear that the underdeveloped countries play a much less important role

[15] Zolotarev, cited, p. 46.

[16] U. S. Department of Commerce, *Business Statistics, 1957 Biennial Edition* (Washington: GPO, 1957), pp. 104-109.

in Soviet foreign trade—and therefore in the whole Soviet economy—than they do in the economy of the United States.

Two possibilities are suggested by this fact. The first is that Soviet trade with the underdeveloped countries might reasonably undergo a considerable increase in the future. If the United States finds it economical to conduct one-fourth to one-third of its foreign trade with the underdeveloped countries, the figure of about 5 per cent for the U.S.S.R. is surely extremely small. There is, of course, no certainty on this point. A detailed resource and commodity analysis of the economic systems of the U.S.S.R. and the underdeveloped countries might bring to light significant reasons why increased trade would not offer large gains. But if it were assumed that the U.S.S.R. had discarded its policy of autarky and were to trade on the basis of the principles of international specialization of labor, it is reasonable to expect that Soviet trade with the underdeveloped countries would expand greatly. That trade might not grow as large, relative to total trade, as that of the United States, but one would expect it to exceed greatly the present level of 5 per cent. By the beginning of 1957, however, despite the promise of expanded trade with the underdeveloped countries, the trade had come nowhere near the level that one might guess to be economically advantageous for the U.S.S.R.

The second possibility is that, since the relatively small size of Soviet trade with the underdeveloped countries probably means that the Soviet economy is not greatly dependent on the commodities involved, the U.S.S.R. is in a good position to use that trade for political purposes. If, for example, the Soviet Union were a heavy importer of a certain commodity, it would be more difficult for it to terminate such imports for political reasons. Of course, it is possible that a commodity imported in small quantities may nevertheless be of great importance to the importer. Moreover, a small total volume of trade could be of vital importance to the importer if that trade consisted of large imports of one or two essential commodities. But, by and large, it would seem that the small volume of trade permits the U.S.S.R. considerable maneuverability in using its trade for political purposes when that is in its interest.

It might appear that if the U.S.S.R. is successful in its objective of expanding trade with underdeveloped countries it would lose the maneuverability it presently enjoys precisely because of the small size of that trade. It is unlikely that trade is expected to grow to such magnitudes. In the case of most of the underdeveloped countries, the U.S.S.R. will always enjoy the advantage of a large trader dealing with a smaller. Even with a considerable expansion of trade, the U.S.S.R. will always enjoy the advantage of the large trader dealing with the smaller underdeveloped countries taken singly.

ROLE OF SOVIET BLOC IN TOTAL TRADE OF UNDERDEVELOPED COUNTRIES

The effective use of trade for political advantage, however, depends not only on the importance of that trade to the U.S.S.R., but also on its importance to the trading partner country. The next question is: How important a place does Soviet Bloc trade occupy in the total trade of the underdeveloped countries? Table 16 shows that in 1956, of all the underdeveloped countries, seven shipped 10 per cent or more of their total exports to the Soviet Bloc, and six bought 10 per cent or more of their imports from the Bloc.[17] Only three sold more than 10 per cent

[17] Iceland and Finland sold 30 per cent and 27.3 per cent of their total exports to the Bloc, but they are outside the geographical area with which this study is primarily concerned. Afghanistan does not publish systematic data on its foreign trade, but it did report that, in the fiscal years 1955 and 1956, 18.8 per cent and 19.1 per cent of its exports went to the U.S.S.R. This included 84 per cent, 58 per cent and 100 per cent of its exports of wool, cotton and oilseeds. See United Nations, Economic Commission for Asia and the Far East, *Economic Survey of Asia and the Far East, 1956* (Bangkok: Author, 1957), p. 61. A later source gives figures that are not consistent with the foregoing, but which show a rise in Afghan trade with the U.S.S.R. From fiscal 1956 to fiscal 1957, Afghan imports from the U.S.S.R. rose from 29 per cent to 36 per cent of total imports, and exports rose from 14 per cent to 28 per cent. International Monetary Fund, *International Financial News Survey*, v. 10, no. 29 (January 31, 1958), p. 233. Thus Afghanistan should be included among the countries with the largest proportion of trade with the U.S.S.R.

of their exports to the U.S.S.R. alone, and only two obtained more than 10 per cent of their imports from the U.S.S.R. Of those that carried on 10 per cent or more of their trade with the Bloc in 1956, only Afghanistan, Egypt and Yugoslavia reached the 20 per cent mark. Only Afghanistan carried on as much as 20 per cent of its trade with the U.S.S.R. alone.

Preliminary data for the first half of 1957 show that the Bloc increased its position as a market for underdeveloped

TABLE 16

Underdeveloped Countries Carrying on More than Ten Per Cent of Their Foreign Trade with the U.S.S.R. and the Soviet Bloc, 1956

U.S.S.R.'s share of national foreign trade			
Exports	*Per cent*	*Imports*	*Per cent*
Afghanistan	14.0	Afghanistan	29.0
Iran	13.7	Yugoslavia	14.9
Yugoslavia	13.0		
Soviet Bloc's share of national foreign trade			
Exports	*Per cent*	*Imports*	*Per cent*
Egypt	34.4	Yugoslavia	23.0
Yugoslavia	24.1	Burma	18.7
Turkey	19.7	Turkey	14.6
Burma	18.6	Egypt	14.4
Iran	16.7	Iran	10.0
Ceylon	10.6	Afghanistan	at least 29.0
Afghanistan	at least 14.0		

SOURCE: Appendix Table J and International Monetary Fund, *International Financial News Survey*, v. 10, no. 29 (January 31, 1958), p. 233. The figures for Afghanistan, which come from the latter source, refer to fiscal 1956 and cash trade with the U.S.S.R. only. As footnote 17 indicates, Afghanistan reported to ECAFE that the U.S.S.R. took 19.1 per cent of its exports in fiscal 1956.

country exports. Two more countries entered the ranks of those shipping more than 10 per cent of their exports to the Bloc, Syria (22 per cent) and Ghana (13 per cent); Egypt and Iran increased their percentages to 49 per cent and 27 per cent, while Burma (in the first quarter) reduced its to 10 per cent. Egypt and Ghana also surpassed the 10 per cent level in their exports to the U.S.S.R. (21 per cent and 13 per cent), while Iran increased its to 20 per cent. But while the Bloc was taking relatively more of the underdeveloped country exports, it did not register a significant advance in supplying the imports of the underdeveloped countries. While Egypt's imports from the Bloc rose to 29 per cent of its total imports, Burma's fell to 7 per cent. And while Egypt's imports from the U.S.S.R. rose to 15 per cent of its total imports, Yugoslavia's fell to 9 per cent. So far as one can judge from the evidence of these few years, the Soviet Bloc's ability to absorb the export surpluses of the underdeveloped countries may prove to be a more effective basis of expanded trade than its ability to supply their import needs.

What do these figures mean? It is not possible, of course, to determine exactly what level of trade would make a country "dependent" on the Soviet Bloc, certainly not with a single percentage figure. Still, broadly speaking, one could reasonably suppose that a country with 10 per cent of its trade with the Soviet Bloc was not dangerously exposed to pressure, except in unusual circumstances. But 20 per cent or more begins to look like an appreciable amount of leverage for the Soviet Bloc, provided it retains its maneuverability and can effectively manipulate the trade. The meaning of these figures, however, depends on how the bargaining power is being used, what ulterior "price" is being asked for continuing the trade, what alternative markets or supplies are available abroad, what degree of adjustment would be involved at home and how well the country can stand it, economically and politically. There is probably a difference, too, between being dependent on export outlets and on sources of imports; other differences result from the character of the goods involved and the degree of concentration on a few key products, especially export surpluses. The obverse of the figures already presented helps give additional perspective.

One of the most striking impressions conveyed by these

data is that of the overwhelming importance of the free world in the foreign trade of the underdeveloped countries. As markets for their exports and as sources of imports, the Soviet Bloc has scarcely made an impact on the underdeveloped countries as a group. In the case of most countries on which an appreciable impact has been made, it is not the U.S.S.R. as much as the other Bloc countries that account for the larger part of the trade. This again underscores the importance of Russia's Communist allies to the success of the trade aspect of the Soviet aid program.

For the underdeveloped countries as a group, Soviet Bloc trade can be expected to make a positive though distinctly marginal contribution. But even a manifold increase in that trade would not alter the fact that the economic future of those countries will continue to be interwoven with the trade of the free world. It is conceivable that Bloc trade may virtually take over the entire trade of a few of the smaller countries. But it is clear that, for the group of underdeveloped countries as a whole, the possibility is too remote to be seriously entertained. However, each country will have to evaluate the increase in Bloc trade in terms of the impact on the rest of its trade. Suppose, for example, that the expansion of a country's trade with the Bloc should place the latter in a position to make demands that would jeopardize that country's trade with the free world. The potential loss of some of the benefits of a relatively large volume of trade with the free world might well exceed the gains from a relatively small volume of trade with the Bloc. A large Western customer of long standing is not lightly to be given up for a smaller Soviet customer recently arrived. If the latter proves to be an unreliable trading partner, the country may find that the old Western customer has found himself a new source of supply and cannot easily be persuaded to return.[18] In the same way

[18] Egypt's experience with Soviet cotton purchases is one of the first illustrations of this possibility. In 1955 and 1956 the Soviet Union offered premium prices for Egyptian cotton, thus bidding up the price to a point that caused other customers to take their trade elsewhere. Western Europe, which took over half of Egypt's cotton in 1953, took less than 30 per cent in 1956. The Egyptians have expressed concern over the

the figures suggest that the free world countries, if they consider it important, are well placed to provide reasonable alternatives for the trade of underdeveloped countries.

An earlier chapter noted that the credit program was remarkable, not so much for its total size, as for the degree of concentration in a few countries. Table 16 suggests that the same statement may be made about the commercial trade program. The degree of concentration may be revealed in another way, by examining the distribution of Bloc trade among the underdeveloped countries. Chart 2 shows that in 1956 five countries accounted for 55 per cent and 58 per cent of total Bloc exports and imports to underdeveloped countries, and 92 per cent and 70 per cent of total U.S.S.R. exports and imports to underdeveloped countries. These were not always the same five; seven countries were involved in all. Yugoslavia, Egypt and India appear in the top group in all four sets of trade relations. Four of the seven (including Egypt and Yugoslavia) are also countries that conduct more than 10 per cent of their trade with the Bloc. Reverting to what was said above about shares of trade and potential dependence, we would emphasize here, not the extent to which these countries are subject to Soviet Bloc pressure,[19] but rather the extent to which the trade program, like the credit program, is noteworthy less for its general size or the large number of countries affected than for its sharp focus on a relatively few countries.

[19] Yugoslavia is clearly a special case, in which trade is unlikely to be the major determinant of "dependence"; for Turkey and Iran, too, political considerations go beyond the trade factor; in the case of India, Malaya and Argentina, their appearance in the top five in Bloc trade is not matched by marked prominence of the Bloc's share of their trade.

---

loss of their old customers, and attribute the loss to high Soviet prices. The U.S.S.R. is thus getting a taste of some of the unanticipated ill will that can come of what was intended to be a gesture of generosity. Allen, *Middle Eastern Economic Relations* . . . , cited, p. 22.

Chart 2

DISTRIBUTION OF SOVIET BLOC TRADE AMONG UNDERDEVELOPED COUNTRIES, 1956

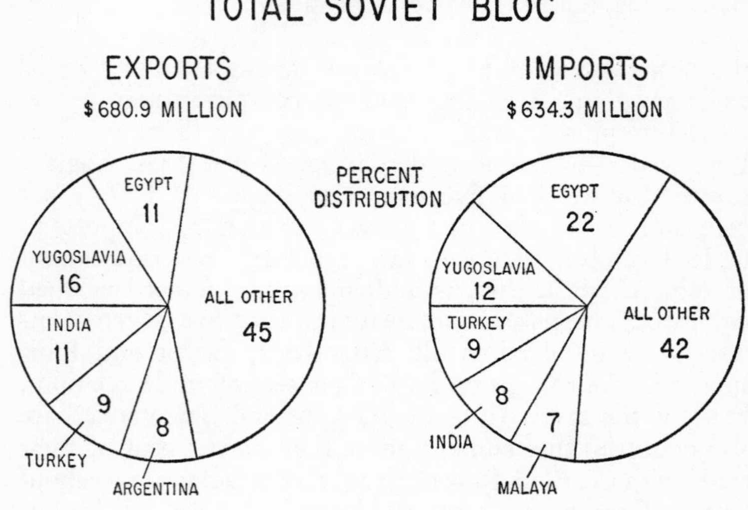

U.S.S.R.

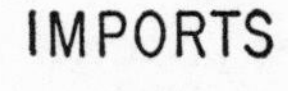

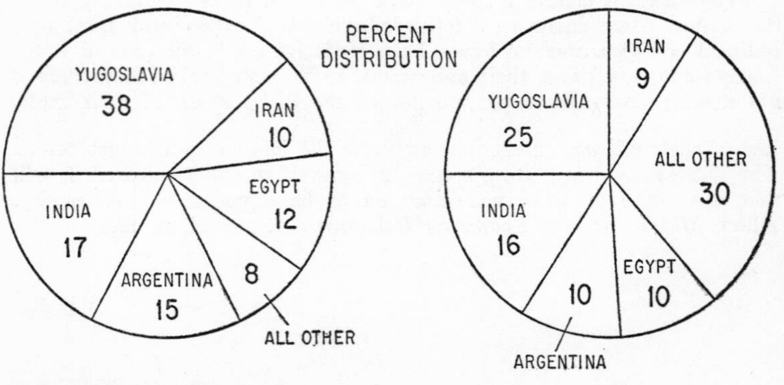

Source: Appendix Table J.

VI

SOVIET CAPACITY TO EXTEND ECONOMIC AID

THE WORLD has learned to respect the industrial achievements of the U.S.S.R. A generation ago, that country was numbered among the underdeveloped countries. Today it is the second mightiest industrial power in the world. Despite the rapid rate of growth, however, Soviet industrial production is still far smaller than that of the United States. Moreover, in view of the oft-repeated objective of "overtaking and surpassing" the United States, it would seem that the Russians can make good use of every ton of steel and every machine they produce. Can they afford to ship these valuable industrial commodities to other countries for the sake of some other advantage? And what of the people who have only lately begun to see some amelioration of a standard of living that scarcely rose at all during Stalin's lifetime? Can a nation with so sharp a need for more housing and more consumer goods be expected to divert much of its resources to helping other countries?

We cannot know what price the Soviet leaders will be willing to pay for whatever advantages they hope to gain from their aid program. But we can try to obtain some sense of what the price is at present, and what it would be if the aid program should be expanded in the future. By comparing the size of the aid program with the size of Soviet economy, we may hope to assess how much of a drain, if any, the aid program is on the economic system.[1]

[1] Although the other Bloc countries have contributed substantially to the Soviet program of aid to underdeveloped countries, this chapter measures the burden of aid against the economy of the Soviet Union

Because of the complexity of the task, we shall begin the analysis by making a drastic, simplifying assumption. The assumption is that every machine and every engineer sent to an underdeveloped country make the Soviet economy just so much poorer. In other words, the annual production of goods and services in the U.S.S.R. is viewed as a pie of fixed size, and any part of the pie shipped abroad means that that much less is available for use within the nation. On this assumption, most of this chapter is devoted to an attempt to determine what the Soviet Union would have to give up if it expanded exports under the credit program by various amounts.

The merit of this assumption is that it provides us with an upper-limit measure of the drain of foreign aid at various levels. In the short run, for example, the Soviet Union's capacity for building steel mill equipment is fairly limited, and any of the current production shipped abroad is so much equipment that will not be installed in new domestic steel mills. In the longer run, however, the U.S.S.R. may expand its productive capacity in certain lines beyond that needed to supply internal needs. Then it may be able to produce all it requires for internal use and still have a surplus available for shipment abroad. Moreover, commercial exports are paid for in imports, and even in the short run the value lost from exports is offset by the value of imports (and more than offset if it is assumed that a nation trades only if it gains thereby). In the case of the credit program, the same consideration applies, although the offsetting imports are deferred for a number of years. For present purposes imports are ignored, until the very end of the chapter. How they may offset the cost of exports is examined in the next chapter. Here the aim is to estimate the gross cost to the Soviet economy of exporting capital goods to underdeveloped countries on credit and thus to

alone. The difficulties of obtaining comparable data for all the Bloc countries and of presenting them in manageable form make this course advisable. It can also be argued that the aid given by other Bloc countries is more than offset by the economic assistance which they receive from the Soviet Union.

form an idea of the Soviet Union's ability to expand its aid program.

THE SIZE OF THE SOVIET NATIONAL PRODUCT

The Soviet government unfortunately does not publish detailed statistics on the size and composition of its national production. It does, however, publish selected financial and production statistics on various sectors of the economy which permit us to develop some gross and approximate measures of resource allocation.

A recent study of the Soviet national product, which was undertaken by the Legislative Reference Service of the Library of Congress in consultation with a number of eminent specialists, estimates the Soviet gross national product in 1955 to have been about 1,090 billion rubles.[2]

[2] U. S. Congress, Joint Economic Committee, *Soviet Economic Growth: A Comparison with the United States*, by the Legislative Reference Service of the Library of Congress, 85th Cong., 1st sess. (Washington: GPO, 1957).

The report does not actually state the total, but we are told that consumption, which accounted for 57 per cent of the gross national product (p. 127), amounted to 620 billion rubles in 1955 (p. 108 fn.). These figures indicate a gross national product of 1,090 billion rubles.

The Economic Commission for Europe has also published an estimate of U.S.S.R. gross national product in 1955. Its total is 1,100 billion rubles, The ECE method differs from that employed in the American study primarily in two quantitatively significant ways:

(1) No attempt was made to eliminate turnover taxes (242 billion rubles) or add subsidies. For this reason the ECE estimate should be about 200 billion rubles larger than the Library of Congress estimate.

(2) Following accepted GNP accounting conventions, the ECE valued agricultural production at prices actually paid to farm producers. Since a large part of agricultural production is purchased by the Soviet government at extremely low prices, it is likely that the ECE procedure understates the real value of agricultural production, although there is no good way of determining what the real value is. The ECE study also fails to include an item for imputed rent of owner-occupied dwellings, which it estimates to have been something less than 20 billion rubles.

The first point of difference tends to make the ECE estimate larger than that of the Library of Congress; the second tends to make it smaller. If the ECE data were adjusted according to the method of the Library of Congress study, the results would probably be fairly close to each other. The ECE study thus increases the confidence that may be placed in the figures employed in the text.

See United Nations, Economic Commission for Europe, *Economic Bulletin for Europe*, v. 9, no. 1 (May 1957), pp. 89-107.

The estimate is based on 1953 Soviet prices, adjusted to bring them into closer accord with factor costs.[3]

As a very rough estimate we may assume that the Soviet national product increased about 6 per cent between 1955 and 1956. Applying this to the figure given above, the 1956 gross national product would be about 1,150 billion rubles. If we make certain crude assumptions about the way in which this increase was distributed among the components of the national product,[4] and allow for a substantial margin of error, the 1956 Soviet gross national product and its major components are as follows:

Gross national product: 1,100-1,200 billion rubles, of which:

Consumption: 630-670 billion rubles
Gross investment: 310-340 billion rubles
National security: 150-170 billion rubles.

These figures are presented with no pretense at precision, but only as a benchmark against which to form some judgment of the relative size of foreign trade and aid.

SOVIET FOREIGN TRADE AND NATIONAL PRODUCT

How does the volume of foreign trade compare with the size of the national product? The total foreign trade turnover of the U.S.S.R. (imports plus exports) is officially

[3] The major adjustments required by this "factor cost standard" of measuring Soviet national income and product are (1) elimination of indirect sales (turnover) taxes, (2) additions of subsidies, and (3) correction for multiple pricing of farm products. See *Soviet Economic Growth: A Comparison with the United States*, cited, p. 130. Since the general price level fell somewhat between 1953 and 1955, the figure would be somewhat smaller if calculated at 1955 prices.

[4] The Library of Congress study yields the following estimates for 1955: consumption, 57 per cent, or 620 billion rubles; gross investment, 26.9 per cent, or 293 billion rubles; national security, 14.2 per cent, or 153 billion rubles; and government administration, 1.9 per cent, or 21 billion rubles. Our rough assumptions of the increases in 1956 are as follows: consumption, 30 billion rubles, or about 5 per cent; gross investment, 30 billion rubles, or about 10 per cent; national security (in view of the Hungarian and Suez crises), 5 billion rubles, or about 3 per cent. See *Soviet Economic Growth: A Comparison with the United States*, cited, p. 127.

reported to have amounted to 29.1 billion rubles in 1956.[5] Thus, the value of foreign trade is equivalent to about 2.5 per cent of the gross national product.[6] By comparison, total exports and imports of the United States in 1956 amounted to $31.5 billion, or about 7.5 per cent of the gross national product ($414.7 billion).[7]

What is interesting about these figures is not that the Soviet percentage is so low, as one would expect, but that it is so high relative to the United States. Here are two countries, quite similar in certain important ways; both have large continental land areas, and both are well endowed with natural resources to the point of potential self-sufficiency. One is a capitalist country that engages in relatively free trade by modern standards; yet its trade amounts to only 7.5 per cent of its national product. The other is a Communist country, traditionally committed to a policy of self-imposed economic isolation from a putatively hostile capitalist encirclement. One would guess that the foreign trade of this country would be a much smaller percentage of its national product than the foreign trade of the former. Yet it turns out to be at least one-third as large.

This comparison indicates something about the limits that might be relevant to expectations of the potential increase in Soviet foreign trade if all trade restrictions were removed. Large nations that have major agricultural, industrial and mineral resources do not engage in trade to the same extent as smaller nations. Even if the U.S.S.R. renounced its devotion to autarky and began to buy in

[5] V. Azov and D. Fokin, "Razvitie vneshnei torgovli SSSR v 1956 godu" (Development of Soviet Foreign Trade in 1956), *Vneshniaia torgovlia*, no. 11 (1957), p. 35.

[6] Soviet foreign trade figures are based on world market prices of its exports and imports converted to rubles at the official exchange rate of 4 rubles to the dollar. This exchange rate probably understates the value at which the traded commodities enter the national accounts. If foreign trade were valued at the real domestic prices of the traded commodities (net of turnover taxes and subsidies), foreign trade might prove to be larger than 2.5 per cent of the national product.

[7] U. S. Department of Commerce, *Business Statistics: 1957 Biennial Edition* (Washington: GPO, 1957), pp. 3, 104-108.

the cheapest markets, at least to the extent that the United States does today, perhaps we ought not to expect much more than a tripling or quadrupling of its foreign trade.[8] If Soviet trade with the non-Bloc world should reach four times the 1956 level, it would still amount only to about $6-$7 billion. This is about the value of the foreign trade of the Netherlands in 1956, and about one-fifth the total trade of the United States (imports plus exports).

The focus of interest at this point, however, is not total Soviet trade, but trade with the underdeveloped countries. Our objective is to gain some insight into the impact on the Soviet economy of a considerable expansion of exports to the underdeveloped countries, without a corresponding increase in imports for several years. We might start, then, by estimating the importance of such exports in 1956. As Table 17 shows, Soviet exports to all underdeveloped countries amounted to insignificant percentages of the principal components of the national product. For example, if defense expenditures were decreased by one-half of one per cent, and an equivalent volume of resources redirected into exports to the underdeveloped countries, the total volume of exports to the underdeveloped countries would be more than double the 1956 level. Thus, in purely quantitative terms, exports to the underdeveloped countries, it would seem, could be greatly expanded without having a perceptible impact on the various uses of the national product.

The same statement cannot be made about exports to the other countries in the Soviet orbit. These exports amounted in value to 1-2 per cent of total consumption and 6-7 per cent of defense expenditures. Any appreciable expansion of exports on long-term credit to the other Com-

[8] If this hypothetical liberalization of trade were also accompanied by removal of political considerations which affect the direction of trade, we might further expect a relative increase in the *proportion* of trade with the non-Communist world, at the expense of the proportion of trade with the Communist countries. Under these conditions, a quadrupling of total Soviet trade would mean an increase of more than four times in trade with the non-Communist world.

munist countries would involve a noticeable drain on the other uses of the national product.

An increase in exports to the underdeveloped countries could conceivably be carried out, not at the expense of the domestic national product, but at the expense of other exports, notably exports to the other Bloc countries. In 1956, exports to the underdeveloped countries amounted to about 7 per cent of exports to Bloc countries. A diversion of Soviet exports from the Bloc countries to the free underdeveloped countries would therefore have an appreciable impact on Soviet exports to the Bloc.

TABLE 17

Soviet Exports to Bloc and Underdeveloped Countries, in Millions of Rubles and as Percentages of Components of Gross National Product, 1956

Exports to:	VALUE (*millions of rubles*)	EXPORTS AS PERCENTAGE OF: *Consumption* (*630-670 billion rubles*)	*Gross Investment* (*310-340 billion rubles*)	*National Security* (*150-170 billion rubles*)
Underdeveloped countries	735	.1	.2	.5
Yugoslavia	282	.04	.09	.2
Near East and Africa	193	.03	.06	.1
Far East	140	.02	.04	.09
Latin America	120	.02	.04	.08
Bloc countries	10,900	1.7	3.4	6.8

Source: Appendix Table G. Dollar figures are converted to rubles at the official rate of four rubles to the dollar. Soviet exports to the Bloc countries are assumed to be roughly equal to imports, i.e., one-half of total trade. Total Soviet trade with the other Bloc countries amounted to 21.7 billion rubles in 1956, according to a tabulation in V. Zolotarev, "Torgovye sviazi s sotsialisticheskimi stranami" (U.S.S.R. Trade Relations with Socialist Countries), *Vneshniaia torgovlia*, no. 11 (1957), p. 46. Absolute figures for components of gross national product are estimated in the text.

ECONOMIC AID AND THE NATIONAL PRODUCT

Rather than talk loosely about an expansion of exports to the underdeveloped countries, we shall formulate several hypothetical programs of economic aid and compare them with the competing uses of the national product. The following are three hypothetical variants of an aid program:[9]

I. A program of exports on credit of approximately the 1957 size.

II. A program of exports on credit of such size that the ratio of total exports to the gross national product would equal the corresponding ratio for the United States.

III. A program in which the Soviet Union undertakes to match the absolute size of the United States aid program to underdeveloped countries.

For the first variant, it was estimated in Table 4 that in 1957 Soviet Bloc deliveries under the present credit program will amount to \$160-\$200 million. It would be useful to take the full amount as our minimum variant, even though much of it was to come not from the U.S.S.R. but from other Bloc countries. On this basis, Variant I amounts to 640-800 million rubles at the official rate of exchange.

For the second variant, the point of departure is the \$1.6 billion of United States economic aid deliveries to the underdeveloped countries in 1957 (Table 10).[10] This was

[9] The discussion is confined to the impact on the Soviet economy of increased aid to non-Bloc underdeveloped countries. A large increase in such aid might well compel the U.S.S.R., for political reasons, to increase aid to its Communist allies also. If this is taken into account, the final impact of aid to non-Communist countries is intensified. The discussion also ignores the matter of Bloc exports to the underdeveloped countries.

[10] The total includes "defense support" of about \$900 million. (For the period July 1-December 31, 1956, defense support funds obligated to the areas listed in Table 10 amounted to \$441 million. International Cooperation Administration, *Operations Report*, December 31, 1956, pp. 16-17. For the fiscal year 1957, the total may be assumed to have been roughly twice that figure, or close to \$900 million. (Defense support funds actually "expended" are not given separately, but the total is not likely to be very different from funds "obligated.") The handling of "defense support" in aid poses difficult conceptual problems. (Cont.)

about 0.4 per cent of the 1956 gross national product ($414.7 billion). If Soviet aid amounted to the same percentage of the 1956 Soviet national product (1,100-1,200 billion rubles), it would come to about 4.5 billion rubles. This provides the second hypothetical variant of an aid program.

For the third variant, American aid of $1.6 billion, translated into rubles at the official exchange rate of four rubles to the dollar, would come to 6.4 billion rubles. Allowing for the overvaluation of the ruble at the official exchange rate, the third variant may be rounded off to 7 billion rubles at Soviet factor costs.

Table 18 shows the relative size of the three variants of an aid program compared with competing uses of the national product. The first column (Variant I) shows that a program the size of estimated actual deliveries in 1957 uses up less than one-tenth of one per cent of the gross national product. If the exported commodities were produced entirely at the expense of a reduction in consumption, consumption would be reduced by slightly more than one-tenth of one per cent. If defense alone were curtailed in order to produce the exports, the reduction would amount to less than one per cent. However, if the exports were made available by the diversion of exports presently going to other Bloc countries, the latter would be sharply affected, by a reduction of 7 per cent in their imports from the U.S.S.R.

If the Soviet aid program were to rise to a percentage of the national product equal to the corresponding percentage for the United States (Variant II), it would require roughly a sevenfold increase over the level of estimated deliveries in 1957. A program of this size would be equivalent to about seven-tenths of one per cent of total consumption,

However, it seems appropriate to include it here for three main reasons: (1) it involves the export of economic goods and therefore competes with other uses for those goods; (2) the distinction in American usage between "defense support" and "economic aid" is often a formality, depending on whether the recipient country gets military aid or not; (3) since the U.S.S.R. also provides military aid, some of its economic aid might come to have the character of "defense support."

TABLE 18

Various Hypothetical Soviet Aid Programs as Percentages of Competing Uses of the National Product

Competing Uses	*Aid as percentage of competing uses*		
	Variant I[a]	*Variant II*[b]	*Variant III*[c]
Gross national product	.06	.40	.61
Consumption	.11	.70	1.1
Gross investment	.22	1.4	2.2
National security	.45	2.8	4.4
Exports to other Bloc countries	6.9	43.0	67.0

a A program of exports on credit of approximately the 1957 size.

b A program of exports on credit of such size that the ratio of total exports to the gross national product would equal the corresponding ratio for the United States.

c A program in which the Soviet Union undertakes to match the absolute size of the United States aid program to underdeveloped countries.

and about one and one-half per cent of gross investment. Variant II would have a sharper impact on consumption in the U.S.S.R. than American aid does in the United States for several reasons: because the ratio of total consumption to gross investment is smaller in the U.S.S.R. than in the United States, because on a per capita basis Soviet consumption is even smaller compared to the United States than on a total consumption basis, and for the related reason that Soviet consumption consists of a larger proportion of necessaries and therefore has a smaller margin of "slack." On the other hand, Variant II would have a smaller impact on gross investment in the U.S.S.R. than in the United States. Variant II is equivalent to almost 3 per cent of defense expenditures, and rises sharply to 43 per cent of the volume of exports to the other countries in the Bloc.

If the aid program were to rise to a level equal in volume to the United States aid program (Variant III), it would require a tenfold increase over the level of estimated deliveries in 1957. A program of this size would still be equivalent to less than one per cent of the national product. While the program looks small in percentages of competing uses of the national product, it does begin to loom larger in the case of investment and defense. A program of this size looks particularly threatening when compared to the present level of total exports to other Bloc countries.

The general impression one gets from examining Table 18 is that in purely aggregative terms a greatly enlarged program of exports on credit to the underdeveloped countries would pose no great problems for the Soviet economy. If the Soviet government spent as much on economic aid to underdeveloped countries as the United States (Variant III), it would still spend no more than it spends on student scholarships and stipends.[11] If a disarmament agreement required the Russians to reduce their 1956 defense expenditures by 5 per cent, the value of the resources released would permit the U.S.S.R. to more than match the total size of United States aid to underdeveloped countries.

How do the three variants compare with the annual increase in the Soviet national product? If we assume that output will increase at about 5 per cent a year, the national product will increase by some 55-60 billion rubles each year. A program of the present size (Variant I) would absorb from 1-1.5 per cent of the annual increase in production. But a program equal in size to that of the United States (Variant III) would absorb about 12 per cent of the annual increase in production. If the aid program should continue to grow in size, the effect is not likely to be an absolute reduction in the supply of goods available for domestic use, but rather a reduction in the annual increase in the supply of goods.

Our conclusion must be further modified to the extent that technological change may continue to ease the burden of supporting an aid program. Capital-saving innovations, reduction in the weight of parts, and similar improvements increase the size of the pool of resources from which the aid program can be supported without a corresponding reduction in resources available for domestic use. One such technological change that could conceivably be of great moment is the shift in military technology away from the

[11] In 1955 outlays on student scholarships and stipends are estimated at 7 billion rubles. See United Nations, Economic Commission for Europe, *Economic Bulletin for Europe* cited, p. 92.

heavy, steel-using matériel of the past toward missiles and nuclear weapons.

While the relative size of even a greatly expanded aid program is small compared to Soviet production capabilities, one must not lose sight of the fact that the funds involved are not small in absolute terms. Their equivalents within the Soviet economy are of appreciable importance. For example, Variant I is equal to about 3 per cent of total state expenditures on housing in 1956; Variant III is equal to about 28 per cent of housing expenditures. Thus, if Variant I is used for housing instead of foreign aid, it could build the equivalent of about 720 thousand square meters of dwelling space; Variant III could build 6,700 thousand square meters.[12] Taking average dwelling space per person at about five square meters,[13] the minimum variant would provide housing for about 145 thousand people, and the maximum variant for about 1.3 million people.

ECONOMIC AID AND SOVIET MACHINERY PRODUCTION

The argument thus far has been carried out under the implicit assumption that a nation's resources are completely mobile, and can be shifted from one use to another at no cost. That is, a million rubles of resources used for producing consumer goods can readily be shifted into the production of an equivalent value of goods for export. This means, in effect, that a million rubles of exports has the same impact on the economy regardless of whether the exports consist of steel or machinery or wheat. While this assumption was useful for obtaining a broad idea of the size of the Soviet economy and of the relation of various hypothetical aid programs to the national product, it gives a greatly exaggerated view of the practicability of a large aid pro-

[12] State housing expenditures in 1956 were 25 billion rubles. Total new housing built in 1956 (state and private) was 36 million square meters of "total" space. (*Pravda*, February 6, 1957, p. 3.) About a third of "total" space consists of closets, toilets, corridors, stairwells, etc.; this portion is usually deducted to arrive at the concept of "dwelling" space. See Timothy Sosnovy, *The Housing Problem in the Soviet Union* (New York: Research Program on the U.S.S.R., 1954), p. 69.

[13] Sosnovy, cited, p. 106; calculated average floor space per person at about 4 square meters in 1950.

gram. In reality, resources are not perfectly mobile, least of all in the short run. If the U.S.S.R. wishes to increase exports of machinery to the underdeveloped countries, it cannot simply reduce consumption or military expenditures by a billion rubles and use the freed resources to produce a billion rubles of machinery. The machinery exports have to come out of machinery production, and the rate at which such production can be expanded is limited. Therefore, a realistic picture of the short-run capabilities of the U.S.S.R. to support an enlarged aid program requires that we take a closer look at those sectors of the economy from which the exports are most likely to come.

The export of industrial equipment would have its sharpest impact on that part of the national product going into fixed capital investment. Fixed capital investments account for roughly half of the gross investment component of the national product, the other half comprising such items as investment in working capital, inventories, stockpiles, collective farm investments and capital repairs. Thus, if we apply the three variants of aid programs to capital investments, the percentages would be roughly double those indicated on the "gross investment" line of Table 18. There is ample evidence that the Soviet economy is encountering difficulties in achieving the rates of investment necessary for the growth called for by the government's plans. Part of the reason for scrapping the original Sixth Five-Year Plan appears to have been inability to achieve the levels of investment in capital goods necessary to meet the 1960 targets. The economic plan for 1958, while providing for an increase in capital investments in housing and in the most important branches of industry, "required a certain decrease in capital investments, compared to 1957, in other branches."[14] Hence, the impact of the aid program on marginal investments in particular industries can be substantial.

If we narrow the focus further, even the value of fixed capital investment overstates the size of the pool of resources from which the aid program must be drawn, for fixed capital investment includes a large quantity of labor

[14] *Pravda,* December 20, 1957, p. 3.

and building materials that are not to be exported. The aid program bears most heavily on one portion of fixed capital investment, namely, machinery and equipment. Unfortunately, the Soviet government does not publish data on machinery and equipment production in money terms, but if we confine the analysis to orders of magnitude it is possible to make an estimate.

In Soviet statistical reporting, the two principal components of "capital investments" are "construction and installation work" and "equipment, tools and stock." The latter component consists mainly of installed machinery such as industrial or power equipment, and noninstalled machinery such as railroad rolling stock, trucks and agricultural equipment. For the purposes of our calculation, we shall assume that the value of the "equipment, tools and stock" component of capital investment is equal to the value of the machinery production of the same year. This assumption is valid if three conditions are satisfied: (1) all machinery production eventually finds its way into "equipment, tools and stock"; (2) the category "equipment, tools and stock" includes nothing but products of the machinery industry; (3) the end-of-year inventories of finished goods held by the machinery industry do not change from year to year. While none of these conditions is perfectly satisfied, they are realistic enough for the purposes of a rough calculation. In 1955, capital investments amounted to 149.9 billion rubles (at prices of July 1, 1955), and "equipment, tools and stock" amounted to 31 per cent of capital investments, or 46.5 billon rubles.[15] On the assumption set out above, this is our rough estimate of the value of machinery production in 1955. A check on this estimate is afforded by another set of calculations. The Library of Congress study, alluded to earlier, estimated the value of production of "industry, mining and construction" at 41 per cent of the 1955 gross national product at factor

[15] Tsentral'noe Statisticheskoe Upravlenie, *Narodnoe khoziaistvo SSSR: Statisticheskii sbornik (The U.S.S.R. National Economy: A Statistical Handbook)*, (Moscow: State Statistical Press, 1956) pp. 159-160.

cost, or about 450 billion rubles.[16] Employment in those three sectors was 20.6 million, while employment in the "machinery and metal-working" industry was 5.4 million.[17] Thus, employment in machinery and metal-working was 26 per cent of total employment in industry, mining and construction. If labor productivity (value of output per man) were the same in machinery and metal-working as in the larger category, total output of machinery and metal-working would amount to 117 billion rubles. In fact, we may assume that productivity was higher in machinery and metal-working, so that the output of that industry should be greater than 117 billion, perhaps about 125 billion. Machinery alone accounts for about one-third of the output of machinery and metal-working, indicating a machinery output of about 40-45 billion.[18] Thus, this second line of calculation yields a result that is not inconsistent with our estimate of machinery production.

Assuming then that machinery production in the U.S.S.R. amounts to nearly 50 billion rubles, how much of this production is required by a program of economic aid? Since Soviet offers stress the wish to aid in the industrializa-

[16] *Soviet Economic Growth: A Comparison with the United States*, cited, p. 133. Since subsidies and turnover taxes were extremely small in the machinery industry in 1955, the factor cost value of machinery production is probably not very different from the market price value as estimated above.

[17] Employment in industry and mining was 17.4 million, and in construction, 3.2 million. Employment in "machinery and metal-working" was 31.5 per cent of employment in industry and mining. *Narodnoe khoziaistvo SSSR: statisticheskii sbornik*, cited, pp. 43, 190.

[18] The three components of the machinery and metal-working industry are "machinery," "metal products" and "repairs." "Repairs" refers mostly to special railway rolling-stock repair plants, which presumably account for a very small proportion of the total. Our estimate of the proportion of "machinery production" to "machinery and metal-working production" is based on the following data on 1955 production as a percentage of 1950 production: "machinery and metal-working," 220 per cent; "machinery," 243 per cent; "metal products," 209 per cent; "repairs," 141 per cent. Tsentral'noe Statisticheskoe Upravlenie, *Promyshlennost' SSSR: statisticheskii sbornik* (U.S.S.R. Industry: A Statistical Handbook), (Moscow: State Statistical Press, 1957), p. 203. If we ignore the "repairs" component, the weighted average increase of 220 per cent for the whole group implies a weight of 1/3 for "machinery" and 2/3 for "metal products."

tion of the underdeveloped countries, it is evident that machinery will make up a substantial proportion. The list of projects contracted for (Appendix A) shows a heavy preponderance of industrial establishments, such as the Indian steel mill, power plants, mining installations, chemical plants, fertilizer plants, cement plants, the Yugoslav aluminum plant, and factories of various kinds. Under the terms of the credit agreements, the recipient countries provide all the building materials that can be produced locally, and the credit covers only materials that need to be imported. Thus, a portion of the credits will cover the costs of some Soviet exports of cement, steel, glass, etc. Another small portion will cover the cost of transportation and of Soviet technical and supervisory personnel. Part of the aid will be used for projects requiring relatively little machinery, such as road building, grain storage facilities, and irrigation dams. The balance of the credits will be used to pay for the machinery and equipment to be installed in the projects.

Unfortunately, the Russians publish no data on the commodity composition of their exports under the credit program, so that we must either abandon this line of inquiry or try to form some rough judgment of the magnitudes involved. It seems reasonable to conclude that the machinery component will not amount to more than 50 per cent of the total credit program. If we take 25-50 per cent as the broad range, what proportion of Soviet machinery production will be required to support the three hypothetical variants of the aid program? Our calculations may be summarized as follows:

	Variant I	*Variant II*	*Variant III*
1. Hypothetical annual volume of credits, million rubles	640-800	4,500	7,000
2. Machinery export component of credit program, million rubles (25-50 per cent of line 1, above)	160-400	1,125-2,250	1,750-3,500
3. Estimated Soviet annual machinery production, million rubles	50,000	50,000	50,000
4. Machinery exports on credit, as a percentage of Soviet machinery production	0.3-0.8	2.2-4.5	3.5-7

Thus, the minimum variant would require less than one per cent of Soviet machinery production. The second variant would require 2-5 per cent of total Soviet machinery production. And the maximum variant, consisting of a volume of credits equal to the present United States aid program, would require 3–7 per cent of Soviet machinery production. This, of course, applies only to machinery shipped as part of the credit program. The expansion of regular commercial trade will require still larger shipments of machinery and equipment on a direct trade basis.[19]

The increase in machinery production during the period 1950-1955 is reported to have been 143 per cent, or an annual rate of growth of about 20 per cent. If we apply this to our estimate of machinery production, the annual increase in machinery production amounts to about 10 billion rubles. Thus, the minimum variant of the Soviet aid program requires from 1.5 to 4 per cent of the annual increase in machinery production. The maximum (Variant III) would require from 17 to 35 per cent of the annual increase in machinery production. Looked at in this light, a greatly expanded aid program could conceivably have a substantial negative impact on the Soviet rate of investment and therefore on the rate of economic growth.

If the data were available, it would be useful to push this

[19] It has been estimated by Alexander Eckstein that in 1954 Soviet capital goods exports to Communist China absorbed about 1.5–2.5 per cent of total Soviet engineering and metals production. For machinery and equipment alone, the range is probably about the same. However, Eckstein's estimate of the value of 1954 Soviet machinery production is $19 billion, or about 76 billion rubles at the official exchange rate. Our own estimate of about 50 billion rubles in 1955 accords roughly with a United Nations estimate quoted by Eckstein. If we take our estimate as the base, machinery exports to China absorb about 2.5–4 per cent of Soviet machinery production. This is about the range of our Variant II. Two conclusions might be drawn from these estimates: (1) while the percentages are small, the export demands for machinery products are probably concentrated in certain branches of the industry, in which the percentages may mount to substantial volume, and (2) while present levels of machinery exports to non-Communist underdeveloped countries are small (Variant I), at the level of Variant II they rise to magnitudes quite competitive with Chinese demand for Soviet machinery. See Alexander Eckstein in *Moscow-Peking Axis*, by Howard L. Boorman and others (New York: Harper, for the Council on Foreign Relations, 1957), pp. 84, 111.

inquiry still further. For certainly not the entire range of Soviet machinery production would be affected by the aid program, but only certain segments of it. It would be useful to know precisely the quantities of each type of machinery exported under the credit agreements, and to compare the exports with Soviet production of each type of machinery. We would undoubtedly find that in certain types of machinery production the export commitments would mount to larger percentages of production than those we have dealt with thus far. For instance, the Indian steel mill agreement obliges the U.S.S.R. to export the equipment for a steel mill of about 1.2 million tons annual capacity. M. Gardner Clark's calculations show that, for a roughly equivalent steel mill in the U.S.S.R., about 46 thousand tons of metallurgical equipment are required.[20] Total production of metallurgical equipment in the U.S.S.R. in 1955 is reported to have been 172.1 thousand tons.[21] Thus, the Indian steel mill will require the export of a volume of equipment (over several years, to be sure) equal to about a quarter of total Soviet metallurgical equipment production in 1955. The reported offer of a steel mill to Pakistan, if accepted, will not materialize until after the capacity allocated for equipment going to the Indian steel mill has been released.[22] Thus, the Russians may be willing to transfer a certain proportion of their metallurgical-equipment-production capacity permanently to the export of steel equipment to underdeveloped countries, but it is likely that any substantial new requests for steel mills will have to wait their turn.

If excess capacity existed in some machinery industries, export requirements could be met without a decrease in domestic consumption of the products of those industries. It is reasonable to expect that in an economy that is planned, even though imperfectly, excess capacity is a marginal phenomenon, but it may nevertheless arise for a number of reasons: on technical and economic grounds an industry

[20] M. Gardner Clark, *The Economics of Soviet Steel* (Cambridge: Harvard University Press, 1956), p. 48.

[21] *Narodnoe khoziaistvo SSSR: statisticheskii sbornik*, cited, p. 56.

[22] *The New York Times*, January 31, 1958.

may be expanded beyond the capacity needed for current consumption, in anticipation of future requirements; or changes in economic policy may leave some capacity idle that would have been used were the discarded policy still in force. But the aid program could not in general be conducted on the basis of such excess capacity as happened to be available. If the composition of aid is to be determined by the needs and wishes of the recipient countries, it is only by chance that excess-capacity Soviet industries should be involved.

The conclusions of these rough calculations of Soviet capacities and foreign aid can be summarized briefly. The size of the Soviet national product is such that even a greatly expanded aid program, such as one equal to the present United States program, would amount to less than one per cent of the national product. But the commodities to be exported under an aid program will not come equally from all sectors of the economy, but primarily from the machinery-producing industries. A program of roughly the present size does not loom large compared to the total volume of Soviet machinery production. But, if the program expanded to the size of that of the United States, a significant proportion of Soviet machinery production would be involved, perhaps as high as 7 per cent. Finally, in specific branches of the machinery-producing industries, such as the metallurgical-equipment industry, even a program of the present composition and size requires the export of a large proportion of current Soviet production.

The answer to the question of Soviet economic capability to support a large aid program must therefore consist of several statements. In over-all monetary terms, the Soviet economy can support a program even as large as that of the United States without entailing a very great sacrifice. But, if the requests from the recipient countries concentrated on a few types of industrial construction projects, Soviet industrial capacity could not satisfy them all. The U.S.S.R. could not undertake to construct hydroelectric plants or iron and steel plants in more than a few countries at a time without seriously cutting into domestic investment. From the Soviet point of view, the ideal economic aid program would consist of a large variety of different types of projects, thus spreading the burden evenly over a large number of Soviet industries. This ideal is probably incompatible with the statements of Soviet spokesmen that they will not influence recipient countries in their choice of projects but will accept any projects the recipients propose. The future course of the program should be watched to see how far the U.S.S.R. finds it necessary to go in refusing requests or dissuading potential recipients from requesting projects similar to those already under way in or promised to several other countries.

The foregoing conclusions apply not only to the extension of credits but also to the possibility of a large expansion in Soviet commercial trade with underdeveloped countries. The last chapter showed that Soviet trade at present is an extremely small proportion of the total trade of the underdeveloped countries. An expansion of exports large enough to make the U.S.S.R. a major supplier to many underdeveloped countries would place a greater strain on the Soviet economy than the most ambitious credit program considered above. While only a detailed commodity analysis could prove the point, it seems highly unlikely that in the near future the U.S.S.R. could come close to assuming the present role of the free world in meeting the needs of the underdeveloped countries. In the longer run, of course, it is conceivable that the U.S.S.R. might restructure its economy to provide for larger exports and to accommodate itself to larger imports. As the next chapter will argue, there is little evidence that the Russians are moving in this direction. The present size and structure of the Soviet economy, however, are such that the underdeveloped countries must expect that for some time to come the free world will remain the dominant market for their exports and the major source of their imports.

Before we leave this discussion, two qualifications must be made explicit. First, we have assumed that exports under the credit agreements are not repaid in the form of imports for an indefinite period. In fact, the volume of imports will begin to rise as repayments of the loans grow larger, and will thus offset to some extent the cost of the original exports. But the extent of the offset will depend on whether the Russians redistribute their resources in such a manner as to reduce the domestic production of imported commodities. For instance, as cotton imports in repayment of earlier credits grow in volume, the U.S.S.R. will be able to withdraw some of its resources from the production of cotton and use them to produce more of the industrial commodities to be exported under the continuing aid program. In this way, the U.S.S.R. might have as much cotton available for consumption as it would have had in the absence of an aid program, while the expanded production of industrial commodities would leave a balance for export over domestic requirements. On the other hand, it is conceivable that the U.S.S.R. will be unwilling to reduce domestic production and thus become "dependent" on imports for certain of its needs. The imported commodities may be re-exported, or may be treated as an unplanned addition to domestic production. In this case, the effect of imports in reducing the drain of the export program on the economy will be greatly modified.

The second qualification, related to the first, is that we have dealt thus far primarily with the short-run impact of an aid program on the economy. In the short run, the nation's resources cannot be shifted easily from industry to industry, so that exports on credit must be supplied out of existing production capacity in the producing industries. Thus we have argued that the over-all size of the economy is no guide to the drain caused by the aid program; the size of the machinery-producing industry and that of its individual branches are the proper basis for judgment. However, in the longer run the economy can adjust to the export requirements. If the demand for metallurgical equipment in the underdeveloped countries is large, the U.S.S.R. can expand the capacity of that industry by reducing investment in other industries. In this way, the initial heavy impact of exports on the machinery industry can be spread to other industries and to other sectors of the economy. Thus, in the longer run the size of the economy becomes the relevant basis for judging the impact of the aid program.

In the case of both of these qualifications, the crucial question is whether the U.S.S.R. will actually redirect its resources in the ways indicated. Will it be willing to cushion the impact of the aid program by reducing investment and production in industries that produce commodities to be imported in increasing quantities? Will it expand the capacity of machinery industries beyond that required for purely domestic production, confident that the expanded aid program will not collapse and leave it with idle capacity?

There is a line of argument that insists that the U.S.S.R. has much to gain by carrying out just such a reallocation of its resources. Even in the absence of a program of economic aid to underdeveloped countries, runs the argument, there are potent economic reasons for the U.S.S.R. to expand its machinery-producing industries and contract many of its raw materials-producing industries. If this argument is valid, it has important implications for an evaluation of the cost of the aid program to the U.S.S.R. It means that, far from being costly to the U.S.S.R., the program of economic aid to the underdeveloped countries makes the U.S.S.R. better off economically. The implications are important enough to warrant a careful consideration of the argument.

VII

SOVIET ECONOMIC GAINS FROM THE AID PROGRAM

THE DOCTRINE of "comparative advantage" is one of the hoariest principles of economics. Simply stated, the doctrine asserts that a nation is better off economically if it imports those commodities that can be produced domestically only at a comparatively high cost, and pays for the imports by exporting commodities produced domestically at comparatively low cost.[1]

Soviet industrialization under the five-year plans may be viewed as a process in which the nation radically changed its comparative advantage. Thirty years ago the U.S.S.R. was a predominantly agricultural country with an abundance of unskilled labor, a generous endowment of natural resources, many of which had scarcely been tapped, and a relatively small industrial base. It lacked the technology and the skills with which to produce the equipment and machinery needed to industrialize the country. By exporting the products of the land that could be produced at relatively low cost, the U.S.S.R. was able to import foreign skills and industrial machinery. In the course of the five-year plans a huge industrial complex was established. Large

[1] The term "comparatively" implies a comparison of domestic cost ratios with world price ratios. For example, if the domestic production cost of grain is three times the production cost of textiles, and the world price of grain is twice the price of textiles, then grain is a comparatively high-cost product and textiles are a comparatively low-cost product. The nation would be better off economically if it exported textiles and imported grain than if it produced all its own grain and textiles.

numbers of engineers were trained and a skilled labor force developed. The productivity of workers was steadily increased by providing them with modern machine tools and equipment, and by putting more and more mechanical and electrical power at their disposal. As small-scale production gave way to large, greater efficiencies were achieved and a large transportation network was established, reducing the costs of moving commodities from one area to another.

In the course of this process, however, many of the cheapest and best mineral resources were gradually used up, and agriculture was pushed into less productive lands in order to supply the food and raw material needs of a growing population and expanding industry. Thus the process of industrialization was accompanied by diverging trends: relatively less of the nation's resources were needed to produce a unit of industrial production, while relatively more resources were required to produce a unit of the products of the land. In the light of this historical change, the doctrine of comparative advantage suggests the possibility that now it may be cheaper for the Russians to export the products of their more efficient industries and to import products of the land rather than produce them all domestically.

THE CASE FOR THE COMPARATIVE ADVANTAGE ARGUMENT

While the broad trends of Soviet economic development fit the pattern of changing comparative costs, the concrete evidence makes for a presumptive rather than a decisive case. What is the nature of the evidence?

There are, first, numerous indications of diminishing returns in several of the extractive and other primary industries. Lest we fall into the Malthusian trap, it should be stated at the outset that in looking to the future we must make allowance for the discovery of new resources and for technological advance. However, the Soviet geologists have been prospecting their land with great diligence over the past decades and, while important finds are certainly to be expected, it is doubtful that many potential Bakus or

Magnitogorsks have escaped the notice of the earth probers. As for technological change, it is certainly possible that new inventions, particularly the development of new synthetic materials and fuels, can for a long time keep well ahead of the rate of depletion of old resources. But from a survey of the recent past, it appears that in a number of important sectors the Soviet Union has been running into rising costs in extracting the products of the land.

In both of the great coal basins, the Donets and the Kuznets, the mines are going deeper, thinner seams are being worked, gas bursts and fire hazard are increasing, and the average quality of coal is decreasing. "The Donbass has been mined for almost a century and a half," writes M. Gardner Clark, "and with every year difficulties of this type [coal bursts] increase, as the English have learned from bitter experience in their own mines." [2] In the Kuznetsk basin the share of low-grade lignite in total coal production rose from 13 per cent in 1937 to 20 per cent just before World War II; larger percentages are anticipated for the future.[3] Transportation difficulties are also compelling Soviet producers to resort to poorer coals; steel plants are under pressure to use local fuels (and ores) rather than transport them from long distances, and local coals are often of poorer quality.[4] In the case of coking coals, vital for steel production, the best source is in the Pechora basin, located above the Arctic circle. Rising demand for coking coal has led to increased reliance on beneficiation, an intermediate process for removing impurities from poorer coals, which adds to total costs.[5]

The falling quality of Soviet iron ores is reflected in various ways. Over the years, production plans have steadily provided for larger quantities of ore to be mined

[2] M. Gardner Clark, *The Economics of Soviet Steel* (Cambridge: Harvard University Press, 1956), p. 124.

[3] Nicholas W. Rodin, "Comments," in Abram Bergson, ed., *Soviet Economic Growth* (Evanston: Row, 1953), p. 186.

[4] Holland Hunter, "Comments," in Bergson, ed., same, p. 161.

[5] M. Gardner Clark, "Soviet Iron and Steel Industry: Recent Developments and Prospects," *The Annals of the American Academy of Political and Social Science*, v. 303 (January 1956), pp. 57-59.

for each ton of pig iron. Not only are ores of lower iron content being mined, but also ores with poorer physical and chemical properties, which require more preliminary processing. Thus, in 1913, practically all ores were charged in the blast furnace with no prior treatment; in 1946, 81.2 per cent of all ores were treated in one way or another. Faced with similar developments, the United States turned to the development and import of high-grade foreign ores. The U.S.S.R., on the other hand, has confined its efforts to developing better ways of utilizing the low-grade domestic ores.[6] While certain types of ore processing are regarded as technically desirable even for the better-grade ores, Soviet ores seem to require additional treatment that may well involve increasing costs.

The present regime in the U.S.S.R., committed to a policy of increasing the food supply, is expanding grain production into the virgin lands of Western Siberia and Kazakhstan. These lands are distinctly marginal in terms of limited rainfall and recurring drought. The program is an ideal example of the Ricardian theory of differential rent—an expanding population pushing into more and more marginal lands. The program has increased total grain production, but over a cycle of years it is highly likely that the cost of grain products in the new lands will exceed the cost in the rest of the U.S.S.R.

A major element in the solution adopted for the livestock problem is Khrushchev's corn-hog program. To bolster the short forage supply, the program originally called for the gradual increase in acreage under corn to about 70 million acres, or only about 10 million acres less than United States corn acreage in 1955. Part of the expansion is at the expense of barley, oats and low-yielding summer grasses. Western experts appear to agree that climatic conditions, particularly the short growing season, do not augur well for the corn program. Khrushchev has admitted that the corn is not expected to reach the grain stage; most of it will be cut in the "milk" stage and used for silage or

[6] Clark, *The Economics of Soviet Steel*, cited, pp. 148-149, 189. For more recent disclosures see *The New York Times*, April 14, 1957.

green fodder. The feed value of corn in the milk stage, however, is much less than in the full-grain stage.[7] The quick and cheap results originally expected appear not to have materialized, and it has become apparent that the program will not work without extensive and expensive reliance on fertilizers. The corn program has since been cut from the original 70 million acres to 40 million, and much greater reliance is being placed on potatoes. Thus, the corn-hog program appears to be a venture into a marginal agricultural process that will indeed increase the meat supply but at an increasing cost.

Illustrations such as the foregoing point to a process that is to be expected in an expanding and industrializing economy: progressively diminishing physical returns in some of the primary industries. The encroachment of diminishing returns, however, is not in itself sufficient to establish a case for a change in comparative costs. It is conceivable that increasing labor productivity and improved technology may have more than offset diminishing physical returns, so that total production costs may have fallen. One must also consider the changes occurring simultaneously in costs of industrial production. To decide the question unequivocally, one would need access to data on production costs of both primary and highly fabricated commodities for some pre-industrial and post-industrial years. The closest one could come to such data are Soviet prices, a questionable substitute because of the uncertainty of the extent to which relative prices reflect relative costs.[8] Such studies as have been made show wide differences in the price trends of various types of commodities between 1928 and 1950. With 1928 taken as 100, the 1950 price index of

[7] Lazar Volin, "Soviet Agricultural Policy after Stalin: Results and Prospects," *Journal of Farm Economics*, v. 38 (May 1956), pp. 284-285.

[8] A recent study of Soviet cost-price ratios concludes that for certain benchmark years (including 1928 and 1950) "wholesale prices bore at least some sort of rough correspondence to production costs." The results indicate that in a rough way relative prices may provide a key to changes in relative costs. Lynn Turgeon, "Cost-Price Relationships in Basic Industries during the Soviet Planning Era," *Soviet Studies* (October 1957).

nonferrous alloys was 1,381, coke 1,186, coal 1,094, blast furnace products 670, iron ore 602. At the other extreme we find that the price index of trucks and automobiles was 88, roadbuilding and construction machinery 116, tractors 173, diesels 258, steam turbines 360.[9] In general, the price rises in machinery products were considerably smaller than the price rises in various primary and first-process products.

Thus, the data are not inconsistent with the proposition that relative costs have risen more in primary production than in highly fabricated production; perhaps this is as much as one can say. And indeed, this is precisely what one would expect on a priori grounds. The natural resources of a nation are a once-and-for-all gift of nature. As the better mineral deposits are depleted and the best lands used up, further extension of economic activity tends to run into increasing costs. The tendency can be slowed and even reversed for periods of time as capital is invested, technology improved, and substitute products developed. But for some periods of time, the primary industries may have to face up to the "niggardliness of nature." It is different with the processing and fabricating industries. Their progress is limited not by nature but by the state of the technological arts and the skill of the labor force. While the mining industry may have to use more and more labor and capital to produce a ton of coke, the steel industry can continue to produce greater and greater quantities of steel from each ton of coke. Similarly, if the cost of steel should rise because of the depletion of the best mineral resources, the steel-using industries such as machinery manufacturing can continue to produce more efficient and more productive machines with every ton of steel. Thus it is to be expected that, as industrialization proceeds, rising costs in

[9] Abram Bergson, Roman Bernaut and Lynn Turgeon, "Prices of Basic Industrial Products in the U.S.S.R., 1928-1950," *The Journal of Political Economy*, v. 64 (August 1956), p. 323; Richard Moorsteen, *Prices of Railroad Rolling Stock, U.S.S.R., 1927/28-1949* (Santa Monica: RAND, 1954), RM-1258, May 27, 1954, pp. 13, 31. Moorsteen presents his indexes for 1949; I have reduced them by 25 per cent as a rough adjustment for the sharp price reduction in 1950.

the primary industries will be accompanied by falling (or more slowly rising) costs in the processing and fabricating industries.

Only one Soviet manufacturing industry has been the subject of a detailed, published study by a Western scholar. M. Gardner Clark's work on the Soviet steel industry bears out the developments described above. While coking coal and iron ore production have been running into increasing costs, the steel industry itself has shown significant increases in productivity. The output of pig iron per cubic meter of blast furnace, and the output of steel per square meter of open-hearth furnace have both been rising steadily over the years. The increase has been the combined result of improvements in the organization and skill of the labor force, and of the continued investment in newer and more efficient industrial processes. Foreign observers have been impressed with the high technological level of Soviet steel plants. In at least one case a revolutionary new technique first developed in the United States was widely adopted in the U.S.S.R. before Western European steel firms had even begun to experiment with it, and indeed before it was in general use in the United States.[10]

In the case of machinery manufacturing, it is difficult to present direct evidence of falling costs. A mass of indirect evidence points in that direction, however. For instance, the best-known study of Soviet investment policy has established that, in comparison with the United States, the U.S.S.R. has consistently channeled a larger proportion of its total investment into industry; and of all investment in industry the Russians have allocated a much larger portion to the metals and metal-products industries.[11] This is perhaps not surprising. Stalin used to refer to machinery manufacturing as the "heart" of the economy, and throughout the period of the five-year plans it retained the highest priority. The industry enjoyed the benefit of ample funds for experimentation, for expansion, and for labor training. Its

[10] Clark, *The Economics of Soviet Steel*, cited, Chapter 15.

[11] Norman M. Kaplan, "Capital Formation and Allocation," in Abram Bergson, ed., cited, pp. 59-64.

rapid growth placed it in an ideal position to make the most of economies of large-scale production. One would expect this industry to have made the greatest advances in efficiency and productivity.

Even if it could be shown conclusively that the ratio of Soviet costs of primary products to highly fabricated products had risen considerably, the case for a shift in comparative advantage would not yet be proved. One would have to examine further the changes that had taken place in world prices during the same period. A United Nations study concludes that from the latter part of the nineteenth century to the eve of World War II "there was a secular downward trend in the prices of primary goods relative to prices of manufactured goods. On the average, a given quantity of primary exports would pay, at the end of the period, for only sixty per cent of the quantity of manufactured goods which it could buy at the beginning of the period."[12] A more recent study compares the change between 1928 and 1952 in the prices of industrial Europe's exports to and imports from the underdeveloped countries. European exports of metals and manufactures in 1952 bought 2.09 times as much raw material and 1.53 times as much food, drink and tobacco as in 1928. European exports of machinery bought 1.93 times as much raw material and 1.42 times as much food, drink and tobacco.[13] Thus the Soviet Union was the beneficiary of a kind of "scissors" movement in price trends. The commodities that were growing relatively more costly to produce domestically were at the same time growing relatively cheaper in the world market.

In the light of the evidence marshaled above, perhaps the strongest judgment that can be rendered is that there is a *prima facie* case for the argument that the comparative advantage of the U.S.S.R. has shifted in favor of highly fabricated commodities. At the least, the evidence is not

[12] United Nations, Department of Economic Affairs, *Relative Prices of Exports and Imports of Underdeveloped Countries* (New York: Author, 1949), p. 7.

[13] Charles P. Kindleberger, *The Terms of Trade: A European Case Study* (New York: Technology Press and Wiley, 1956), pp. 49-50.

inconsistent with the proposition. To go beyond statements of this kind one would need a good deal of additional information. For one thing, not all primary products have risen sharply in relative cost, nor have all highly fabricated commodities fallen sharply. To determine precisely which primary products would be most suitable for import and which manufactured products for export, one would need detailed world-price and Soviet-cost data, commodity by commodity. All that can safely be said is that there is reason to believe that the U.S.S.R. today is in a position to benefit economically by exporting certain types of manufactured commodities and importing certain types of primary products.

OTHER ECONOMIC ADVANTAGES

Quite apart from the direct gains to be enjoyed, there are two additional advantages for the Soviet economy from expanded trade. The first is a mitigation of the great transportation problem posed for the U.S.S.R. by its huge continental mass. Many regions of the U.S.S.R. could be provided with materials more cheaply from neighboring foreign countries than from remote areas within the country itself. Before the revolution, for instance, Leningrad industry used to import most of its coal by sea; the policy of autarky during the five-year plans caused a shift to the use of domestic coal hauled a thousand miles. Similarly, grain shortages in the Far East used to be met by imports from Manchuria; in the Soviet period grain has often been brought by rail from Siberia, a distance of 3,000 miles. An expansion of foreign trade could confer distinct economic advantages on the border regions of the U.S.S.R. and lighten the strain on the nation's transportation system.[14]

The second advantage may be explained by imagining alternative policies that might be adopted over the next decade. The first is the autarkical policy in which the U.S.S.R. produces as much of its own primary products

[14] James H. Blackman, "Transportation," in Abram Bergson, ed., cited, p. 141. Also Demitri B. Shimkin, "Comments," in same, p. 183. Recent Soviet purchases of grain from Canada for shipment to Siberia indicate Soviet concern over the cost of autarky in terms of transportation.

(foodstuffs and raw materials) as it needs, and as much machinery and equipment as it needs. The second is the policy of foreign trade: the U.S.S.R. retrenches on the production of primary products, uses the freed resources to expand the stock of capital in the metal-fabricating industries, exports the surplus of machinery production thus generated, and uses the proceeds to replenish by imports the shortage of domestic primary products. Suppose there were no net gains from trade, so that both policies left the U.S.S.R. with the same quantities of primary products and machinery each year. Nevertheless, the second policy should recommend itself to the U.S.S.R. for at least two reasons. First, at the end of ten years the second policy would have resulted in a slower rate of depletion of domestic natural resources. And second, the U.S.S.R. would possess a larger capacity for producing machinery and equipment. Thus even if there were no immediate gains from foreign trade, a policy of expanded trade would have distinct advantages in furthering both the military potential of the nation and the pace of industrialization. To that extent it would enhance the military potential of the country, though at the cost of greater dependence on imports.

The growing advantages for the U.S.S.R. of exporting capital goods and importing raw materials have attracted the interest of observers for some time. Over a decade ago Alexander Gerschenkron, in a remarkably prescient pamphlet, anticipated that within a generation Russia would become a grain-importing country, and would export semimanufactures, equipment and technical assistance to the Near and Middle East.[15] M. Gardner Clark, noting that the new Soviet steel mill on the shore of the Azov sea "is struggling to smelt some of the world's worst ores from the Crimea," pointed to the favorable results that might be obtained from the import of high-grade Algerian, Turkish,

[15] Alexander Gerschenkron, *Economic Relations with the U.S.S.R.* (New York: Committee on International Economic Policy, 1945), pp. 36, 56, and *passim.*

or even Indian ore.[16] More important, Soviet economists have begun recently to discuss the advantages of international specialization in production, and the idea has even found its way into the speeches of Khrushchev.[17] It is true that such pronouncements usually refer only to specialization within the Communist group of nations. But the thought is there, and its implications for trade with the underdeveloped countries are not easily missed.

THE ECONOMIC INTERPRETATION OF THE AID PROGRAM

What light do the foregoing considerations shed on Soviet economic policy toward the underdeveloped countries? The temptation is great to leap to the conclusion that economic motivations are an important, and perhaps a major, factor in explaining why the program was undertaken. To be sure, there were gains to be enjoyed from trade in the past, and if the attraction of autarky outweighed them then, why, it may be asked, should this no longer be so? For one thing, during the thirties Soviet industry benefited from certain overriding temporary advantages, such as the siphoning off of agricultural labor into industry and the borrowing of foreign technology. Compared to the contribution that these factors made to rapid growth, the potential additional gains from trade were perhaps quite marginal. The task of consolidating the economic and political structure of the nation during those years of rapid structural change was challenging enough, without introducing the additional structural changes necessary to incorporate the U.S.S.R. into the highly volatile world market of those years. But the rapid rates of growth of the nineteen thirties have since slowed down. In the early fifties the government reported annual rates of growth of industrial production ranging from 11 per cent to 16 per cent, distinctly less than in the pre-

[16] M. Gardner Clark, "Comments," in Abram Bergson, ed., cited, pp. 179-180.

[17] *Voprosy ekonomiki*, no. 3 (1956), p. 32. Also Khrushchev's speech at the XX Communist Party Congress, in *Pravda*, February 15, 1956, p. 2.

war period. In 1957 the government announced the unprecedentedly low planned rate of growth of only 7.1 per cent. It was reported that the rate actually achieved was 10 per cent, but for 1958 the planned rate is again down to only 7.6 per cent.[18] This downward tendency conforms to the expectations of Western scholars that certain forces within the Soviet economy were increasing the likelihood of retardation in the rate of growth. If the downward trend continued the Soviet leaders would have to relegate further and further to the future the long-standing goal of "overtaking and surpassing" the United States. Something had to be done to shore up the sagging rate of growth. The high cost of autarky, it might be thought, would begin to loom larger and larger in the eyes of the Soviet leaders. According to this interpretation, mounting economic problems within the U.S.S.R. provided a strong impetus to expand foreign trade, especially with countries that produced raw materials and food. This logically led to the program of economic aid to underdeveloped countries.

While the argument has a plausible ring, there are several reasons for believing that it overstresses the economic motivation. For one thing, it is doubtful that the possible scale of trade could have an overriding or critical effect. Moreover, the argument does nothing to explain the credit aspect of the aid program. That is, it may be expedient for the Soviet Union to export capital goods in exchange for primary products, but there is no economic advantage to the policy of extending long-term credits. The credit provisions mean that it will be several years before the Russians begin to enjoy the benefits of the imports, and surely capital is not so abundant in the U.S.S.R. that the 2½ per cent interest charge compensates for the sacrifice of the immediate use of the exported commodities. Unless long-term credits were extended, however, the underdeveloped countries would be unwilling or unable to purchase Soviet capital goods. The extension of credit may thus be interpreted as a necessary cost that the Soviet Union must bear for the sake of the longer-run exchange

[18] *Pravda*, December 20, 1957, p. 2.

of goods to which the aid program will lead. This may be a valid appraisal, but it would require an extremely close calculation for a nation in the economic situation described above to decide that, for economic reasons, it is worth making such short-run sacrifices for the sake of gains to be enjoyed several years hence.

A more significant reason for doubting the importance of economic motivations emerges from an examination of the commodities figuring as the eventual imports to be received in payment for current exports of capital goods. One of the features of the Soviet program that attracts underdeveloped countries is that the U.S.S.R. is willing to accept repayment in the commodities the borrowers traditionally export. When published credit agreements specify the commodities in which repayment may be made, the lists look like a catch-as-catch-can of whatever the recipient country has to sell. Imports from India will consist of jute, tobacco, shellac, textiles, copra, spices, cinchona, tea, and oil seed. Rice predominates in the exports of Burma, but we also find reference to hardwoods, nonferrous metals, and rubber. From Egypt it is to be cotton and rice. From Syria, the commodities mentioned are cotton, oil seeds, vegetable oils, dried fruits, vegetables, wool, tobacco, skins, hides, hemp, textiles,[19] It is evident that such lists are drawn up more with an eye to what the partner needs to sell, than to what the U.S.S.R. could most profitably import. This is natural enough, but it casts doubt on the idea that obtaining these commodities is a primary aim of the Soviet policy.

This is not to deny that the commodities to be imported are useful to the U.S.S.R. Vegetable oils have long been in short supply in the Soviet Union and imports of oil seeds and copra could help meet the need. Consumer goods and foodstuffs, such as textiles, coffee, tobacco, spices and dried fruit, could help relieve some of the pressure on the economy caused by the increased attention to living standards

[19] U. S. Senate, Subcommittee on Technical Assistance Programs, *Soviet Technical Assistance*, 84th Cong., 2d sess., Staff Study no. 7 (Washington: GPO, 1956), pp. 13, 28, 42, 44, and *passim*.

following Stalin's death. Nonferrous metals and rubber from Burma would rank fairly high in industrial priority, although it is clear that Burmese exports will consist mostly of rice, and except for the Moslems the people of the Soviet Union do not eat rice as a staple food. But one misses in the enumerated commodities those mentioned earlier as illustrations of rising costs: such commodities as coal, iron ore, grains. It is doubtful that the underdeveloped countries could supply significant quantities of the primary commodities most needed to relieve the burden on the rising-cost sectors of the Soviet economy. Certainly countries such as Afghanistan, Burma, Egypt and Syria, that are among the chief foci of the aid program, are not the ones most able to contribute significantly to easing the strains in the Soviet economy. If economic considerations were fundamental to the aid program, these are not the countries one would expect to find the Russians cultivating most diligently.

But the strongest doubts about the economic interpretation of the aid program arise from an examination of recent developments within the Soviet economy. If the aid program is designed to take advantage of potential gains from trade, a reallocation of the nation's resources must occur. Investment would be curtailed in the high-cost sectors, and labor would be channeled away from them in anticipation of increased imports of those commodities. Investment and production would be increased in the metals and metal-fabricating industries in anticipation of the need to produce an export surplus beyond domestic requirements. Has a reallocation of this kind actually occurred? An attempt to answer this question on the basis of empirical evidence could probably never reach conclusive results; because the volume of trade is so small relative to the size of the economy, statistical data are likely to be too crude to permit detection of the small changes that would be involved. Thus, empirical evidence must be taken as suggestive rather than decisive. Such evidence as one does find seems to show that the Soviet planners, far from making room for import surpluses, are in some ways making it more difficult to absorb large imports from the underdeveloped countries. Consider, for example, the increases in cotton and wool fibers and textiles called for by the Sixth Five-Year Plan (1956-1960). By 1960 Soviet production is supposed to show the following percentage increases over 1955:[20]

	Fiber	*Textile*
	(in per cent)	
Cotton	56	23
Wool	82	45

Cotton is a major export of Egypt and the Sudan, and an important export of Afghanistan and Syria. Yet the Soviet plan provides for an increase in domestic cotton fiber production about 2½ times as large as the increase in cotton textile production. Part of the discrepancy can be explained by the fact that the 1955 cotton harvest was relatively poor, about 8 per cent smaller than in 1954 (although it was 9 per cent larger than in 1950).[21] Since the 1960 target is expressed as a percentage increase over 1955, it would tend to be large. But it is doubtful that the full discrepancy is explained by this fact. In 1956 the Soviet Union continued to export cotton to other Bloc countries and to Western Europe.[22] In 1957, however, the Russians greatly increased their purchases of Egyptian cotton, and for the first time entered the Sudanese cotton auction as a purchaser.[23] Possibly more detailed information on types of fiber involved in these transactions would make the pattern more understandable. The least one can say about this confusing picture is that there is no clear evidence of Soviet intentions to prepare its economy and those of the

[20] Tsentral'noe Statisticheskoe Upravlenie, *Narodnoe khoziaistvo SSSR; statisticheskii sbornik (The U.S.S.R. National Economy: A Statistical Handbook)*, (Moscow: State Statistical Press, 1956), pp. 61, 102.

[21] Same, p. 101.

[22] *The New York Times*, May 28, 1957.

[23] Same, June 28, 1957. Soviet cotton purchases from the Sudan, following persistent reports of Bloc re-exports of Egyptian cotton, have given rise to speculation that the Soviet Union may be stockpiling cotton surpluses. The threat of dumping such surpluses could serve as a powerful weapon against Egypt. They could also serve to frustrate United States efforts at preventing its own surpluses from disrupting the world cotton market.

Bloc for greatly increased cotton imports from abroad.

Rice has figured prominently in Soviet negotiations with Burma and is also imported from China (which turned from a net importer to a net exporter after the Communist victory). But rice is important to the diet of only some of the minor nationality groups in the Soviet Union. While large purchases may be made from non-Communist Asia for political reasons, rice is not likely to be imported in growing amounts for its contribution to the Soviet economy. Steps such as the Soviet grain purchases from Canada might be interpreted as having broader economic implications, but not the import of Asian rice.

Wool is one of the major exports of Afghanistan and an important export of Syria. As in the case of cotton, the planned increase in Soviet fiber production is about double that set for textile production. Since the Soviet wool clip in 1955 was exceptionally large, the difference in the two plan targets is even larger than it appears.[24] While the U.S.S.R. continues to import large quantities of wool, the indications are that it is trying to reduce rather than expand its external supplies of wool.

The Soviet national economic plan for 1957 gives further indications of an increase rather than a retrenchment in agricultural investment. While the production of all machinery is to increase 10.2 per cent, production of agricultural machinery is to increase 24 per cent. Nor can it be argued that the agricultural machinery is to be exported as part of the aid program. The largest planned increases are clearly in those types of machinery needed to further Khrushchev's agricultural policy: grain combines are to increase 65 per cent, corn combines 110 per cent and silage combines 80 per cent. These figures do not suggest a nation about to solve its food problem by becoming an importer. The foreign trade targets of the 1957 plan specify increased exports of grain, lumber products and petroleum products, all products of the land. Machinery exports are mentioned as a sort of afterthought.[25]

[24] *Narodnoe khoziaistvo SSSR: statisticheskii spravochnik*, cited, p. 101.

[25] Report by M. G. Pervukhin in *Pravda*, February 6, 1957.

Natural rubber is one industrial raw material that all temperate zone countries must import from the few places in the tropical world that produce it. It has been mentioned as one of the commodities the U.S.S.R. might import from Burma. The production of synthetic rubber, however, has been increasing rapidly in the U.S.S.R., though it is a high-cost operation. During the Sixth Five-Year Plan production is to increase by another 120 per cent. While expanding demand for rubber may be expected to lead to continuing import requirements, the U.S.S.R. is trying to reduce the gap between requirements and domestic production by resort to high-cost synthetics.[26]

These scraps of evidence, while not conclusive, cast strong doubts on the economic interpretation of the aid program. The argument that the U.S.S.R. could gain economically by changing its pattern of resource allocation so as to import primary products and export capital goods remains valid, and imports may be desirable even in amounts too small to make a detectable difference to resource allocation. But the Soviet leaders seem not yet to be willing to surrender the costly independence they enjoy because of their high degree of autarky (at least with respect to the non-Communist world). Their unwillingness to make room for the imports generated by their exports reduces the gains they might enjoy from expanding that trade. The exports of capital goods involve a decrease in the supply of capital goods available for domestic use, a decrease that could be avoided if a shift in resource allocation were made.

This conclusion applies only to the U.S.S.R. There are reasons to believe that for the countries of Eastern Europe the aid program and particularly the expansion of trade may bring substantial economic gains. We have noted that the other Bloc countries have played a more important role than the U.S.S.R. in the expansion of trade with the underdeveloped countries, and that trade looms larger in their economies than in that of the U.S.S.R. Since they are small countries, the potential gains from specialization and trade are greater. For highly industrialized countries like

[26] United Nations, Economic Commission for Europe, *Economic Survey of Europe in 1955* (Geneva: Author, 1956), p. 183.

Czechoslovakia and East Germany, the export of capital goods may well confer distinct economic advantages. But to pursue this question further would require that we explore the intricacies of intra-Bloc trade as well as the natural resource endowments of each of the member countries, a task which is beyond the scope of this study.

What then remains of the comparative advantage argument? At most, it warns us against overestimating the drain on the Soviet economy that the aid program entails. To the extent that any substantial volume of imports is absorbed into the economy, some reallocation of resources must occur. If the Soviet leaders plan for a certain rate of improvement in the standard of living, imports of foodstuffs and consumer goods from the underdeveloped countries will permit that rate to be attained with a somewhat lesser use of domestic resources. Re-exports of imports raise certain difficulties to be discussed presently; to the extent that those difficulties are overcome, re-exports can be used to satisfy the requirements of the other Bloc countries or to be traded to non-Bloc countries for more urgently needed commodities. Thus, the cost of the aid program to the U.S.S.R. is not to be measured by the full value of the machinery and equipment exported under the credit agreements. The cost is offset to some extent by the imports eventually received in repayment. But the main conclusion of the discussion is a negative one. The Russians have not demonstrated an intention of changing the structure of their economy in ways that would permit them to enjoy the full advantage of the potential gains in trade resulting from a capital-export aid program. The pursuit of economic advantage does not appear to be an important motive behind the Soviet aid program.

VIII

GREEKS BEARING GIFTS?

AMERICANS OFTEN find it difficult to understand how certain nations that profess a commitment to international morality can insist on remaining "uncommitted" in the struggle between Soviet communism and Western freedom. How can one be "neutral" in the conflict between good and evil? Those who view international politics in these terms must wonder at the blindness of the underdeveloped countries in their failure to see that the Soviet engineers and technicians are Greeks bearing gifts. Is it some subconscious urge toward self-destruction that has led the leaders of the underdeveloped countries to accept millions of dollars of Soviet aid?

It is difficult enough for any nation to "see ourselves as others see us." How much more difficult it is to see a second nation as a third sees it! And yet not to make the effort could lead to a disastrous failure to appreciate the full appeal of Soviet aid to the recipient nations. For a variety of reasons, Soviet aid is much more attractive to the underdeveloped countries than Americans might imagine, if we failed to substitute their viewpoint for our own. The very novelty of the Soviet program is itself an advantage; it offers promising new prospects and breaks what many recipient nations saw as the United States' virtual monopoly of aid-giving. Moreover, to many people in the underdeveloped countries, the U.S.S.R. does not appear to be the aggressive villain of the world drama usually portrayed in the West. The Soviet authorities have fashioned the terms of their aid program so as to mitigate the latent fears of the recipients and to appeal to many of their aspirations. As a donor of aid, the U.S.S.R. also enjoys certain advantages (as well as disadvantages, to be sure) because of the totalitarian character of its government.

THE ADVANTAGE OF NOVELTY

For many years, the underdeveloped countries were almost entirely dependent upon the West for aid in economic development. Whether the aid was given through an international agency, or in the form of private investment, or through bilateral agreements between governments, the source was almost always the wealthier capitalist nations of the West, and predominantly the United States. No one likes to be beholden to another for help, least of all if the recipient is a young nation that has very recently won its political independence, and, worst of all, when a single nation is the dominant source of large-scale aid. However tactful the donor strives (and often fails) to be, the recipient understands that ultimately it must accept the aid on the donor's terms or not at all. In these circumstances, it is readily understandable that the underdeveloped countries must be elated to find another powerful nation now entering the competition with enthusiastic offers. The existence of the Soviet program strengthens the bargaining power of the recipient countries in their negotiations with the older sources of aid. Thanks to the Russians, the underdeveloped countries are now able to say to an irritating Western negotiator, "Very well, if you won't give us the steel mill on our terms, we know someone who will!" Some countries may accept Soviet offers, not because of their intrinsic advantages, but in order to demonstrate their independence or their neutrality in the East-West conflict. Or some may accept Soviet aid on a trial basis, simply in order to test how it works out.

The new program has advantages just because it is new. Prospects and promises create happy anticipations; the test of performance is in the future. An older program is bound to have accumulated a burden of disappointments, compromises and irritations that are likely to be remembered more vividly than the accomplishments that have become part of ordinary life.

A realistic evaluation of Soviet aid to date must keep the newness of the program prominently in view. After all, not one of the really large projects has been completed yet; not the Indian steel mill nor the Yugoslav aluminum plant. Of the $100-million credit to Afghanistan, only a meager $10-15 million have been spent.[1] It is not certain that any detailed projects have yet been formulated under the $100-million credit to Indonesia. Countries that have "tried it once" have hardly had time to decide whether they will try again. The Soviet Union has not yet had to face the diplomatic problems of trying to play the friend of two competing countries. If, for example, the U.S.S.R. should succeed in making a large-scale aid agreement with Pakistan, how will Soviet relations with India be affected? The effect on Egypt of increased Soviet purchases of Sudanese cotton is something for the future to tell. The debtors' problems of repaying loans and the Soviet Union's problem of absorbing imports have not yet been faced. The administrative problems of running a large-scale aid program take time to develop. The rapid rate of growth of Soviet credit agreements during the first few years of the new policy is in part a reflection of the fact that the program started from zero. There is no reason to assume, as is sometimes done, that the rate of growth will continue.[2] It is equally possible that, once all the countries originally disposed to accept Soviet aid have done so, the program from then on will maintain a constant size. But in the first few years the rate of growth is impressive.

Thus, the very newness of the Soviet aid program is an aid to the U.S.S.R. in the paramount matter of attracting potential recipients of aid. The more important test of the success of the program is yet to come.

[1] *The New York Times*, September 2, 1957.
[2] Same, July 29, 1956.

THE IMAGE OF THE U.S.S.R.

It is perhaps not sufficiently appreciated in the Western world that the U.S.S.R. evokes a highly favorable image in the eyes of many people in the underdeveloped countries who are not Communists. The political attitudes of those lands toward the West are compounded of many sentiments that breed suspicion and distrust. Although the tradition of anti-imperialism has lost some of the intensity it had before independence, it still colors the attitudes of the former colonial lands in their dealings with the West. The religious and social traditions of many of the underdeveloped countries contain strong anticapitalist elements such as a contempt for the merchant and money-lender and for the spirit of individualism and profit-seeking. Even keener is the antagonism toward the racial discrimination practiced in various sections of the Western world.

These deeply felt political sentiments are not directed in the same way against the U.S.S.R. The U.S.S.R. has historically defended the cause of anti-imperialism, and has thus always been the enemy of the enemy and therefore a friend. The latter-day colonialism by which the U.S.S.R. has maintained political control over its European satellites may be admitted when it is thought about, but it does not carry the same emotional punch as the memory of colonialism at home. The Yugoslav defection, the East German, Hungarian, and Polish uprisings, and the new Soviet regime's denunciation of Stalin have undoubtedly made an impact on some circles in the underdeveloped countries. Any future troubles within the Communist camp may serve further to mar the image that the U.S.S.R. wishes to present of itself. But, by and large, the U.S.S.R. has succeeded in identifying itself with opposition to imperialism.

Similarly, by representing itself as a socialist nation, the U.S.S.R. avoids identification with rapacious, profit-seeking and individualist materialism. Marxism has had a considerable influence on intellectuals in the underdeveloped countries, and the association of capitalism with struggles for markets, with war, and with exploitation serves to whiten the image of the U.S.S.R. There is plausibility in the Soviet claim to have no need for foreign markets and to be motivated entirely by friendship in extending economic aid. The claims are strongly reinforced by such devices as the low interest rate and the refusal to criticize the proposals of the underdeveloped countries. In contrast, the higher interest rate on American or International Bank loans and the close financial control and irritating inquisitions that sometimes accompany Western aid sharpen the distinction between dealing with a socialist and a capitalist country.

The U.S.S.R. is also able to present itself as free from the taint of white supremacy by emphasizing its role as a part-Asian nation. Those who take the trouble to look under the carpet will find numerous features of Soviet nationality policy that would hardly fit the image of a nation of equally free peoples. But with its rigid control over the information that the outside world obtains about itself, the U.S.S.R. has managed to impress on the Asian and African world its antiracist character. To be sure, experience with Japanese occupation during World War II has driven home to some the lesson that Asian imperialism can be as harsh as Western. Nevertheless, in solid alliance with China, the U.S.S.R. can claim that it has a closer spirit of brotherhood with the colored peoples of Asia than the Western nations have.

If these facets of the Soviet image were not enough, there is one further facet that alone would provide the U.S.S.R. a favorable audience among the underdeveloped countries. For the U.S.S.R. is a good example of a nation that in a relatively short time has achieved what all the underdeveloped countries aspire to, a high level of economic development. In one generation the Communists have transformed the world's image of Russia from that of the ignorant, downtrodden *mujik* to that of the nation that launched the interplanetary age. In the view of the leaders of the underdeveloped countries, such a nation has much to teach them. In Stalin's day, political and economic isolation kept the Soviet teachers and engineers at home, but now the U.S.S.R. has opened its universities and factories and offers its wares and talents to all who would make use of them. In a way, the U.S.S.R. may be thought to have more to teach the underdeveloped countries than the United States; the latter seems always to have been an advanced nation, but the U.S.S.R. has the special quality of a nation that has very recently gone through all the stages of development.

For these reasons, the Soviet aid program may be expected to receive a warmer reception and to carry more conviction of being devoid of ulterior motives than a Western aid program can. But we must not overstate the case. It is doubtful that one can go as far as to argue that, if identical offers were made by the U.S.S.R. and the United States or the International Bank, the Soviet offer would always be preferred because of the attitudes described above. This would seem to give too much weight to the role of political attitudes. In any case, the choice for the recipient country is not Soviet *or* Western aid. It is rather how much to accept, or perhaps to seek, from both.

While the U.S.S.R. enjoys a generally favorable reception in the underdeveloped countries, there are several features of the Soviet image that handicap it in its relations with at least some groups in those countries. In the Moslem countries, for instance, the antireligious tradition of Soviet dogma is the source of latent hostility among some sections of the population. The pose as a part-Asian nation does not obscure the fact that the U.S.S.R. is dominated by Europeans; Mao, for example, seems to have succeeded in making a stronger emotional impact on Indian leaders than did Khrushchev and Bulganin. The totalitarian and repressive features of Soviet history are not lost upon those groups in Asia who spring from the Gandhian spiritual tradition of nonviolence or who have accepted the values of European humanism and law. While rapid industrial growth ranks high on the list of objectives of the underdeveloped countries, the "welfare state" ideology of the mid-twentieth century has placed rising living standards of the masses on an equally high level of urgency; and there are growing indications that the leaders of the underdeveloped countries are questioning whether the Soviet model, however successful it might be for the achievement of industrial growth, is at all consistent with the objective of rising consumption standards.

But perhaps the most significant handicap faced by the U.S.S.R. is the suspicion of Soviet adventures in domestic subversion and political domination. We might distinguish two kinds of potential threats apart from espionage; support of domestic mass Communist movements for the overthrow of existing governments, and support of pro-Soviet military and political cliques for political control. With respect to the former, it was pointed out earlier that the policy of friendly relations with the governments of the underdeveloped countries was preceded by a change in tactics of Asian Communist parties from violence and insurrection to the policy of a peaceful "voting revolution." The Soviet government has been extremely correct in avoiding overt support of domestic Communist parties. Under such conditions, latent suspicion of Soviet subversive intentions is not likely to dissuade a nation from accepting Soviet aid. Egypt and Burma have continued to deal vigorously with domestic Communist subversion, despite their economic relations with the U.S.S.R.[3]

The outstanding instances of Soviet political domination of foreign governments are the countries of Eastern Europe. It is inevitable that the political tribulations of distant lands do not carry the same emotional impact as the struggles in which one is directly involved. In the intensity of the Indian-Pakistani conflict over Kashmir or the Arab-Israeli conflict, the notions of "good" or "bad" tend to be defined primarily according to whether one's own position is strengthened or not. It is true that the Hungarian uprising forced upon the leaders of some of the underdeveloped countries the need to reflect on the techniques of Soviet domination of foreign countries. "Look at Hungary!" is the reported remark of the former Premier of Cambodia in explaining to his party his sharp shift to an anti-Com-

[3] *The New York Times*, August 31, 1957; July 1, 1957.

munist position.[4] But the lessons of the Hungarian tragedy have only the remotest bearing on the question of the acceptability of Soviet aid by a free, non-Communist country.

The Syrian events of the summer of 1957 are another matter. When a nation is seized by an intense political issue, and an existing government contains powerful military and political groups that wish to force the issue with Soviet help, it is clear that the U.S.S.R. is prepared to assist those groups in gaining control of the government. But it should be emphasized that in the Syrian case the economic aid program as such had little to do with the Soviet political victory. Where an unstable government has cause to fear overthrow by a military group, economic aid is the least of the methods whereby the U.S.S.R. might support such groups. And where a government feels relatively secure against a coup of this sort, Soviet aid may be thought to carry little danger. It therefore seems that, with the exception of unstable governments, neither the revolutionary nor the aggressive aspects of the Soviet image are likely to seem prominent enough in most underdeveloped countries to motivate a refusal of Soviet aid. There are probably exceptions to this statement. Turks are apt to view the U.S.S.R. differently from Indonesians. One country will be more cautious than another in looking the Soviet gift horse in the mouth. Longer experience may demonstrate implications of Soviet aid for internal politics less obvious than the revolution and *coup d'état*. To a considerable degree the Soviet Union has it in its power to preserve and even extend the initial advantage which the warm reception of the aid program provided, but it remains to be seen whether a "correct attitude" in these matters always seems correct foreign policy to the men in the Kremlin.

THE TERMS OF SOVIET AID

To the other assets of its aid policy the U.S.S.R. has added terms and conditions that are well designed to make Soviet offers attractive and acceptable to the underde-

[4] Same, January 12, 1958.

veloped countries. As the following discussion indicates, the terms are also designed to protect the U.S.S.R. from getting involved more deeply than it might wish, but the overt emphasis is on features attractive to the underdeveloped countries. We may be sure that the Soviet strategists have carefully studied the troubles that afflict Western economic aid administrators, and have fashioned their own program so as to exploit those difficulties.

Credits versus grants

One of the outstanding features of Soviet aid is the almost exclusive reliance upon long- and medium-term credits, compared to the heavy use of grants in the United States program. One wonders why, if the Russians wish to make their aid offers as attractive as possible, they do not rely more heavily upon grants. Recipients would then not have to calculate their future ability to repay, as they must before accepting loans. They could safely accept more aid in the form of grants than as loans. If Soviet purposes are served by a large aid program, grants would seem more effective instruments than loans.

The first answer that suggests itself is that Soviet officials believe that a grant program would be too expensive. Loans will eventually be repaid and the imports will offset at least a part of the cost of the exports, whereas grants are a complete economic loss. But this answer is not fully convincing. It seems to place excessive emphasis on cold economic calculation. The billion-and-a-half-odd dollars worth of aid thus far negotiated will be repaid over a period of perhaps ten to fifteen years. The annual imports will thus amount to something like $100-$150 million. And a large part of these imports will consist of such things as dried fruits and cinchona bark, along with the cotton and the rice. It is hard to believe that such sums, so paltry in terms of the magnitudes with which the Soviet leaders customarily deal, were decisive in the determination to offer loans rather than grants. Moreover, the picture one gets from the scanty reports of how the Russians negotiate their aid offers hardly suggests a profound interest in the imports to be received eventually. The approach seems to be: tell us what you want and we will take anything you wish to sell us in exchange.

Not all the evidence supports this impression of easy-going open-handedness. Reports from Burma allege that the Russians engaged in hard price-bargaining with the Burmese under their barter exchange agreement.[5] In Egypt, we read that the Russians, after underbidding Western firms on construction contracts, proceeded to raise their prices by 40 per cent; this report is consistent with later evidence that in negotiations on the $175-million loan the Egyptians were pressing the Russians hard for detailed information and advance guarantees on prices.[6] Negotiations with Ceylon bogged down for a while over Soviet insistence on an agreement based on a "swing credit," which might have placed the Ceylonese in the position of supplying credit to the U.S.S.R. for periods of time.[7] The Russians apparently relented and accepted an agreement more favorable to Ceylon. These reports conflict with the notion that the U.S.S.R. has no interest in the returns it receives from its aid program.

With so little reliable information on the details of Soviet negotiations, and with contradictory reports at that, one can offer only a compromise conclusion. Perhaps the policy is, first of all, to place aid and trade contracts in recipient countries, but then to take advantage of the recipients' great need and desire for aid to press for terms as advantageous as can reasonably be secured. Thus, there may be economic reasons for the decision to employ loans rather than grants as the basis of the aid program, but they do not appear to be decisive. Several other reasons may be suggested.

First, Soviet aid to countries in the Bloc consists primarily of credits. A number of instances have come to light revealing the existence of tensions between the U.S.S.R. and its allies over the aid program. A Communist Chinese general has demanded that the U.S.S.R. write off the Soviet loans to China, citing the United States cancellation of war loans

[5] Same, January 6, 1957.
[6] Same, June 5, 1957; December 18, 1957.
[7] Same, January 22, 1958; January 29, 1958.

as an example of a proper attitude. He further demanded a "drastic cut in foreign aid" extended by China to neighboring countries.[8] The United Press quotes Khrushchev, on the other hand, as having complained that China is "milking us dry" in its demands for economic aid.[9] We do not know how the Bloc countries react to the Soviet agreement to build an institute of nuclear physics in Cairo, but the following year the U.S.S.R. agreed to construct an atomic power station and an institute of nuclear physics in Czechoslovakia.[10] The very launching of an aid program to non-Communist countries must have been greeted with mixed feelings in the underdeveloped countries within the Soviet Bloc itself.[11] Under these conditions, it would be awkward to extend more generous terms of aid to non-Communist countries than those extended to other Communist countries.

Second, credits apparently have a distinct psychological advantage over grants in the minds of many people in the underdeveloped countries. Loans seem to do less violence to the sense of dignity and independence of the recipients. A borrowing country feels, not like an object of charity, but rather like an equal, engaging in a normal economic exchange in which he is paying fairly for what he receives. Soviet propaganda has made the most of this factor, stressing the *mutual* benefit of the economic aid program, and the friendly but businesslike character of the agreements. The strong desire of the governments of the underdeveloped countries to pay their own way was reflected dramatically in Burma's insistence upon paying, with a "gift" of rice, for the technological institute the Soviet Union offered as a "gift" to the Burmese people.[12] In discussing

[8] Same, June 24, 1957.
[9] *Syracuse Herald-Journal*, July 14, 1957.
[10] *The New York Times*, January 30, 1957.
[11] For an evaluation of Chinese reaction, see G. F. Hudson, "Moscow and Peiping: Seeds of Conflict," *Problems of Communism*, v. 5 (November-December 1956), p. 22.
[12] U. S. Senate, Subcommittee on Technical Assistance Programs, *Soviet Technical Assistance*, 84th Cong., 2d sess., Staff Study no. 7 (Washington: GPO, 1956), p. 29.

the resumption of aid from the United States, the Burmese Premier stated, "We prefer to pay for it, as this forms a more solid basis of friendship than acceptance of gifts." [13] By extending loans rather than grants, the Russians are less vulnerable to depiction as "Greeks bearing gifts," a charge they often hurl at the United States.

While this argument has merit, it should not be overstressed. One could make a fairly good case for the psychological advantages of a grant program as well. What better way to dramatize the economic might and the peaceful intentions of the U.S.S.R. than a large-scale extension of gifts of factories and technical assistance to the underdeveloped countries? If the immediate purpose of the aid program is to create good will, could not gifts be depicted in a much more favorable light than loans? "The chains of debt" are, after all, traditional symbols of the subservience that the new nations reject. If the Soviet aid program had emphasized grants rather than loans, few would have argued a priori that this was a psychological blunder. Yet, in the present state of the world it appears that the psychological advantage lies—perhaps only temporarily—with loans, and the Soviet policy exploits the fact.

A third advantage of credits is that they limit the number of requests for aid to more or less reasonable proportions. The need to repay loans is a sober reminder to the recipients that requests for Soviet aid must be kept within bounds and reduces the number of occasions on which the Soviet negotiators might have to turn down applications for aid. (They have managed to give the impression that they almost never do this; they could hardly expect people to believe that factories were to be had free for the asking.) In the negotiations over the large Indonesian loan, we witnessed the curious spectacle of the Soviet Union seeking to persuade the Indonesians to accept a loan of unlimited size while the Indonesians insisted on limiting it to $100 million.[14] If the roles had been reversed, with the Indonesians asking for more and the Russians offering less, the propa-

[13] *The New York Times,* March 13, 1957.

[14] Same, September 20, 1956.

ganda value of the transaction for the U.S.S.R. would have been decreased.

It may be argued that reliance on credits is disadvantageous to the Soviet Union precisely because credits limit the amount of aid recipients are willing to accept. The validity of this argument depends upon the scope of the aid program the Russians have in mind. If they would like to establish a truly mammoth program, designed virtually to saturate the target countries with Soviet technicians and Soviet construction projects, then it is true that the use of credits would hamper their objective. On the other hand, if their objective is to "penetrate" rather than to "saturate" the recipient countries, then credits serve their purpose better. For reasons to be discussed later, it is probable that the U.S.S.R. has the less ambitious kind of program in mind.

Loans may also appeal to the Soviet policymakers because they offer more opportunities than grants for future manipulation of the aid relationship in pursuit of Soviet objectives. An outright grant establishes an economic relationship that exists only during the period it is being drawn upon. Only some minor continuing economic relationships develop, such as the continued import of replacement parts. But loans inaugurate relationships that continue for the full period of repayment and therefore establish a broader and longer-lasting foothold in the underdeveloped countries. The Indian steel mill, for instance, will provide occasion for Soviet purchasing agents to operate in India for twelve years after the completion of the project, negotiating for commodities to be imported into the U.S.S.R. with the proceeds of the loan repayments. Thus, as a basis for the long-run maintenance or expansion of trade, a credit program offers more to the Soviet Union than a grant program.

Grant aid permits greater flexibility in the original transaction; it can be used without regard to a country's ability to support the burden of repayment. But a loan involves a whole series of transactions over a period of time, and thus permits greater flexibility on various occasions subsequent to the loan transaction itself. Suppose some recipient country should be unable to meet its payments of interest and principal, perhaps because of a poor harvest or because it had overcommitted its exports. The U.S.S.R. would then be in a position to make a magnanimous gesture, by reducing or even forgiving the interest or principal, or postponing the payment until the recipient is in a better position to pay. Credits are thus twice-blessed; they bless by maintaining the sense of dignity of the recipient when first extended, and they bless by securing the gratitude of the recipient if payments are reduced or forgiven. Grants would serve neither of these ends.

On balance, then, the use of credits serves Soviet interests at least as well as grants and possibly better. In the short run, at least, the offer of credits has not proved to be a serious obstacle to the acceptance of Soviet aid. Credits must eventually be repaid with interest, however, and repayment may give rise to certain difficulties. If the rate of increase of new Soviet lending tapers off, the value of repayments, plus interest, will eventually exceed the volume of new lending. The debtor countries will find their exports to the U.S.S.R. growing larger than their imports under new loans. With large proportions of their foreign exchange-producing exports going to the U.S.S.R. they may face difficulties in buying from Western countries. The U.S.S.R. will therefore be under some pressure to expand loans to underdeveloped countries at a time when it may no longer feel disposed or prepared to do so. Yet, to refuse to increase lending would place the Soviet Union in the uncomfortable, and very unsocialist, position of a Shylock living off the fat of the poor nations on the basis of past investments. By extending loans, rather than grants, the Russians are, in effect, giving a hostage to fortune that may one day create as much bad feeling as the present program creates good will.

A second problem to which the repayment of credits may give rise is the absorption of a mounting volume of imports into the U.S.S.R. It was shown earlier that the Soviet planners give little evidence of an intention to modify greatly the autarkical pattern of their economy. Of course, there is no absolute barrier to absorbing imports. In the extreme, cotton and rice can simply be burned; even sensible capitalist nations have at times found this an expedient political solution to an economic problem. More realistically, the surplus imports could be employed in uses in which their real economic value is low. If the Soviet (and Bloc) populations did not wish to consume the rice and dried fruits in the quantities offered at the going prices, prices could be lowered to levels at which the imports would eventually be consumed. To the extent that imports are absorbed in this way, they represent a much smaller value to the Soviet economy than the capital goods once exported.

As long as imports are absorbed in this way, only an economic loss is involved. The question is whether the Soviet Union and the other Bloc countries will be content to accept the loss, or whether they will seek to make the best of a bad thing by re-exporting the surplus imports. Reports persist that this has actually been done with some of the goods obtained by barter between the Bloc and the underdeveloped countries. Burmese rice, bartered for Chinese goods at a time when the world market for rice was low, was later resold by China to Ceylon for cash, and at a higher price, a deal which aroused the ire of both the Burmese and the Ceylonese. Indonesian goods, sold under barter to Bloc countries, were later reported to have been resold in the European market for cash, in competition with direct Indonesian exports. West German importers assert that they have bought Egyptian cotton from Czechoslovakia and other Bloc countries at ten per cent below the market price.[15] Even exports from Communist China to the U.S.S.R. are reported to have been resold in West European markets at low prices.[16] Whether or not these reports are all true, as the volume of imports shipped in repayment of development loans begins to rise, the

[15] *The New York Times*, January 6, 1957; August 21, 1956; March 8, 1957. The last report was denied by Egyptian authorities.

[16] Alexander Eckstein in *Moscow-Peking Axis*, by Howard L. Boorman and others (New York: Harper, for the Council on Foreign Relations, 1957), p. 83.

pressure to re-export the surpluses will grow. The problems to which this practice would give rise could be avoided if the aid program took the form of grants rather than loans.

A more reasonable adjustment to the problem of absorbing surpluses would be a partial relaxation of autarky if imports from the underdeveloped countries became large enough to pose serious problems. We can imagine the U.S.S.R. deciding to become "dependent" upon the underdeveloped countries for imports in excess of a certain minimum domestic production deemed necessary in case of a sudden cessation of such imports. For example, the Russians would continue to produce enough cotton so that, if political or military developments interrupted the flow of imports, they would still be able to supply their minimum needs from domestic sources; requirements in excess of this minimum would be met through imports. This new concept of a limited autarky would greatly ease the problem of absorbing imports, while preserving the nation's basic invulnerability to a cessation of imports in times of emergency.

The rationale of the Soviet use of credits instead of grants for the aid program is therefore fairly clear. The policy offers a number of advantages, at least in the short run. In the long run, however, the credit program may be expected to create difficulties which, while not insurmountable, might undermine some of the favorable results obtained during the first few years of the program.

Aid with no questions asked

The Soviet spokesmen stress their willingness to approve any project the government of the recipient country wishes to undertake. "Just tell us what you want and you can have it," the Soviet mission is reported to have told the Indonesian negotiators.[17] We read also that the U.S.S.R. first offered the Egyptians a loan of $147 million, but when President Nasser expressed dissatisfaction with the amount,

[17] *The New York Times*, September 20, 1956.

the Russians on the following day raised the offer to $175 million.[18] In determining how the money is to be spent, the Soviet negotiators refuse to assume responsibility for telling other sovereign nations what is good for them and what is not. They do not demand a wide range of statistical information about the economy of the recipient country in order to judge the desirability or even the economic sense of the project requested. They do not require a detailed "economic justification" of a project as a condition of granting a loan. Only if requested by the recipient country, will they suggest projects that might be useful or evaluate a project proposed by the recipient.

This position is in deliberate contrast to that taken by Western agencies dispensing economic aid. The International Bank for Reconstruction and Development, for example, uses the capital markets of the world as the source of the funds lent to underdeveloped countries. Its ability to borrow depends upon the wisdom with which it places loans, and an important part of that wisdom is the ability to select those projects that are economically and financially sound. The Bank, therefore, insists that a project proposal be accompanied by a detailed technical and economic analysis. If the Bank is not persuaded of the soundness of the project, the request is refused. The Bank has assisted various underdeveloped countries by carrying out detailed economic analyses of their economies, gathering a large body of statistical data about the country. Similarly, the United States aid program requires its administrators to pass on the economic soundness of project proposals, and to refuse those requests it considers unjustified.

The defense of this kind of "interference" in the affairs of the underdeveloped countries is that the goal of economic development is not well served by a squandering of limited funds on useless projects. Many of the underdeveloped countries lack the trained personnel to evaluate the economic suitability of individual projects or development programs. Or their governments may wish to undertake flamboyant projects that would enhance their political

[18] Same, November 22, 1957.

positions or their country's international prestige, but that would contribute little or nothing to genuine economic growth. To accede to such requests, it is felt, would win a cheap prize of good will, but would in the long run tend to undermine the economic development of the country. It is believed to be the unpleasant duty of the donor or lender to restrain the governments of the underdeveloped countries from what are conceived to be costly acts of folly.

Inevitably, this policy kindles resentment and discord. Jordan has expressed its displeasure with United States aid officials' insistence upon participating in the execution of the aid program, and has demanded that they confine themselves to technical and supervisory functions.[19] Syria turned down an offer by the International Bank for Reconstruction and Development to finance a number of development projects, stating as one of the reasons that the conditions imposed were a threat to Syrian sovereignty.[20] The Soviet policy, in contrast, avoids the danger of trampling on the sensibilities of the recipient governments. Naturally the Soviet approach receives a much warmer reception. After battling with the hardheaded bankers, skeptical lawyers and insistent economists who run Western and international aid programs, it is a welcome relief for the negotiators of the underdeveloped countries to deal with the openhanded and eager Russians. The vaunted American administrative efficiency melts away when negotiators bog down in what appear to be endless surveys and reports. Soviet negotiators emphasize speed. Thus, a report from Cairo states that only four months after the signing of the Soviet credit agreement some of the machinery contracted for was already on a ship bound from the U.S.S.R. to Alexandria. "The United States," Arab critics say, "first sends in a big survey team that must certify economic justification for a project before it is approved. It sometimes has been years before any concrete results were seen."[21]

[19] Same, August 26, 1956.
[20] Same, August 28, 1957.
[21] Same, February 8, 1958.

One major issue on which Western economists often find themselves in conflict with the representatives of underdeveloped countries is the place of industrialization in economic development. Under certain circumstances, there are potent economic reasons for arguing that a country's economy would advance more rapidly if agriculture or mining or light industry were developed ahead of, or in place of, heavy industry. But heavy industry sometimes has an important symbolic value to the underdeveloped countries; it represents power, progress, achievement, prestige, independence, and other values that may outweigh the economic cost. The Soviet Union has consistently supported the view, sometimes to a ludicrous extent, that heavy industry is virtually synonymous with economic development. In the Economic and Social Council, for example, a Soviet delegate has argued that the failure of the United Nations to support the industrialization of Tanganyika illustrates the opposition of the West to a genuine economic development in underdeveloped countries.[22] Thus, regardless of the merits of the individual case, the underdeveloped countries find their aspirations strongly supported by the U.S.S.R. while the West is in the position of pushing them in a direction in which they may not wish to move.

Two points may be made in evaluating this aspect of the Soviet program. The first is a question of fact, namely, whether the Russians are actually as unquestioning in their approach to aid requests as they represent themselves to be. Unfortunately, very little published information is available on the details of negotiations, and official announcements must be expected to paint a rosy picture. We can readily imagine cases in which Soviet negotiators would feel compelled to refuse requests because the item requested is not available in the U.S.S.R., or because the recipient has already received too much aid, or because the item requested is of a kind that would yield the Soviet Union

[22] Alvin Z. Rubinstein, "Soviet Policy toward Underdeveloped Areas in the Economic and Social Council," *International Organization*, v. 9, no. 2 (May 1955) p. 234.

little propaganda advantage. In fact, the negotiations do sometimes take a long time, and newspaper reports indicate considerable and sometimes heated haggling. Nevertheless, it is significant that no important case has come to light in which the U.S.S.R. turned down a request for aid on the grounds that it was to be used for economically unsuitable purposes. The most obvious apparent exception is the High Dam at Aswan that the Egyptians thought the U.S.S.R. might finance when the United States, Britain, and the International Bank withdrew their offer. This episode is too obscure for the outside observer to be quite sure exactly what happened, what was asked, offered, or refused, and who was persuaded of the soundness of what judgment. But the case at least shows that the Soviet offers of aid were not unlimited and indiscriminate. This seems obvious, yet Soviet spokesmen continue to convey the impression to many people that they never refuse a reasonable request and that their concept of what is "reasonable" is much closer to that of the governments of underdeveloped countries than are the views of Western aid-givers. It will be of great interest to see if the U.S.S.R. is able to maintain this reputation as the Soviet aid program gets older and, perhaps, bigger.

The second point is the possibility that in acceding to any requests for aid, regardless of economic justification, the U.S.S.R. may run into some of the problems that the Western policy seeks to avoid. If the U.S.S.R. should build an iron and steel plant that subsequently proves to be a high-cost and uneconomical operation, it may well have to bear the blame, justifiably or not. A monumental hydroelectric plant that has few customers for its power or a gleaming highway that bears little traffic would be constant irritants to the recipients, especially during the years when precious exports were flowing out in repayment of the loan. Perhaps some such consideration lay behind the Soviet unwillingness to embark on the Aswan Dam project.

The picture must not be overdrawn. It would be foolish to assume that the underdeveloped countries do not know what they are doing. Indeed, critics of the Western policy have argued that the bad feeling caused by refusals to support requests for marginal projects have done more harm than the projects would have done had they been supported. Every country is entitled to the honor of having at least one steel mill, is the argument. And there are few countries, advanced or underdeveloped, that accept optimum economic performance as the sole guide to action. Moreover, the experience that economic planners in underdeveloped countries have gained from having had to justify their proposals to such institutions as the International Bank will be applied in their proposals to the Russians. Thus, both the Russians and the underdeveloped countries owe a debt to the International Bank. And it is likely to be the rare project that becomes a clear and obvious failure; more often it is a matter of resources being applied to one use when another use might have been more effective. The misallocation of resources in such cases is not apparent to the eye, but can be demonstrated only by sophisticated economic analysis. Aside from a few "impact" projects, the credit agreements thus far made by the U.S.S.R. are of the kind one would expect to find in carefully planned programs of economic development.

If we put these bits of argument together, the proper conclusion seems to be that the Soviet policy of accepting whatever projects are proposed may result in somewhat less than the maximum efficient use of Soviet economic aid by the recipient countries. But it is likely to be the rare case in which an obviously unwise project remains a rankling source of irritation to the recipient. Against this possibility, the Russians enjoy the undisputed advantage of the favorable reception that comes of respecting the dignity of the governments with which they deal.

The interest rate

Soviet loans typically carry an interest charge of 2 to 2½ per cent, compared with rates of about 4 to 5 per cent charged by the International Bank and the United States government. The Indian government, for example, is paying the U.S.S.R. 2½ per cent on the Bhilai steel mill, whereas the Tata Iron and Steel Company, Ltd. and the Indian Iron and Steel Company are paying the International Bank 4¾ per cent on their loans. Soviet propaganda represents the West as striving to exploit the poverty of the underdeveloped countries by charging so much. Its own low interest rate is presented as evidence of the fact that its aid program is of *mutual* benefit, and not designed to squeeze as much as possible out of the poor peoples of the world. The low interest rate also strikes a vital chord in the traditional and religious attitudes of many peoples of Asia and the Middle East, where the money-lender is an object of scorn. Some may happen to know that a large proportion of United States aid consists of grants which not only carry no interest at all, but need not even be repaid. But when loans are arrayed against loans, the comparison is favorable to the U.S.S.R. The low interest rate thus serves to increase the attractiveness of the lender as well as the loan.

In view of these advantages, one may well wonder why interest is charged at all. If the economic motive is of doubtful significance in explaining the choice of credits rather than loans, it has even less significance as an explanation of an interest charge. More important is the fact that Soviet loans to other Bloc countries normally carry an interest charge, sometimes of 2 to 2½ per cent and sometimes less. An interest charge serves further to lend conviction to the Soviet claim that their aid is based on businesslike and friendly negotiations between equals, shorn of political motivations. Thus, the interest rate of 2 to 2½ per cent accomplishes several purposes. It is low enough to undercut Western rates and make Western lenders seem rapacious by comparison. And it is high enough to support the claim that Soviet aid is based on mutual economic interest.

In an estimate of the total cost of Soviet loans to the recipients, the significance of the interest rate depends upon the prices charged for the projects. Consider, for example, the Bhilai steel mill, for which the Russians are charging the Indian government $115 million. Repayments are to be made in twelve equal annual installments, with 2½ per cent interest charged annually on the unpaid balance. Total interest payments will therefore amount to about $18.7 million. If the interest rate were 4¾ per cent, as the International Bank might charge, total interest payments would amount to about $35.5 million. Thus, India appears to be saving $16.8 million in interest charges because of favorable Soviet financing. But the question of how much the Indians will save on the entire project depends upon the kind of steel mill that is built for the $115 million. If the mill they build could have been built by Western firms for $100 million, the entire saving on interest would be lost by the overcharge on the price.

This illustration is presented only in order to demonstrate the relevance of price to the question of the significance of the interest rate. There is too little published evidence upon which to base a general statement about the competitiveness of Soviet pricing. We have only such information as a news report from Cairo that Soviet Bloc negotiators raised their prices 40 per cent on various development projects after underbidding all Western private firms,[23] or the Burmese complaint that they were being overcharged on all their purchases. On the other hand, the reports from Yemen state that the U.S.S.R. constructed roads, ports and factories there at 30 per cent below world prices.[24] It would be unwise to leap to a general conclusion on the basis of so little evidence. In any case, it is extremely difficult to form an accurate judgment on the fairness of a price for a construction project. One would first need a complete set of blueprints of the project, to be submitted to Western firms for bidding purposes. Even this would tell us only what a fair price of the project in blueprint form would be; one must also consider the quality of the final product—of the equipment actually installed and of the construction and installation work. For lack

[23] *The New York Times*, June 5, 1957.

[24] Council for Economic and Industry Research, Inc., *Foreign Assistance Activities of the Communist Bloc and Their Implications for the United States*, in *Foreign Aid Program*, Senate Doc. no. 52, 85th Cong., 1st sess. (Washington: GPO, 1957), p. 760.

of such information, it is difficult to make any but the most general statements about Soviet pricing of their projects.

A country such as India has a sufficient number of experienced government officials, engineers and businessmen to hold its own in negotiations with the Russians. This may be less true in some other underdeveloped countries. Even in the case of India, there were reports that the Soviet Union had sought, at first, to sell a dismantled Czech steel mill and later a second-rate mill that had previously been rejected by China,[25] instead of building a new mill. In general the borrower is at a disadvantage when the lender is at the same time the contractor. Negotiations over price are intermingled with negotiations over financing terms, and more attractive financing terms create a disposition to accept a less favorable price. On this account, one would expect that Soviet prices may be somewhat higher.

On the other hand, if the U.S.S.R. is eager to expand its activities in underdeveloped countries through its aid program it would make little sense for the Soviet negotiators to quibble over price. A million dollars means a great deal to a Western engineering firm bidding on a contract, but in terms of the whole Soviet program it is a small sum. It would hardly seem worth risking the enormous damage that could come from a scandal involving price-gouging. The circumstances were entirely different in Soviet dealings with the countries of Eastern Europe, for the latter were under the firm thumb of Moscow and had no choice but to accept Soviet price terms. Trade between China and the U.S.S.R. has taken place at prices fairly close to the world level.[26] To be sure, we may expect instances of ignorance or of bureaucratic fumbling. In negotiating over a construction project, Soviet engineers may set a price honestly in terms of their own costs; but, ignorant of foreign costs, they may set a price considerably in excess of the foreign price. Or individual Soviet negotiators in credit or trade agreements, having their own plan targets to meet and their own departmental budgets to be reckoned

[25] *Soviet Technical Assistance*, cited, p. 17.
[26] Eckstein, cited, pp. 86-88.

with, may seek to squeeze a little more out of the negotiations than they should. On the basis of United States experience, we should also expect some defamatory reports of Soviet activities by disgruntled negotiators of underdeveloped countries who have tried unsuccessfully to force completely unacceptable terms on the Russians. But it would be erroneous to interpret such reports as evidence of a general policy of price-squeezing, or of the importance of economic considerations among the motivations of the aid program. On balance, then, one would expect Soviet prices to be competitive with world prices, with some exceptions.

Repayment in local currencies and commodities

One of the most difficult problems in international lending is the "transfer problem." A borrower may be well prepared to repay the principal and interest on a loan in his own currency, but may encounter difficulties in transferring these funds to the lender in the lender's currency. Thus, Burma may have enormous quantities of rice with which to repay a United States dollar loan but, unless United States importers wish to purchase the rice, the Burmese cannot obtain the necessary dollars. As an alternative, Burma could sell the rice to a third country that is able and willing to pay dollars for it, but unless the seller's bargaining position is strong he is likely to have trouble persuading countries to use their dollars in this way. The Russians have cut straight to the core of this problem and announced their willingness to accept repayment of their loans directly in the form of the customary exports of the recipient countries.

As the system works in practice, the recipient country makes its annual repayments of interest and principal in the form of cash deposits in its Central Bank, to the account of the Soviet government. The U.S.S.R. thus accumulates sums of local currency that may be used to pay embassy and other costs and to purchase commodities, on sale within the country, to be exported to the U.S.S.R. A question that arises is the extent to which domestic inflation in the underdeveloped countries will reduce the real value of the accumulated currencies. It is believed that the agreements generally contain "gold clauses" providing that, in the event of inflation, the amounts due would be revised upward to maintain the original purchasing power of the local currency.

One can hardly overemphasize the attractiveness of the local currency provisions of Soviet credit agreements. An underdeveloped country, facing a choice between a loan that must be repaid in dollars or sterling and one that can be repaid in its own currency, has much to gain by choosing the latter. The burden of solving the transfer problem is in effect taken over by the Russians. It becomes their responsibility to find the commodities to be purchased with the local currencies and exported to the U.S.S.R. The appeal of the local-currency provision was emphasized when Turkey, after several years of refusing Soviet offers, accepted Russian aid in the construction of a $10-$14 million sheet glass factory because the loan could be repaid in local currency and not foreign exchange, of which Turkey is critically short.[27]

In the long run, the practice of accepting repayment in local currencies and local commodities may not be without difficulties. For the Soviet Union the problem of absorbing imports that was discussed above remains. There will be additional problems as word gets around among merchants in the debtor countries that the Russians have large sums of money that have to be spent locally; it is to be expected that this knowledge will be reflected in the prices quoted to Soviet purchasers. Repayment in local currency may not prove as painless for a debtor country's balance of payments as appears at first glance. Unless the U.S.S.R. uses these funds to buy goods that would not otherwise have been exported, the debtor is really paying in foreign exchange. There is also a risk that Soviet buyers will bid up prices so that the debtor country loses export markets in other countries. But, if the future will not all be smooth sailing, the immediate impact of the local-currency provision is highly favorable. However, the U.S.S.R. has no

[27] *The New York Times*, August 14, 1957.

monopoly on this practice. The United States, too, offers loans that are repayable in local currencies, both out of aid funds and out of the proceeds of sales of surplus agricultural products.

Absence of political "strings"

Of all the advantages the Russians advertise in their aid program, perhaps the one that has made the greatest impact is the assertion that aid is given with absolutely "no strings attached." The very expression has become part of a formula used by leaders of underdeveloped countries in public statements on their aid negotiations with the U.S.S.R. Thus, President Sukarno of Indonesia accepted Soviet aid only because it was given "without any strings attached"; Minister of National Economy Kallas of Syria praised the U.S.S.R. for having given aid "with no conditions attached"; Premier Khalil of Sudan is prepared to buy arms from the Soviet Bloc because Czechoslovakia sold arms to Egypt "without political strings." [28] The very repetition of the phrase testifies to its vitality as a political issue.

In stressing the absence of political strings in their aid program, the Russians accomplish two things: they face up directly to the issue over which many countries may balk at accepting Soviet aid; and they indirectly level a potent charge against Western aid programs, particularly that of the United States. This is not the place to discuss the merits of the United States aid programs. It is important to note, however, that influential groups within the underdeveloped countries consider that United States aid involves political strings. Neutral countries note that most United States aid goes to countries that have accepted military alliances or allowed United States air bases to be constructed on their territories. Responsible United States officials have called attention to our policy of using the aid program to strengthen capitalism in the underdeveloped countries, at the expense of the socialized sectors,[29] and it is felt that United States influence in the International Bank for Re-

[28] Same, September 12, 1956; September 1, 1957; July 26, 1956.
[29] Same, September 13, 1957.

construction and Development works to the same end. Recommendations from Western sources designed to stimulate the flow of private capital to the underdeveloped countries, and particularly criticism of the restrictive measures taken by underdeveloped countries, have evoked resentment in some quarters. By proclaiming a "no strings attached" policy in its aid program, the U.S.S.R. has capitalized on the jealousy with which the underdeveloped countries cherish their newly won sovereignty.

It is difficult to evaluate the extent to which the Soviet Union has actually lived up to its "no strings" policy. It is clear that political loyalty is not a condition of granting aid, for aid offers are open to such countries as Pakistan and Turkey, which are members of Western military defensive alliances. As evidence of their wish not to interfere in the political balance between capitalist and socialist sectors within the recipient countries, the Russians can point to the steel file plant they built for the Hindustan Gas Company, a private firm in India. They have invited a delegation of leading Turkish businessmen to Moscow to discuss the financing of future projects.[30] They have championed the right of underdeveloped countries to erect tariff barriers to protect infant industries, and to employ exchange controls for the promotion of domestic economic development.[31] Perhaps the most telling argument is the fact that industrial establishments constructed under the Soviet aid program become the property of the recipient country. This contrasts sharply with foreign private direct investment, in which foreign companies construct plants and then continue to own and operate them for profit. The Russians thus represent themselves as making a genuine contribution to the economic independence of the underdeveloped countries, while the presence of foreign capitalist firms serves as a constant reminder of economic dependency. When it serves the political interest of groups in the underdeveloped countries to hurl the charges of "exploitation" and "imperialism," foreign capitalist firms

[30] Same, September 4, 1957.
[31] *Vneshniaia torgovlia*, no. 3 (1948), p. 25.

are ever present targets, but the Russians have left their monuments of aid and have gone back home.

It would not be difficult to show the ways in which Western aid has been misrepresented in the above characterization. United States aid has been given to socialist countries such as Yugoslavia, and to state-owned projects in such countries as India. Substantial quantities of aid have gone to neutral countries that have made no political or military commitments to the United States. There have been economic requirements attached to American aid, but this is different from political strings, and after all the need to repay Soviet "aid" with interest is a fairly respectable string in itself. Aid by the United States government and also private United States lending through the International Bank do not involve ownership of property in the recipient countries. It can be shown that private direct investment by United States firms has made significant contributions to economic growth in the underdeveloped countries, not only in production and employment but perhaps more in the training in technical and managerial skills.[32] This is recognized in many underdeveloped countries that have said they would welcome private investment subject to reasonable limitations. However, the free public discussion and annual Congressional debates in the United States provide ample reason for the underdeveloped countries to feel that United States aid is a tool designed to serve United States interests, and is thus inevitably tied to political ends.

There have been instances in which Soviet aid has been used as a direct lever for political gain. The experience of Yugoslavia, as a renegade Communist country, cannot perhaps be generalized for the underdeveloped countries as a group; but it is worth noting the sharp halt in aid to Yugoslavia because of Soviet dissatisfaction with the Yugoslav position during the Hungarian uprising. In the case of

[32] Emilio G. Collado and Jack F. Bennett, "Private Investment and Economic Development," *Foreign Affairs*, v. 35, no. 4 (July 1957), pp. 631-645; American Enterprise Association, Inc., *American Private Enterprise, Foreign Economic Development, and the Aid Programs*, in *Foreign Aid Program*, cited, pp. 539-618.

Syria, however, it would be an error to interpret the events in the late summer of 1957 as evidence of the use of political strings in the economic aid program. The Syrians apparently came asking for military aid, and the rise to power of pro-Soviet forces in the military establishment is to be explained primarily by domestic political factors. It does not at all appear to be a case of economic aid being used by the U.S.S.R. to install pro-Soviet military leaders and to force military aid upon an unwilling government.

Thus, we might conclude that, except for a few instances, Soviet aid has not been used so far as a weapon for securing political gains. But the Yugoslav exception is important because it suggests something to be looked for in the future. If we are right in believing that a major objective of the Soviet aid program is to influence the foreign policies of the underdeveloped countries, then the Soviet Union cannot forever maintain the policy of renouncing political strings. As the aid program grows and political events move on, more and more cases may be expected to arise in which the Russians will want a recipient country to take a certain action favorable to their interests. It will be increasingly difficult to abstain from saying, in effect, "Look, we are pouring a lot of aid into your country. We would hate to stop giving aid, but you are not being as friendly to us as we are to you." This puts the matter bluntly; it may be to the advantage of the U.S.S.R. to try to prevent such situations from arising. And other pressures are likely to be more effective. Direct pressure may not work unless heavy dependence on Soviet aid has been established. The particular action on which the U.S.S.R. might want to insist would have to be very important to risk giving up the position gained by the aid program if the recipient should reject the pressure and cancel Soviet aid. To the extent that the political aim of the Soviet aid policy is a broad one, comprising a picture of the U.S.S.R. as a friend and real supporter of underdeveloped countries which does not "interfere" as the United States does, its successful pursuit may inhibit political pressure on specific issues. The U.S.S.R. benefits from offering an alternative to American aid, but the American alternative to Soviet aid has not disappeared.

There is no way of knowing what political use the U.S.S.R. will be able to make of its aid program in the long run. Soviet officials may feel that unless they can apply effective pressure, the aid program will not be yielding the results it was designed for. If the recipient countries actually felt that Soviet aid would continue to be available, regardless of the international moves they made, the Soviet leaders might well feel they were getting little benefit from their aid program. They are surely seeking primarily political advantage. The problem is to know what form it will take and how successfully they can use their aid program to secure it. One condition of success seems to be to deny any political objective, at least at the outset.

The first few years of the Soviet aid program may be looked upon as the period of "infiltration," as it were. It is necessary first to induce the underdeveloped countries to accept Soviet aid and to expand trade relations. Then a position will be created that has various possibilities. If a sufficient measure of "dependence" has been established, the withdrawal or withholding of aid may be used as a lever for obtaining political concessions. Short of that, the new economic intimacy still offers political possibilities. It is, therefore, not surprising that in the first few years the Russians should be extremely careful to avoid attaching political strings to their aid, lest they not be able to do so later on.

Advantages of totalitarian government

The Asian friend of the United States has an unenviable job in trying to defend American economic aid to his people. America speaks with many voices, and the words that come through to Asia are not only those of the internationalist and the humanitarian, but also those of the isolationist, the racist, the military-minded, and the budget-cutter. The Asian friend of Russia has a much easier job of it. The Soviet press, the radio and the pronouncements of all public and private citizens constitute a single chorus of support for the government's brotherly assistance to all underprivileged peoples. If Asians are suspicious of ulterior motives behind economic aid, America feeds much more fuel to the fires of suspicion than does the U.S.S.R.

It has often been remarked that the government of a totalitarian state possesses a number of advantages in political activity over governments of democratic states. With total control over press and radio, the Soviet leaders can ensure that the public pronouncements of officials and citizens support the policy of the moment. The government operates in secrecy, and the less attractive motivations of policy are never discussed in public. By contrast, Congressional hearings and debates in the United States reflect a full cross section of public opinion, some of which has an unfortunate propaganda effect. Nor need the Soviet leaders be embarrassed by published utterances of dissident citizens and the sometimes unfortunate statements of public officials. Thus, the Soviet Union is well placed to make political capital out of its aid program.

In the administration of its economic aid program, the U.S.S.R. is able to operate more flexibly than the United States. The Soviet leaders can plan their strategy a number of years ahead, without having to reconsider their program every year on the basis of annual appropriations by the legislature. They also have greater short-run maneuverability because they are not bound by detailed budget appropriations, and can therefore capitalize quickly on favorable situations that arise suddenly. Policy changes can be made with rapidity, and may be considered on their merits, without regard to their impact on special political and economic interests within the nation.

The Soviet government is less restricted in its action by the demands of vocal pressure groups. There are no farm blocs, no organized nationality groups, no articulate anti-socialist organizations, no powerful economy-minded tax-payers' associations. Of course, the Soviet leaders do have pressures of their own to contend with. Popular demand for a higher standard of living, and the pressures in the satellite countries for a revision of the economic relationships of the past, must certainly be taken account of in party deliberations over the size of the aid program. It may even be argued with some justice that a totalitarian regime is at a disadvantage in coping with resistance from its own people. A democratic regime provides, through public debate, a means whereby a policy can be explained and defended against outspoken criticism, and opponents who are not persuaded find release for their passions. A totalitarian regime cannot tolerate open debate on, say, the relative merits of foreign aid versus a higher standard of living, and therefore resistance remains underground, passive, ignorant and sullen. But it also remains unorganized and diffused, so that it poses a lesser problem for the government.

With its total control over the national economy, the Soviet government can channel resources in those directions that are most important for its own purposes. Although the total Soviet national product is smaller than that of the United States, a larger proportion of it is allocated to the production of capital goods than to consumer goods. Therefore, the difference between the two nations is smaller in capital goods production than in total production. Moreover, it is easier to allocate more of the machinery and capital goods production for export, if this suits policy. Thus, totalitarian control over the economy enables the Soviet Union to enjoy relatively more maneuverability with an absolutely smaller national product.

Not only goods but people are subject to this control. All Soviet engineers and technicians above a certain level of skill have until recently been subject to job transfer at the pleasure of the state. Soviet engineers are accustomed to the idea that they may one day be ordered to move to a new job in some remote section of the country. There is no need to induce skilled people to accept an appointment in a technical mission abroad by offering them high salaries. If policy requires that only the best people be sent, there is no problem of some of the best people not wishing to go abroad at any price. For instance, when prospects brightened for the extension of economic aid to Turkey, the

Soviet leaders were able to dig out of mothballs the man best suited for an ambassadorship. He is Nikita Rizhov, the engineer who supervised the construction of the textile mill built for the Turks by the Russians twenty-three years ago.[33] Since Soviet citizens are not free to travel abroad at their own pleasure, the opportunity to join a technical mission may be expected to arouse keen interest in many technicians. The role of totalitarian control is evident in the very size of the corps of engineers and technicians from which the government may select the personnel of its technical missions. The yearly production of engineers and technicians is perhaps the first significant instance in which the U.S.S.R. has achieved its aim of "overtaking and surpassing" the United States. A totalitarian regime can deploy its technicians even more easily than it can produce them.

Since the Soviet government need not be ruled by commercial considerations in its aid and trade programs, it can compete effectively against private Western firms and such organizations as the International Bank. It can, for instance, sell below world prices, or absorb a loss to make the lowest bid on a construction contract that it particularly wants. However, Soviet policy pronouncements do not emphasize price concessions as one of the advantages of Soviet aid and trade. The emphasis is rather on "mutually favorable terms," usually signifying trade at world prices. It is paradoxical that the Russians, on the one hand, criticize Western monopolists for deliberately depressing the prices of exports from the underdeveloped countries, yet, on the other hand, offer trade at world prices as the basis of mutually advantageous terms. The pattern seems to be that, where trade and construction contracts can be secured on favorable terms, the Soviet Union strives to operate on those terms, but where it seems necessary to subsidize trade offers or contract bids, economic loss can be accepted for political gain. Whenever Western transactions follow normal commercial patterns, the Soviet Union, if it wishes, can offer better terms just as it can let politics guide its eco-

[33] *The New York Times*, August 14, 1957.

nomic policy, as it did when it withdrew from the Australian wool market for purely diplomatic reasons.

Successful administration of a large aid program, however, requires more than that the government be able to operate freely. It depends as well upon the initiative and resourcefulness of the many people at the lower levels who actually apply the policy established at the top. The serious problems faced by the Soviet government in industrial management suggest some of the difficulties they may face in the administration of foreign aid. The poor quality of construction and production, for instance, is a chronic problem in Soviet industrial administration. Not even the harsh penalty of imprisonment has offset the factors that impel managers to produce substandard output. Only where the government has concentrated its efforts, as in military production, has it been able to maintain consistently high standards. But the central government cannot be everywhere at once, and in the sectors of the economy that do not have priority the problem of obtaining high quality continues.[34]

Quality may be particularly important in foreign trade, which involves larger amounts of goods than the credit program. While mounting in volume, foreign trade has already given rise to disappointment by purchasers of Soviet goods. Reports from Egypt alleged dissatisfaction with the quality of crude oil and wheat shipments and with delays in deliveries. Negotiations over the $175-million loan were apparently held up because of Egypt's irritating insistence on advance guarantees on prices, quality and delivery.[35] From Burma, too, have come reports of dissatisfaction with the quality of Soviet goods received and offered as part of the barter exchange deal.[36] The extent to which quality will be a problem in the capital goods exported under the credit program depends on the level of

[34] Joseph S. Berliner, *Factory and Manager in the U.S.S.R.* (Cambridge: Harvard University Press, 1957), Chapter 9.

[35] *The New York Times*, June 5, 1957; December 18, 1957.

[36] Same, January 6, 1957.

priority and the degree of attention that the central government gives to this matter. As the program expands, less and less of it can command the direct attention of high government officials, and it is reasonable to expect that the normal processes of the Soviet economy will manifest themselves. Thus, the Soviet plants producing the equipment for the Indian steel mill, which is so much in the public eye, will certainly strive for as excellent products as they can, even if the effort and cost are such that they fail to fulfill their general production quotas and to stay within assigned cost. But not every export can be treated this way. Operating under tight production schedules, Soviet managers may be expected to turn to those practices they have found necessary in the past to obtain successful performance, one of the most prominent of which is deterioration of quality. The problem is particularly serious for the U.S.S.R. since the low quality of some Soviet products is well known in many of the underdeveloped countries, and the recipients may therefore be hypercritical.[37]

Substandard production is most evident in the Soviet construction industries. Travelers in the U.S.S.R. repeatedly report the poor condition of Soviet buildings only a few years after their construction. Again, this is partly the consequence of the low priority assigned to residential construction, and of the poor materials and labor apportioned to it. To the extent that the technicians sent abroad are the best in the country, foreign construction work may prove superior to the average quality within the U.S.S.R. But traditional habits of work and standards of quality may well be transferred, especially if the aid program grows to a size that requires the export of less and less competent technical personnel.

It is important to distinguish between two types of substandard production: that which merely involves poorer styling, finish and trim; and that which involves lesser durability and efficiency, obsolete models and heavier weight of parts. The lower quality of Soviet production in the former sense may actually be an advantage. Such com-

[37] *Soviet Technical Assistance*, cited, p. 25.

modities may be more suitable to the living standards, tastes and budgets of the underdeveloped countries than the highly styled and finished products that United States purchasers, both individual and industrial, seem to demand. It has indeed been argued that, because the U.S.S.R. has only recently emerged from economic backwardness, it has a better intuitive understanding of attitudes and values in the underdeveloped countries than does the Western world. Because of the lower Soviet standard of living, Soviet missions abroad tend normally to live much more modestly than Western missions. The high salaries demanded by Western engineers to go abroad, and the seemingly ostentatious conditions in which they and their families live,[38] reportedly arouse resentment in the planners of the underdeveloped countries, especially when the costs are charged to a loan that has to be repaid. Similarly, Soviet technicians have a better understanding of the work habits of people not yet accustomed to the rhythm of highly efficient, mechanical factories and construction processes.

The relative advantage of backwardness in this sense may therefore cause the more poorly styled and modestly finished Soviet products to be quite acceptable in the underdeveloped countries. This does not apply to poor quality that affects the length of life, the efficiency and the general utility of the products. The tendency toward low-quality production in the U.S.S.R., which reflects both the system of industrial organization and the relative recency of industrialization, may therefore be expected to prove a handicap to the aid program.

A second prominent feature of the totalitarian economy is its bureaucratic structure. A familiar theme in Soviet writings on the subject is the tendency of officials to seek the safest course of action by following instructions to the letter. This is not to say that initiative is entirely lacking on the lower levels of Soviet administration, but only to emphasize the wide prevalence of caution and the avoidance of responsibility that might get one into trouble. As

[38] See the discussion in Hamilton Fish Armstrong, *Lebanon, Jordan and Iraq*, in *Foreign Aid Program*, cited, p. 1233.

long as the economic aid program is small enough so that senior people can conduct all negotiations and make all decisions, the problem of initiative need not be serious. But as the program expands, a larger number of people will be engaged in the operation of the program, and the habits of work in Soviet society are bound to be reflected in the aid program. There is no better illustration than the Burmese cement case, so typically Soviet that it might have come right out of an article in *Pravda*. The Burmese purchasing agents in the U.S.S.R. ordered a large quantity of cement to be shipped to the port of Rangoon. The Soviet ship carrying the cargo set out just in time to arrive during the monsoon season. Rangoon lacked the warehousing facilities for storing the cement out of the rain, so the Burmese tried to delay its arrival. The Burmese reportedly offered the cement to India at a reduced price, but the Soviet ship's captain had his orders and would not consider delivering it to any place other than the officially designated port. The consequence was that the cement cargo was largely ruined by the rains, and the piers were turned to great blocks of cement.

This is not an isolated instance. Delays in deliveries, a perennial source of irritation to Soviet managers themselves, have created difficulties of various kinds. Egypt ordered a large quantity of badly needed cement from the U.S.S.R. shortly after the Suez fighting ended. The Russians accepted the order, but delivery was so long delayed that the Egyptian cement industry finally caught up with the demand. Then the Egyptians sought to cancel the cement order, but the Soviet trade official refused. When the cement was received, one of the largest cement plants in Alexandria had to shut down for a month.[39]

Oral reports tell of acts so petty and yet so irritating that they must reflect, not general policy, but rigid and unimaginative execution. The Cambodians are said to have discovered that the Chinese sought to deduct the expenses of their good-will mission, including a football team, from their economic development grant to Cambodia. Burma

[39] *The New York Times*, June 5, 1957.

was distressed because it was unable to purchase Soviet goods equal in value to the rice it had shipped to the U.S.S.R.; so what was supposed to be a Soviet credit to Burma turned into a Burmese credit to the U.S.S.R. At this critical juncture, it was discovered that Soviet economic aid missions, instead of paying their own way, sought to charge their expenses to future Soviet deliveries, thus further increasing the Soviet debt to Burma. In view of the paltry sums involved in these incidents, it is clear that the fault is in the bookkeeping and administrative systems, not in the guiding policy.

As the aid and trade programs expand, there will be more ship captains and more trade officials, and the "sea of ink" between senior policymakers and lowly bureaucrats will widen. Following normal administrative procedures in the U.S.S.R, the low-level officials who carry out the day-to-day work of an agency have long lists of plans, targets, quotas and directives, which serve both to map out their work and to measure the success of their performance. If the plan calls for so much cement to be sold, we cannot expect junior officials to assume the responsibility of holding up the cement and thus underfulfilling their plans because the Egyptians or the Burmese have changed their minds. If a better price can be obtained from a sale, or if a lot of second-grade textiles needs to be disposed of, a buyer from Djakarta will do as well as one from Peiping or Kiev. The senior aid officials may groan at the political stupidity of such decisions, but years of Soviet experience and experiment have failed to eliminate the considerable slippage between policy and execution.

This is not to say that the Russians cannot build an excellent steel mill or hydroelectric plant. In the most highly publicized projects, which will command the direct attention of top officials and be staffed by people with considerable skill and authority, performance may well be outstanding. But the larger and more spread-out the program becomes, the more we may expect some of the inefficiencies of Soviet administration to show themselves.

The Soviet system of economic planning suffers from

numerous deficiencies, some of which may be expected to affect the aid program. For instance, one of the ways in which enterprises are motivated to exert a major effort is by setting their production targets at extremely high levels. The consequence is that plans are often not fulfilled; and when one producer fails to fulfill his plan, some of the enterprises he supplies will not receive the materials they need, so they too fail to fulfill their plans. The striving to avoid underfulfillment of production plans leads to many of the characteristic practices of industrial management, such as the deterioration of quality and the production of unplanned commodities that happen to be easy to produce and thus tend to show a spuriously good record of performance.

As long as it is possible for the Soviet foreign aid agencies to keep close watch over the production of machinery, equipment and other goods designated for export, these items can be rescued from the pitfalls of Soviet production processes. But again, as the aid program expands, it will increasingly be caught up in those processes and one may anticipate a mounting incidence of late deliveries, shortages of spare parts, changes in specifications, and other deficiencies about which Soviet managers typically complain.

* * * * * *

To bring together the strands of argument: the terms of Soviet aid are sufficiently attractive for the Russians to encounter no serious obstacles in placing aid contracts. Moreover, the U.S.S.R. enjoys a good reputation in the underdeveloped countries, and the latent suspicion of Soviet subversive and aggressive intentions has been lulled by the very correct behavior of the U.S.S.R. in its dealings with those countries. The totalitarian character of the Soviet government gives it certain advantages in the administration of the aid program, but problems may arise from the rigidities inherent in the Soviet system of administration. Other problems that may be anticipated arise from the terms of Soviet aid, such as the use of repayable credits and the acceptance of repayment in local currencies. The common characteristic of these problems is that they are a function of the size of the aid program; that is, they are likely to become serious only if the program assumes large proportions. If the program remains one of modest proportions, as we shall presently argue it may, they are not likely to be a major obstacle to the effective administration of Soviet foreign aid.

IX

PROSPECTS

THE SIZE and character of Soviet aid and trade can be described with some accuracy. The effect on the Soviet economy of expanding these activities can be estimated on a reasonable basis. But two questions remain that are not susceptible of close analysis. How much influence can the Soviet government exercise as a result of its trade and aid program? How large a volume of aid is the Soviet Union likely to provide during the next few years?

The questions are closely related. A clear answer to one would throw light on the other. Unfortunately we have a clear answer to neither. The consideration of influence leads to scanty evidence and inextricable combinations of multiple causes and effects. For judging the future size of the program, the period of Soviet activity is too short to provide much guidance, though there are some suggestive bits of evidence. Perhaps the most that one can do is to sketch some of the elements of these problems and thus suggest where an observer should look for indications of how the answers may be evolving.

If the principal aim of the Soviet aid program is to increase the influence of the U.S.S.R., then neither the size of the program nor the efficiency with which it is conducted is decisive in determining its success. The crucial question is how the extension of economic aid contributes in practice to influence over the recipients. But "influence" is an extremely difficult concept to analyze, and an even harder condition to detect with certainty. One of its forms is the creation of what we generally call "good will." There is abundant reason to believe that the aid program has thus far succeeded in spreading good will toward the U.S.S.R. There are now several thousand Soviet engineers, agronomists, scientists, and other technical personnel who have traveled in the underdeveloped countries in the company of local people and have given useful technical advice and assistance. Many now reside in those countries, building monuments to Soviet industrial power and to Soviet brotherliness, for all to see. We know little about the actual relations between the Soviet technicians and the local officials and population, but there are no reports of undue friction. If Soviet economic missions live as Soviet diplomatic and other delegations do, in their own compounds apart from the local populations, the chances for friction are reduced.

At the same time thousands of people from the underdeveloped countries have visited the U.S.S.R. for various periods, some for short tours, others for longer training programs. Undoubtedly they have been given the royal treatment. For most, the great Soviet industrial cities and factories are the only ones they have ever seen. If Western visitors find many signs of a lower level of industrialization in the U.S.S.R., the visitors from the underdeveloped countries see a stage of economic achievement they can aspire to reach only after many years. It is to be expected that many of these people will return home with strong pro-Soviet attitudes, even though they may never become Communists.

The aid program has undoubtedly helped to sharpen the image of the U.S.S.R. as a mighty industrial and military power intent upon avoiding war and continuing the building of its country. But we must be careful not to give the economic aid program sole credit for this achievement. Imagine that the post-Stalin government of the U.S.S.R. had conducted its foreign affairs exactly as it did in every respect except that it had no program of foreign loans and increased trade. We would still witness the policy of friendship with the governments of the underdeveloped countries and state visits among their leaders. We would still have the program of "cultural exchange," and those inexpensive activities that we call technical assistance in the United States, such as public health aid, agricultural advice, and so forth. Soviet diplomacy would still win friends in the East at little or no cost to the U.S.S.R. by the positions it took on international issues such as Goa. These policies alone would have done much to create the kind of cordiality that has developed. It is obviously impossible to evaluate the separate contribution of the economic aid program, but it is clear that we must not overstate its importance by ascribing all successes to it.

Just how "good will" gets translated into "influence" is another vexing question. Perhaps this is mostly a matter of an increasing number of people in positions of power in the underdeveloped countries who are favorably disposed toward the U.S.S.R. and would tend of their own volition to support Soviet policies in international affairs. Further, those in power who remain friends of the West may be more constrained by a popular opinion that has grown more favorably disposed toward the U.S.S.R. We might expect that domestic Communist parties have also gained in prestige. In these ways good will has undoubtedly contributed to greater influence.

But if we look for more concrete evidence in the form of acts of policy that can be attributed directly to the good will generated by the aid program, they are hard to find. One of the outstanding events of the past few years was the brutal Soviet suppression of the Hungarian uprising. India and Yugoslavia, the two largest recipients of Soviet economic aid, condemned the Soviet action, though in a rather reluctant manner. The economic aid program certainly did not succeed in deterring them from criticizing the U.S.S.R., and it is doubtful whether economic aid was an important factor in mitigating the force of their criticism.

It is hard to imagine that developments in the Middle East would have been very different in the absence of the economic aid program (if we assume that the other features of Soviet policy remained unchanged). The same cannot be said of the military aid given by the Soviet Bloc—in the absence of military aid the course of events would probably have been far different. It is true that the existence of the Soviet economic aid program lent credence to the report that the U.S.S.R. would finance a large portion of the High Aswan Dam project in Egypt. But if the Soviet leaders actually made or hinted at such an offer and later withdrew it, this could certainly not have endeared them to the Egyptian government.

In certain of the underdeveloped countries political affairs are taking a turn that may be construed as increased acceptance of Soviet political and economic models, in preference to the Western or the Indian models. Thus, in Indonesia there is talk of "guided democracy," and in Syria of a "progressive directed economy." But surely the economic aid program cannot claim more than a small part of the credit for spiritual conversions of this kind. The available accounts of the negotiations suggest that in fact the Indonesians displayed a considerable sense of caution in the amount of Soviet aid they would accept. Domestic political and economic difficulties appear to be sufficient to explain the course of Indonesian events.

Perhaps this line of inquiry does not do full justice to the gains the Soviet Union has secured thus far through the economic aid program. "Good will" and "influence" are both rather amorphous concepts; the separate contribution of economic aid to a complex political process can hardly ever be ascertained. General analysis may have to rest content with the statement that the aid program creates good will that increases the chances that the governments of the recipient countries will wish to adopt policies that would accord with the interests of the U.S.S.R.

Influence can also result from pressure. What can we say about the possible use of economic aid as an instrument of pressure to influence a government's policy?

If economic aid is to be effective in this way, the recipient must be made to understand that failure to adopt a position favorable to the U.S.S.R. would result in a withdrawal of aid. It is precisely here that the Soviet leaders may encounter the most formidable obstacle to the attainment of the goals of the aid program. For the governments of the underdeveloped countries are passionately nationalistic and jealous of their political independence. It would be a grave error to believe that the need for economic aid is so dominant that they would submit to great indignities rather than forgo it. One may recall the suddenness with which Burma canceled its economic aid agreement with the United States in 1953 in protest against various United States actions. The $22-million Chinese grant did not deter Cambodia from veering to a sharply anti-Chinese and anti-Soviet position when the leaders of the nation felt threatened by Communist influence emanating from their embassies and trade missions.[1] The cancellation of all Soviet aid to Yugoslavia because of its independent line during the Hungarian crisis did not deter it. One can well believe that an attempt to exert this kind of pressure on a nation like India would result in a quick invitation to "take your old steel mill and go home."

If the pressure is less blunt and less sweeping than these examples suggest, the U.S.S.R. may be better able to use its aid program to influence policies. Certainly the multiplication of economic contacts increases the opportunities to use lesser pressures. It would be easy to suggest how this might be done, but it would be pure speculation to indicate when or where it might be successful. Again, economic aid functions only as one element in a complex. One of the strongest attractions of Soviet aid is the promise that it is given with "no political strings" attached. Overt use of the aid program to blackmail a country into adopting a certain policy would give the lie to this promise. Perhaps it might be used once or twice in this way, but repeated actions of this kind would irritate the underdeveloped countries in their most sensitive place, their newly won sovereignty. It would undoubtedly increase resistance to the acceptance of Soviet aid.

Thus the aid program presents a dilemma to the Soviet

[1] *The New York Times*, January 12, 1958.

leaders. They have expended substantial quantities of economic aid in order to be in a position to influence policy in the recipient countries. But if they attempt to exert that influence directly, they risk a setback to the whole aid program. This would perhaps not be the case if a country were so dependent on Soviet aid and trade that it had almost no choice but to submit to pressure. How large a volume of aid and trade would the Soviet Union have to provide to reduce a substantial number of countries to this state of dependence? Certainly much more than it has shown any signs of providing so far. If the experience of the United States is any guide, economic aid can play a vital role in supporting the policies of allied countries, but it is of dubious use in bringing about a change in the policies of uncommitted countries. There is no reason to believe that the Soviet Union would be more successful in forcing the hands of reluctant recipient countries even if its aid program was expanded to the size of that of the United States. Therefore, an attempt to insure "total dependency" of a number of countries would require a very large volume of aid indeed.

Our discussion of economic capabilities has shown that an aid program the size of that of the United States would constitute a substantial drain on the Soviet economy. The impact would be felt most heavily in the Soviet investment program, and would probably be greatest in the machinery industries supplying those capital goods most in demand in the underdeveloped countries. It would be irresponsible to say simply that the Russians could not support a program of those dimensions; they could if they were willing to pay so high a price. But a program of this kind would require a rather extensive reallocation of the nation's resources designed, among other things, to expand the production of capital goods for export and to retard the production of those commodities that would be imported in mounting quantities. As we have seen, there is no evidence yet to suggest that such a reallocation is contemplated. Future developments within the Soviet economy will have to be examined closely for evidence of such a shift, for that would be a signal of one possible line of development.

A second possibility is that the Soviet Union does not intend to apply this "strangle-hold" concept across the board, but selectively in a few of the smaller and more vulnerable countries. Economic capability would be less of a limiting factor in this case, and perhaps not at all. The simple arithmetic of the case makes it clear that Soviet trade and aid could totally dominate the economy of a country like Afghanistan without making any appreciable impact on the Soviet economy. The issue is not, however, whether the Russians can make a substantial economic impact on a number of smaller countries. This they clearly wish to do and have done. The issue is rather whether they can establish a *dominating* economic position and then use it as a lever for forcing political concessions that are repugnant to the recipients. Both results may be possible, but there are barriers. Few countries are likely to permit their economic ties with the U.S.S.R. to reach the point of such heavy dependence. Even if they should, the question would remain whether significant political concessions could always be extracted. While a policy of economic pressure may work in one or a few countries, it could hardly work as a general proposition. For, as indicated earlier, the overt use of economic aid for such purposes would compromise the entire program in the eyes of other recipient countries. This is a danger that the U.S.S.R. is likely to keep in mind.

There is at least one important instance in which the Soviet Union was apparently presented with the opportunity of reaching for a strangle-hold position and did not take it. Withdrawal of Western offers to aid in the building of the High Aswan Dam gave the U.S.S.R. a chance to increase greatly its role in the Egyptian economy. It seems highly likely that Egypt would have welcomed a generous Soviet offer at that crucial time. We do not know why it was not made. The job may have been too big, failure too likely, or the Soviet policymakers may have doubted that such a step would in fact have given them a great hold over Egypt (debtors also get a hold over their creditors). The Egyptians may have been more reluctant than has appeared. Or the Soviet tacticians may have seen better targets elsewhere. In any case, the episode shows that—at least at that time—the U.S.S.R. was either unwilling or unable to use its aid program to pursue every possibility of securing a "strangle-hold" even in countries of considerable political importance to it.

A third possibility is that the Soviet leaders will be satisfied with a "modest" program, falling far short of an attempt to make recipient countries completely and irreversibly dependent on the U.S.S.R. This alternative resembles the Soviet program of the last few years. Aid on this scale has several advantages for the U.S.S.R. It ensures that the field is not left clear for the United States, and provides a sufficient material basis for magnification by propaganda. The difficulties the Soviet Union might anticipate in carrying out an aid and trade program are mostly connected with a program of great size; a "modest" program might avoid many of them. For instance, a program of the present size can be entrusted to a relatively small number of top-flight administrators, who are able to keep close watch over many details. Those bureaucratic rigidities of the Soviet system which would inevitably increase as the aid program grew in size can be kept to a minimum in a smaller program. Popular discontent at home and jealousy among the satellites, which could become troublesome under the large program, are less serious under a smaller one. The problem of absorbing surpluses is less taxing. If Soviet objectives can be attained by a "modest-sized" program, there would be clear advantages for the U.S.S.R. in keeping aid at that level.

That an aid program of this size is well within the economic capabilities of the U.S.S.R. has been shown in earlier chapters. Indeed, the U.S.S.R. has the capacity—particularly when it is supplemented by the resources of other countries in the Bloc—to sustain a much larger program of deliveries on credit than it has undertaken thus far. A doubling or even trebling of the program of recent years would be feasible without causing great trouble for the Soviet economy, provided the goods to be delivered were spread over a reasonable number of supplying industries. Even a program that large, growing apace over a number of years with the growth of Soviet industrial production, would still constitute a "modest-sized" program within the meaning described above. A much larger program, on the other hand, one comparable to that of the United States, would become fairly costly for the U.S.S.R. in terms of forgoing alternative domestic uses for the same resources (or perhaps of forgoing opportunities of trading with more advanced countries).

It is, of course, impossible to say how far the Soviet leaders intend to press their aid and trade program. They may not know themselves. But if we try to form some judgment of what the most likely line of development is, most of the indications point to something like a "modest-sized" program. The argument is by no means compelling, and tomorrow's headlines could conceivably require a sharp revision of this judgment. To summarize the position: most of what appear to be the aims of the U.S.S.R. could be satisfied by a program of roughly the present size or by one growing moderately over the next few years. It provides an adequate basis for influence in a large number of countries, and opportunity for expanding the program greatly in a few smaller countries if the chance to establish total domination should arise. The program is small enough to avoid some of the problems that would become serious under a massive program. And the U.S.S.R. is well able to sustain a program of this size without great strain and without requiring a broad restructuring of its economy.

This judgment of the balance of considerations as they appear at this writing should be viewed not as a prediction but rather as a means of focusing attention on what ought to be looked for in the future. While the over-all size of the aid program is not the only dimension of importance, it is surely of vital interest to ask whether we are dealing with an aid program of massive proportions or one of relatively modest size. The great concern felt in the West over the growth of Soviet aid has been due in considerable measure to the rapid rate at which the program was expanding in its initial years. Table 3 (p. 39) showed that the volume of loans placed by the Soviet Bloc in the underdeveloped countries grew slowly in 1954 and 1955 but rose to a peak of about $960 million in 1956. Then, during the first three quarters of 1957 only a few small loans were placed. It was not until the last quarter of the year that the two large loans to Syria and Egypt were made, and as of the end of the year the Egyptian loan agreement had not yet been finally settled. The total for 1957, including the Egyptian loan, was less than half the volume of loans placed in 1956.

What interpretation ought to be placed on the decline in new lending in 1957? Part of the explanation may be that the countries initially disposed to accept Soviet aid have by now accepted all that their economies can absorb and that their future exports can pay for. Other countries either may be unwilling on political grounds to accept any Soviet aid, or may be cautiously waiting to see how those countries fare that have accepted it. The Soviet government has by no means abandoned its efforts to place new loans. Offers continue to be made: to all and sundry, as at the Cairo Asian-African Peoples Solidarity Conference in December 1957, and the 1958 meeting of the Economic Commission for Asia and the Far East in Bangkok; and to individual countries, such as Ceylon, Pakistan and Iran.[2] The reduction in the volume of loans placed in 1957 may mean simply that the Russians had begun to run out of willing takers for the time being. But it may also be that the Soviet leaders are now satisfied with the volume of aid already given to some countries. They may feel, for instance, that aid to India is serving its purpose while one steel mill and a number of smaller industrial projects are being built. When, in September 1957, India announced its intention of seeking one billion dollars in additional

[2] *The New York Times*, December 28, 1957; January 23, 1958; January 29, 1958; January 5, 1958; January 31, 1958.

foreign loans, the U.S.S.R. made no public offer to supply part of the funds. Nor did the Indian government publicly ask for more aid from Moscow. This may mean that the Soviet leaders are satisfied to limit their aid to the $360 million of loans already accepted by India for use during the next several years. Or it may mean that the Indians prefer not to increase their Soviet aid. Alternatively this may be a matter of timing that will lead to a new Soviet offer or Indian request at a psychologically suitable moment.

It is quite possible that the Soviet leaders have no intention of persuading governments to take more and more aid each year. They may deem it sufficient for their purpose to keep a reasonable number of impressive projects going at all times. Thus the record of 1957 may mean that the rapid rate of growth up to that year was not the beginning of an endless progression, but rather a quick building up to a certain plateau and a leveling off after that. The plateau may be the "modest-sized" program alluded to above. The height of the plateau may well continue to rise somewhat as new countries accept Soviet aid. Another possibility is that in the countries already receiving aid we may witness a shift in emphasis from construction loans to technical assistance services, a shift that would make sense from a Soviet viewpoint in the light of the rapid annual growth in the number of graduate engineers and technicians. Because the period is so short, the drop in lending in 1957 can be no more than suggestive, but it does point to the importance of studying the volume of Soviet lending in succeeding years.

It is beyond the scope of this study to explore the implications of the Soviet aid program for United States foreign economic policy.[3] But the character of Soviet aid and some of the successes it has enjoyed suggest areas of United States policy that might be reviewed, whether or not they ought to be revised. Certain advantages of the

[3] An analysis of the implications for United States foreign economic policy of the Soviet aid and trade program is now being carried out by William Diebold, Jr., at the Council on Foreign Relations.

Soviet program are based on differences between the two nations about which little can be done. For example, the chorus of unanimity with which the Soviet press endorses the successive gyrations of Soviet policy is a decided propaganda asset. But as a free nation we cannot contemplate muzzling the dissenting views of those who oppose foreign aid in general or our foreign policy in specific areas. The harm that comes to our relations with the colored peoples of the world because of violence accompanying the retreat of the segregationist forces is not something that can be easily remedied. There are other facets of our foreign economic policy, however, which we might wish to reconsider.

The specific features of the Soviet aid program provide a convenient point of departure. It has been shown that the almost exclusive reliance upon loans rather than grants seems to have been an advantage to the Soviet program. This, of course, is not sufficient reason to suggest that our program shift more toward loans. The burden of repayment on the recipient and the problems of absorbing the imports into the United States economy may argue against more loans, despite Soviet experience. But there may be other alternatives. For example, while recipients may resent the necessity of having to accept grants from a single country, there may be no such resentment if the grants were made by an international agency.

By charging a rate of interest below that of the World Bank or the Export-Import Bank, the Soviet leaders have managed to convey an impression of socialist generosity on the one hand and yet correct businesslike comportment on the other. It is perhaps worth considering whether interest-free loans might not be an effective device for free-world lending policy. Since the loans must be repaid, they are not charity, while the interest-free provision reduces the burden of repayment and constitutes an act of proper generosity, particularly when undertaken by an international agency.

The success with which the U.S.S.R. has identified its program with the absence of political strings suggests what has been a major source of irritation with aid from the free world. It may not be possible to separate totally our military from our economic aid programs, but it would seem wise to push the separation as far as practicable. Again, since United Nations auspices are generally considered in the underdeveloped countries to be much less self-interested than individual country auspices, our aid might find a better reception if carried out through international sponsorship.

Perhaps the most significant feature of the Soviet program from an economic point of view is the willingness of the U.S.S.R. to accept repayment in the local currencies or commodities of the recipient countries. The enormous attractiveness of this arrangement is undoubtedly due to the desire of the raw materials-producing countries to protect themselves from price fluctuations (particularly price drops) in world markets. The Soviet program offers them an assured market for a part of their export commodities over a number of years, a prospect that aids greatly in development planning. In the view of many observers, the greatest service the free world can perform for the underdeveloped countries, exceeding perhaps the importance of economic aid, is to assure them a stable and profitable market for their principal exports over a number of years. Perhaps by a broader encouragement of and participation in international commodity agreements, and in other ways, the United States could make a major contribution toward the solution of one of the most vexing problems of underdeveloped countries. Relieved of the fear of sharp falls in the prices of their exports, the latter would enjoy much more freedom of action in pursuing their development plans and in selecting the sources of economic aid.

The export problems of the underdeveloped countries are also tied in with the trade policy of the United States and the other advanced countries. There is perhaps no other area of American political life in which sectional and group interests are more in conflict with the national interest. Clearly, the problem of economic aid is but one of many that must find reflection in a national trade policy. But in the evolution of that policy, the positive contribution that a more liberal approach could make toward the economic development of the raw materials-exporting countries ought to be kept prominently in view.

At several places above it has been pointed out that an international agency appears to offer certain advantages as a dispenser of aid, compared with direct aid from the United States. Multilateral aid is, of course, not a panacea that will solve all problems. But it is here that the really hard look ought to be taken at our present policy. It is by now a truism that for a complicated set of reasons the giver of aid often makes more enemies than friends in the process. Yet economic development in the poorer countries is in our national interest, whether or not the recipients of our aid love us. Since we must give aid, it might be better to do it in a way that would at least not create hostility against us, if we cannot do it in a way that would create firm friends. By channeling more of our aid through international agencies, we can conceivably do just this. The more recourse we have to multilateral aid, the greater will be the pressure on the U.S.S.R. to do the same. Otherwise, it would become increasingly difficult for the Russians to reconcile their almost exclusive reliance on bilateral aid with their professions of noninterference. If our example led the Soviet Union to channel more of its aid into international agencies, the free world's fears of the implications of Soviet aid would be greatly and properly reduced.

In a review of United States policy in the light of the Soviet aid program, there is one final consideration that should be kept prominently in view. The success of the Soviet aid program in achieving its objectives depends not only on what the U.S.S.R. does. It depends in considerable measure on what the United States does. Two broad courses are open to us. We might regard the countries that have accepted Soviet aid as debased by the act and as ineligible for assistance from the United States. If such countries are later subjected to Soviet pressure by the threat of the loss of Soviet aid and trade, they face considerable domestic economic difficulties if they resolve to resist that pressure. The unavailability of United States aid would enhance Soviet ability to use economic aid as a lever for forcing political concessions. On the other hand, if the United States remains willing to extend aid on the same terms as before, with no penalty for having accepted Soviet aid (and no premium for having rejected it), victims of Soviet pressure might be able to resist Soviet incursions on their sovereignty. In this important sense, the political fate of the Soviet economic aid program is as much in our hands as in the hands of the U.S.S.R.

We cannot deprive the U.S.S.R. of such good will as the extension of economic aid normally brings (and sometimes destroys), or of the influence that such good will creates in the free decisions of governments. But we can, by our policy, support the recipients of Soviet aid in their resistance to the pressures that the U.S.S.R. may seek to exert in order to attain the ultimate objectives of the aid program.

APPENDIX A

SOVIET BLOC CREDIT AGREEMENTS WITH UNDERDEVELOPED COUNTRIES, 1953–1957

NEITHER THE governments of the Soviet Bloc nor those of the recipient countries have published fully detailed accounts of all their credit agreements. A full picture of the Bloc credit program must therefore be pieced together from many sources. The most reliable are the official communiqués issued by the contracting parties. Fortunately most of the large credit agreements have been reported in such communiqués, although not always in complete detail. The flow of information on smaller agreements is rather haphazard. Data have been gathered by combing through newspapers and reprints of monitored radio broadcasts in many countries. These accounts often lack such essential details as the size of the agreement, and it is not always clear whether the agreement alluded to has actually been concluded or is merely an offer. Because of the unreliability of the sources of information, the following summary of the Bloc credit program must be viewed as an attempt to shed as much light as possible on a rather obscure business.

The author has not undertaken the enormous task of sifting through the back files of the newspapers and monitored broadcasts of all the countries involved in the credit agreements. Primary reliance has been placed upon the work of two organizations that have performed this task and have published their results. One of the reports was prepared by the staff of the Senate Subcommittee on Technical Assistance Programs; the other was prepared at the request of the Senate Special Committee to Study the Foreign Aid Program, by the Council for Economic and Industry Research, Inc.[1] All the data contained in Tables A, B and C below are taken from the two reports (principally from the last named which is the later of the two), except where otherwise indicated.

All the agreements listed in Tables A, B and C provide for the extension of credits, except four Chinese agreements which provide for nonrepayable grants. Under the "amount" columns of the tables are a number of figures followed by question marks and printed in brackets. The bracketed figures are hypothetical amounts representing a rough guess about the order of magnitude of the credit in those cases in which the amount was not reported. In some cases the hypothetical amount was arrived at by comparing the agreement with a similar one for which the amount is known. For example, the Czech loan to India for the construction of a cement plant of 100-ton capacity is known to amount to $2.1 million. No figure is available on the Czech loan to Egypt for the construction of a 700-ton cement plant. By analogy to the Indian loan, the Czech loan is assumed to be of the order of magnitude of $4 million. In many cases, however (e.g., the Hungarian loan to Egypt for the construction of seven bridges), the figure is simply a guess. The hypothetical figures represent a relatively small proportion of the total, $109 million out of a total of $1,581 million.

In an evaluation of the data in Tables A, B and C the following cautions should be kept in mind:

1. Because of the "dragnet" procedure by which these data were assembled, it is likely that some agreements escaped inclusion in the total. But one might guess that the Soviet Union has no interest in secrecy about these agreements;

[1] U. S. Senate, Subcommittee on Technical Assistance Programs, *Soviet Technical Assistance*, Staff Study no. 7, 84th Cong., 2d sess. (Washington: GPO, July 12, 1956); Council for Economic and Industry Research, Inc., *Foreign Assistance Activities of the Communist Bloc and Their Implications for the United States* in *Foreign Aid Program*, Senate Doc. no. 52, 85th Cong., 1st sess. (Washington: GPO, 1957), pp. 619-764.

on the contrary, one would expect that it would wish to publicize them, particularly the large ones. The data are therefore probably fairly complete.

2. A further difficulty is that the reports of agreements are often deficient in details. It is not always clear whether a construction agreement involves a credit or not. Indeed, there are various projects under construction in underdeveloped countries by Bloc technicians which are not included in the above data because they are thought to involve a current payment and not a credit. The data in Tables A, B and C, therefore, do not include all construction work but only that financed under Bloc credits.

3. The meaning of a sum expressed in U. S. dollars is sometimes obscure. The original credit agreements may be expressed officially in one of three ways. Sometimes they are expressed directly in U.S. dollars, and are entered as such in our tables. Sometimes they are quoted in the currencies of the recipient countries (e.g., India); such quotations are entered in our tables after they have been converted into U. S. dollars at the official rate of exchange certified to the International Monetary Fund. Finally, in some cases the loan is expressed in Soviet rubles (e.g., in the agreement with Yugoslavia); the procedure in this case is to convert rubles to U. S. dollars at the official Soviet foreign exchange rate of four rubles to the dollar.

A number of objections may be raised to this system of conversion. If the rupee is officially valued at $0.21, does this signify that a loan of 1 million rupees is equivalent in value to a loan of $210 thousand? Because the dollar is a fully convertible currency acceptable for a purchase anywhere in the world, whereas the rupee is of limited convertibility, the dollar loan should be considered as more valuable. On the other hand, if a dollar loan were repayable in dollars, whereas the Soviet loans are repayable in rupees (to be used only for the purchase of Indian commodities), the rupee loan is more valuable. On balance, the use of the IMF rate of exchange seems to be a reasonable compromise.

The use of the official Soviet exchange rate is more questionable. It has long been evident that the rate of $0.25

per ruble overvalues the ruble. In partial recognition of this fact, the Soviet government decided in early 1957 to convert rubles for tourist use at the rate of $0.10 per ruble. For what the evidence is worth, the value of the ruble among foreign exchange dealers outside the U.S.S.R. was quoted at less than $0.03 in the spring of 1957.[2] Have we not, then, overvalued the Soviet-East German loan to Yugoslavia of 700 million rubles by making it equivalent to $175 million (at $0.25 per ruble)? Should it rather be equivalent to $70 million (at $0.10 per ruble) or even $21 million (at $0.03 per ruble)? If the last-named decision is taken, it would lead to significant changes in the picture shown in Table 1 in the text. Yugoslavia, for one thing, would no longer be the largest recipient of Bloc aid.

Unfortunately, there is no simple answer to a question of this kind. It would seem, however, that an exchange rate appropriate to tourist expenditures is not necessarily appropriate to trade in industrial commodities. That is, the consumer goods and services that a tourist could buy in the U.S.S.R. for 100 rubles might cost about $10 if bought in the United States. But industrial commodities which would cost 100 rubles in the U.S.S.R. might well cost much more than $10 in the United States. At least two reasons may be cited for this difference: consumer goods in the U.S.S.R. are subject to a rather heavy sales tax; and the Soviet regime has concentrated its best resources on the production of industrial commodities, so that the cost of producing them is probably relatively less than the cost of producing consumer items (relative, that is, to these two types of production in the United States.)

How do Soviet prices of industrial commodities compare with United States prices of corresponding commodities? The most ambitious attempt that has been made to answer this question found that no simple pattern exists.[3] In twenty-five industries studied, it was found that in 1950 the median

[2] *The New York Times,* May 30, 1957.

[3] Norman M. Kaplan and William L. White, *A Comparison of 1950 Wholesale Prices in Soviet and American Industry* (Santa Monica: Rand Corporation, 1955), RM-1443, p. 33.

ruble/dollar ratios ranged from 19.9 (in the coal, gas, and electric-power industry) to 2.4 (in the metal-working machinery industry). The median of all price ratios (based on 1,902 commodities) was 7.9. When the iron and steel, railroad transportation equipment, and construction industries were eliminated (these industries accounted for almost half of all the commodities in the total), the median of the remaining price ratios was 8.5. Since 1950, U. S. wholesale prices have risen somewhat while Soviet wholesale prices have been reduced on several occasions, so that the median ratio may be somewhere between 6 and 7 in 1956. But an unweighted average is of doubtful usefulness for our purposes. Under the circumstances, no course of action is clearly superior to the simple choice of accepting the official ratio of four rubles to the dollar. To the extent that this ratio overvalues the ruble, the dollar figures on the value of Soviet credits are exaggerated.

4. If we could somehow find an ideal solution for the exchange-rate problem, we would still have to face up eventually to the equally vexing problem of the prices charged by the U.S.S.R. for the equipment and services provided under the credit agreements. For example, we have translated the 550 million-rupee Indian steel mill into $115 million at the rate of $0.21 per rupee. But is that particular steel mill worth $115 million? Perhaps the Soviet Union is overcharging the Indians, and selling a steel mill which could be built for less under competitive conditions? Or, as is more likely, perhaps in their wish to receive the contract the Soviet negotiators are undercharging, and are selling for 550 million rupees a steel mill which a competitive Western firm could not build at that price. If the latter is the case, then a credit of 550 million rupees should be considered as worth more than $115 million.

The evidence on Soviet pricing policies is sparse and contradictory. For lack of reliable information, we can only note that the totals presented in the tables can have quite different meanings depending on the prices paid by the recipients for the equipment and services purchased under the agreements.

TABLE A

U.S.S.R. Credit Agreements Signed, 1953-1957

Amount (million dollars)	*Date Signed or Reported*	*Purpose*
		Recipient: Afghanistan
3.5	1/54	Two grain elevators of $4 million each, electric flour mill of 60 tons per day, mechanized breadbaking plant. Completion date, 1956.
1.2	7/54	Sixty-mile gasoline pipeline, 30 million gallons capacity. Oil storage tanks. Construction begun 11/55.
2.0	8/54	Road-building machinery.
2.1	10/54	Equipment for asphalt factory and concrete-mixing plant, paving street in Kabul. Reported completed, 5/55.
[1.0?]	12/54	Cotton processing equipment. Reported built, 12/54.
100	1/56	Two hydroelectric plants, three motor repair shops, a physical chemistry laboratory, chemical fertilizer plant, highway over the Hindu Kush, three irrigation dams, road maintenance units, construction of airport at Bagram, reconstruction of Kabul airport. Repayment is to begin after 8 years.
		Recipient: Argentina
[5?]	8/53	Original agreement for $30-million credit for the purchase of coal-mining and oil-drilling equipment, transportation equipment, power plants and agricultural machinery. It was reported that actual deliveries by the U.S.S.R. proved to be negligible. It is arbitrarily assumed that $5 million of equipment was delivered in 1954.

TABLE A *(Continued)*

Amount (million dollars)	*Date Signed or Reported*	*Purpose*
		Recipient: Burma
[20?]	12/55	Industrial enterprises, irrigation projects, agricultural development. Specific agreement signed in 6/56. No figure on amount ever released. Burma to pay in current rice exports to U.S.S.R. If in any year rice exports do not equal value of Soviet construction, then a Soviet credit will be extended for the difference. Thus it is impossible to judge how large a credit will result from this agreement, or indeed whether any credit will result. It has in fact been reported that Burmese exports to the U.S.S.R. have exceeded the volume of Soviet aid, so that the Burmans are actually extending credit to the U.S.S.R. (*The New York Times*, January 6, 1957.) But in order to err on the high side, it is arbitrarily assumed a Soviet credit of $20 million will eventually be generated.
		Recipient: Egypt
[2?]	2/56	Nuclear physics laboratory. U.S.S.R. to provide nuclear reactor, technicians, atomic specialists, uranium. Egyptian scientists to train in U.S.S.R. U.S.S.R. to carry out geological research.
175	11/57	Marine workshops and drydock, an automotive assembly plant, building materials plants, petroleum and mining projects. Offer made during visit of Egyptian military commander in Moscow. The formal agreement was not yet concluded as of the end of 1957, but, since oral agreement was reached, the loan is

TABLE A *(Continued)*

Amount (million dollars)	*Date Signed or Reported*	*Purpose*
		included here as of 1957. (*The New York Times*, November 22, 1957.)
		Recipient: India
[2?]	1/55	File manufacturing plant for a private Calcutta firm, the Hindustan Gas Co. No amount or credit terms announced.
115	2/55	Million-ton steel mill at Bhilai.
0.5	12/55	Twenty Soviet drilling rigs for coal mining.
16.8	5/56	Sale of 60,000 metric tons of structural steel for Bhilai steel mill.
3.6	5/56	Three Soviet oil-drilling rigs, training of Indian personnel. (*The New York Times*, January 15, 1958.)
10	6/56	Equipment for diamond mine. Geological survey and training of Indian personnel. Repayment to be made in industrial diamonds.
126	11/56	Machinery, coal-mining equipment, fertilizer plants, oil refinery. Details not completed until November 1957. (*The New York Times*, November 10, 1957.)
63	11/56	Oil-prospecting project with aid of 174 Soviet technicians. Plants for manufacture of oil-drilling equipment. Agreement reported signed but not fully confirmed.
		Recipient: Indonesia
100	9/56	Various projects in coal mining, ferrous metallurgy, building materials, power plants, other industries. Aid in peaceful use of atomic energy, training of Indonesian personnel.

Table A *(Continued)*

Amount (million dollars)	*Signed or Date Reported*	*Purpose*
		Recipient: Sudan
[5?]	4/56	General economic and technical aid.
		Recipient: Syria
[3?]	3/56	Grain storage facilities, oil tanks, cement plant.
170	10/57	Eighteen projects that are part of a large Syrian economic development program. Include exploration and prospecting, fertilizer factory, oil storage facilities, railroad, bridges, irrigation networks, hydroelectric stations. The size of the Soviet contribution is still conjectural, and will not be known until each of the projects is worked out in detail. (*The New York Times*, October 30, 1957; November 2, 1957; January 4, 1958.)
		Recipient: Turkey
12	7/57	Sheet glass factory, to cost $10-14 million. It is not clear whether a credit is involved and, if so, whether the stated figure represents the full size of the credit. (*The New York Times*, August 14, 1957.)
[5?]	9/57	Caustic soda and calcium plant. Not known if credit is involved or how much. (*The New York Times*, September 4, 1957.)
		Recipient: Yemen
[2?]	6/56	Roads, ports, various factories.
		Recipient: Yugoslavia
110	1/56	Nitrogen plant, super-phosphate plant, sul-

TABLE A *(Continued)*

Amount (million dollars)	*Date Signed or Reported*	*Purpose*
		phuric acid plant, thermo-power station, lead-zinc mines, mercury plant, shipbuilding, oil and gas extraction, agricultural development.
54	2/56	Purchase of Soviet raw materials during 1956-1958.
30	2/56	Loan in gold or free exchange, to be used during 1956-1958.
87.5	8/56	Loan of 700 million rubles, or $175 million at the official Soviet rate of exchange. To be shared equally by the U.S.S.R. and East Germany. To be used to increase Yugoslav aluminum capacity by 100,000 tons a year. Construction to take place 1956-1961. On February 26, 1957, Yugoslavia reported that as a result of ideological conflicts with the U.S.S.R. the Soviet Union wished to postpone the construction until 1960. Later reports indicate that the loan was reinstated. (*The New York Times*, July 31, 1957.)

Note: The figures in brackets are hypothetical amounts representing a rough guess about the size of the credit in those cases in which the amount was not reported.

Source: See the discussion of source materials, pp. 193-197.

TABLE B

Other Bloc Credit Agreements, 1953-1957

Amount (million dollars)	*Date Signed Or Reported*	*Purpose*
		I. CZECHOSLOVAK AGREEMENTS
		Recipient: Afghanistan
5	8/54	Three cement plants, cotton textile mill, leather processing plant, roadbuilding machinery, agricultural machinery.
		Recipient: Argentina
[1?]	1953?	Distillery for production of grain alcohol. Completed, 1954. No amount announced.
15	1/55	Coal mine conveyer and coal washing plant, presumably other projects.
		Recipient: Ceylon
[10?]	8/56	General economic development loan. First projects agreed upon are sugar refinery and cement factories. Refinery to cost $3,360,000, construction started. Cement plant still under discussion. (*The New York Times*, January 15, 1958.)
		Recipient: Egypt
0.5	12/55	Ceramics plant, to be completed in 1957.
[4?]	3/56	Cement plant of 700-ton capacity. To be completed in 1958.
[15?]	1957	Plant for the manufacture of leather footwear, rolling mill for nonferrous metals, and a textile factory. (*The Eastern Economist*, October 25, 1957, p. 634.)
[2?]	1957	300-kilowatt transmitter, to be erected in the Cairo area.

TABLE B *(Continued)*

Amount (million dollars)	*Date Signed Or Reported*	*Purpose*
		Recipient: India
[1?]	7/56	Sugar refinery for a private Indian company.
2.1	8/56	Cement plant of 100-ton capacity.
[10?]	1956	Three sugar mills and three steam power plants. (*The Eastern Economist*, October 25, 1957, p. 634.)
		Recipient: Indonesia
1.6	5/56	General industrial development loan, including rubber and tire factory.
		Recipient: Lebanon
[2?]	3/56	Cement plant and auto repair shop.
		Recipient: Paraguay
15	1955	For the purchase of capital equipment.
		Recipient: Syria
10	1957	Oil refinery, to be completed by July 1, 1959. (*The New York Times*, March 22, 1957; December 1, 1957.)
[1?]	1957?	Machinery and equipment for a sugar mill. (*The Eastern Economist*, October 25, 1957, p. 634.)
		Recipient: Turkey
[5?]	1956?	Textile factory was put into operation in 1956 and work proceeding on a ceramic factory. (*The Eastern Economist, October* 25, 1957, p. 634.)
		Recipient: Yugoslavia
50	2/56	Electric power plants, chemical factories, paper and woodworking machinery plants.

TABLE B *(Continued)*

Amount (million dollars)	*Date Signed Or Reported*	*Purpose*
25	2/56	Commodity credit to be used during 1956-1958.
		II. EAST GERMAN AGREEMENTS
		Recipient: India
6.3	8/56	Establishment of a raw film manufacturing plant.
		Recipient: Indonesia
9.2	2/55	Sugar mill of 2,500-ton capacity per day, trucks, rails, alcohol plant.
		Recipient: Yugoslavia
87.5	8/56	East German share in the $175-million aluminum industry development, financed jointly with the U.S.S.R.
		III. CHINESE AGREEMENTS
		Recipient: Burma
[2?]	1956?	Equipment and technical assistance for the expansion of a government-owned textile mill. Not clear if a credit is involved. (*The New York Times*, January 15, 1958.)
		Recipient: Cambodia
22.4	6/56	Grant to be spent over two-year period for construction of textile mills, cement plants, paper mill, plywood plant, universities, hospitals, roads, bridges, power plants. Reported that $17 million was to be spent in 1956.
		Recipient: Ceylon
16	1957?	Grant to Ceylon, details not available. (*The New York Times*, January 4, 1958.)

TABLE B *(Continued)*

Amount (million dollars)	*Date Signed Or Reported*	*Purpose*
		Recipient: Egypt
5	8/56	Grant to Egypt. (*The New York Times*, August 23, 1956.)
		Recipient: Nepal
12.6	10/56	Grant of one-third in money and two-thirds in machinery and capital goods.
		IV. HUNGARIAN AGREEMENTS
		Recipient: Egypt
[3?]	6/55	Seven bridges with revolving mechanisms.
[4?]	8/56	Iron works, 800-meter bridge across Nile to supply iron works with materials, power plant. To be ready in 1957.
		V. POLISH AGREEMENTS
		Recipient: Egypt
[2?]	12/55	Enamelware factory in Alexandria.
		Recipient: India
5	6/55	2,500 railway cars.
		VI. RUMANIAN AGREEMENTS
		Recipient: India
1	3/56	Purchase of an oil-drilling rig and training of twenty-two technicians for six months.
		Recipient: Indonesia
[2?]	3/55	Cement plant.

Note: The figures in brackets are hypothetical amounts representing a rough guess about the size of the credit in those cases in which the amount was not reported.

Source: See the discussion of source materials, pp. 193-197.

TABLE C

Total Bloc Credit Agreements, 1953-1957, by Donor and Recipient

(millions of U.S. dollars)

	Donor							
Recipient	*U.S.S.R.*	*Czecho-slovakia*	*East Germany*	*China*	*Hungary*	*Poland*	*Rumania*	*Total*
Afghanistan	110	5						115
Argentina	5	16						21
Burma	20			2				22
Cambodia				22				22
Ceylon		10		16				26
Egypt	177	22		5	7	2		213
India	337	13	6			5	1	362
Indonesia	100	2	9				2	113
Lebanon		2						2
Nepal				13				13
Paraguay		15						15
Sudan	5							5
Syria	173	11						184
Turkey	17	5						22
Yemen	2							2
Yugoslavia	281	75	88					444
Total	1,227	176	103	58	7	7	3	1,581

Source: See the discussion of source materials, pp. 193-197.

APPENDIX B

THE ANNUAL RATE OF UTILIZATION OF BLOC CREDITS

As a guide to the rate at which development loans are utilized, we might glance at the experience of the International Bank for Reconstruction and Development. Appendix Table D shows that experience varies from loan to loan, as one might expect. The period of utilization of the sixteen electric-power development loans varies from about two-three years to six-seven years. In the three instances of loans for the construction of grain-storage facilities, the two smaller ones (in Nicaragua and Panama) took about three years, but the larger loan (to Turkey) was not fully utilized after six years. The small loan for a pulp and paper mill in Pakistan was fully utilized within a year of the conclusion of the agreement, while the large loan to Chile for a similar project was only about one-third utilized after almost three years.

The considerable differences in utilization periods for loans for similar projects should provide ample warning that any estimates of utilization periods for Soviet loans may be far wide of the mark. However, the Bank's experience suggests some broad generalizations which might be used in estimating Soviet utilization periods. The Bank, for instance, requires a detailed economic justification and a carefully prepared set of estimates before it will grant a loan. Soviet negotiators, on the contrary, make a virtue out of their willingness to grant a loan without requiring such detailed information. Presumably, the detailed planning must be done some time before construction is commenced. In the case of Soviet loans this work must be done after the loan agreement is signed, rather than before, as in the case of Bank loans. Hence we should expect Soviet loans to require a longer period between the conclusion of the agreement and the full utilization of the loan than is required in the case of Bank loans. Thus, the Bank loans to Yugoslavia for a series of economic development projects took about five years to be fully utilized. Those loans were roughly similar to the $100-million Soviet loans to Afghanistan and Indonesia. Since the latter loans were only allotted and not yet obligated for specific projects at the time of signing, we should expect the utilization period to be somewhat longer.

The Bank's experience shows that, for loans of a similar type, the larger loans often take somewhat longer to utilize than smaller ones. Certain Bank loans are roughly similar in nature to Soviet loans for which utilization periods are to be estimated. In a number of cases, such as the Indian steel mill, the date of completion is stated in the agreement, so that we need estimate only the year-by-year allocation of the principal amount; in this case it is assumed that most of the machinery will not be delivered until the later years of the construction period, after the basic construction has been completed. Where information is available on the actual period of utilization of Soviet loans, such information provides a basis for estimating the utilization period for other roughly similar loans. The United States Department of State study released in January 1958 (*The New York Times*, January 4, 1958) provides some information on the status of various projects as of that time.

Appendix Tables E and F present estimates of the utilization periods for each of the known Bloc credit agreements. Obviously there is no claim to accuracy here, but only an attempt to obtain a rough answer to an important question. The results are summarized in Table 4 in the text.

Table D

Annual Rate of Disbursements for Various Loans by the International Bank for Reconstruction and Development

Project	Country and loan number	Principal amount (million dollars)	Months in first fiscal period[a]	Percentage of principal amount disbursed by fiscal year: 1[a]	2	3	4	5	6	7	8
(A)	(B)	(C)	(D)	(E)	(F)	(G)	(H)	(I)	(J)	(K)	(L)
Electric Power Development	Brazil (95BR)	18.8	4	69	90	100					
	Brazil (76BR)	7.3	11	62	97	100					
	Brazil (93BR)	10.0	6	8	19	44					
	Ceylon (101CE)	19.1	11	11	19						
	Chile (5CH)	13.5	3					57	83	98	100
	Colombia (38CO)	3.5	7		47	79	90	100			
	Colombia (113CO)	4.5	3	0	39						
	Colombia (39CO)	2.6	6		83	100					
	Colombia (54CO)	2.4	7	56	79	100					
	El Salvador (22ES)	12.5	6			45	84	100			
	Mexico (12ME)	24.1	5				64	83	93	97	100
	Mexico (24ME)	26.0	2			75	95	100			

Table D (Continued)

Project	Country and loan number	Principal amount (millions dollars)	Months in first fiscal period[a]	Percentage of principal amount disbursed by fiscal year							
				1[a]	2	3	4	5	6	7	8
(A)	(B)	(C)	(D)	(E)	(F)	(G)	(H)	(I)	(J)	(K)	(L)
Electric Power Development (cont.)	Mexico (56ME)	29.7	5	20	30	45	62	75			
	Nicaragua (121NI)	7.1	11	12							
	Pakistan (120PAK)	13.8	12	70							
	Uruguay (132UR)	5.5	10	32							
Grain Storage Facilities	Nicaragua (52NI)	0.55	8	19	95	100					
	Panama (87PAN)	0.29	9	0	29	100					
	Turkey (27TU)	3.9	11		17	31	56	75	86		
Cement Plant (100,000 tons per year)	Peru (116PE)	2.5	2	0	46						
Pulp and Paper Mills	Pakistan (125PAK)	4.2	10	100							
	Chile (83CH)	20.0	9	1	10	34					
Natural Gas Pipeline (350 mi.)	Pakistan (99PAK)	14.0	12	93	100						

TABLE D (*Continued*)

Project	*Country and loan number*	*Principal amount (millions dollars)*	*Months in first fiscal period*[a]	*Percentage of principal amount disbursed by fiscal year*							
				1[a]	*2*	*3*	*4*	*5*	*6*	*7*	*8*
(A)	(B)	(C)	(D)	(E)	(F)	(G)	(H)	(I)	(J)	(K)	(L)
Iron and Steel Expansion	India (71IN)	31.5	*b*	4	27						
Various	Yugoslavia (51YU)	28.0	8	18	63	91	97	100			
Development Projects	Yugoslavia (73YU)	30.0	4	14	61	82	91				

a The Bank reports disbursements by fiscal year. Hence the first reported disbursement on any loan covers less than a full year; it covers the period between the signing of the agreement and the following June 30. Column D shows the number of months in this period. The percentages given in column E are therefore for different lengths of time.

b The data on which the loan went into operation is not made explicit in the annual reports.

Source: International Bank for Reconstruction and Development, *Annual Reports*.

TABLE E

Estimated Rate of Utilization of U.S.S.R. Credits, 1954-1957

Country	*Amount (millions of U. S. dollars)*	*Date*	*Estimated utilization period in years*	*Estimated utilization per year (millions of U. S. dollars)* 1954	1955	1956	1957	After 1957
Afghanistan	3.5	1/54	5	0.5	0.5	1.0	1.0	0.5
	1.2	7/54	2			0.5	0.5	0.2
	2.0	8/54	1	0.5	1.5			
	2.1	10/54	1	0.5	1.6			
	[1?]	12/54	1	1.0				
	100.0	1/56	8			5.0	10.0	85.0
Argentina	[5?]	8/53	5	5.0				
Burma	[20?]	12/55	4				5.0	15.0
Egypt	[2?]	2/56	2			0.5	1.0	0.5
	175.0	11/57	8					175.0
India	[2?]	1/55	2		1.0	1.0		
	115.0	2/55	5		5.0	10.0	20.0	80.0
	0.5	12/55	1			0.5		
	16.8	5/56	3			3.0	7.0	6.8
	3.6	5/56	2				1.2	2.4
	10.0	6/56	2			2.0	5.0	3.0
	126.0	11/56	5					126.0
	63.0	11/56	3				15.0	48.0
Indonesia	100.00	9/56	5				10.0	90.0
Sudan	[5?]	4/56	2			1.0	3.0	1.0
Syria	[3?]	3/56	2			1.0	2.0	
	170.0	10/57	6					170.0
Turkey	12.0	7/57	2					12.0
	[5?]	9/57	2					5.0
Yemen	[2?]	6/56	1			1.0	1.0	
Yugoslavia	110.0	1/56	4					110.0
	54.0	2/56	3			18.0	18.0	18.0
	30.0	2/56	3			10.0	10.0	10.0
	87.5	8/56	5					87.5
Total	1,210.2			7.5	9.6	54.5	109.7	1,045.9
Ranges				5-10	8-12	45-65	100-120	900-1,100

Note: The figures in brackets are hypothetical amounts representing a rough guess about the size of the credit in those cases in which the amount was not reported.

Source: See the discussion of source materials, pp. 193-197.

TABLE F

Estimated Rate of Utilization of Other Bloc Credits, 1954-1957

Creditor	Recipient	Amount (million dollars)	Date	Estimated utilization period in years	Estimated utilization per year (millions of U. S. dollars) 1954	1955	1956	1957	After 1957
Czechoslovakia	Afghanistan	5.0	8/54	2		2.0	3.0		
	Argentina	[1?]	1953?	1	1.0				
		15.0	1/55	3		5.0	5.0	5.0	
	Ceylon	[10?]	8/56	3				1.0	9.0
	Egypt	0.5	12/55	1			0.5		
		[4?]	3/56	2			1.0	2.0	1.0
		[15?]	1957	3					15.0
		[2?]	1957	2				1.0	1.0
	India	[1?]	7/56	1			0.5	0.5	
		2.1	8/56	2				1.0	1.1
		10.0	1956	3			3.0	3.0	4.0
	Indonesia	1.6	5/56	2			0.6	1.0	
	Lebanon	[2?]	3/56	2			0.5	1.0	0.5
	Paraguay	15.0	1955	2		7.5	7.5		
	Syria	10.0	1957	3				2.0	8.0
		[1?]	1957	2				0.5	0.5
	Turkey	[5?]	1956?	4		1.0	1.0	1.0	2.0
	Yugoslavia	50.0	2/56	4			10.0	10.0	30.0

TABLE F (*Continued*)

Creditor	*Recipient*	*Amount (million dollars)*	*Date*	*Estimated utilization period in years*	*Estimated utilization per year (millions of U. S. dollars)* 1954	1955	1956	1957	After 1957
		25.0	2/56	3			8.0	8.0	9.0
East Germany	India	6.3	8/56	2			2.0	2.0	2.3
	Indonesia	9.2	2/55	2		2.0	3.0	4.2	
	Yugoslavia	87.5	8/56	5					87.5
China	Burma	[2?]	1956?	2			1.0	1.0	
	Cambodia	22.4	6/56	3			10.0	8.0	4.4
	Ceylon	16.0	1957?	3				5.0	11.0
	Egypt	5.0	8/56	2			3.0	2.0	
	Nepal	12.6	10/56	2			2.6	5.0	5.0
Poland	Egypt	[2?]	12/55	1			1.0	1.0	
	India	5.0	6/55	1		5.0			
Rumania	India	1.0	3/56	1				1.0	
	Indonesia	[2?]	3/55	2		0.5	1.0	0.5	
Hungary	Egypt	[3?]	6/55	2		1.5	1.5		
	Egypt	[4?]	8/56	1			1.0	3.0	
Totals		353.2			1.0	24.5	66.7	69.7	191.3
Range					0-5	20-30	55-75	60-80	175-215

Note: The figures in brackets are hypothetical amounts representing a rough guess about the size of the credit in those cases in which the amount was not reported.

Source: See the discussion of source materials, pp. 193-197.

APPENDIX C

BLOC TRADE WITH UNDERDEVELOPED COUNTRIES

Table G

Soviet Trade with Underdeveloped Countries, 1948, 1953, 1955, 1956

(millions of U. S. dollars)

	Soviet Exports				*Soviet Imports*			
Trading Partners	*1948*	*1953*	*1955*	*1956*	*1948*	*1953*	*1955*	*1956*
Egypt	46.2	14.1	6.6	22.7	49.8	11.9	20.2	16.0
Ghana (Gold Coast)	—	—	—	—[a]	10.1	10.1	11.5	4.7[a]
Iran	1.8	9.2	20.3	17.5	4.0	8.9	17.1	14.9
Iraq	.1	—	.1	—	—	.1	—	n.a.
Israel	.1	—	.2	.4	n.a.	1.1	1.7	1.6
Lebanon	.1[e]	—	.8	1.1[b]	—	—	1.0	.5[b]
Morocco	.3	—	.2	.1	n.a.	—	1.7	.2
Nigeria	—	—	.1	—	n.r.	—	n.r.	—
Sudan	—	.4	.1	.4	—	—	—	—
Syria	.1[e]	.1	.2	.9	—	—	—	1.1
Turkey	—	—	8.3	5.2	.2	2.4	5.2	6.6
Yugoslavia	34.1	—	14.4	70.4	45.5	—	17.9	41.6
Burma	—	—	.1	2.8[c]	—	—	5.2	10.1[c]
Ceylon	—	—	.1	.2	.2	—	—	n.r.
India	11.1	.9	6.0	31.3	11.5	.8	5.2	26.2
Indonesia	—	.1	.2	.3[a]	—	n.r.	n.r.	—
Malaya	—	—	—	.1	47.4	—	.4	11.5
Pakistan	2.7	8.0	.1	.3	13.4	7.4	—	—
Vietnam[d]	—	n.r.	n.r.	n.r.	—	n.r.	n.r.	n.a.
Argentina	.6	—	32.2	26.7	1.7	11.3	29.7	16.5
Brazil	—	n.r.	n.r.	—	—	n.r.	.7	—
Cuba	—	—	—	—	—	.8	36.4	14.2
Uruguay	—	—	.1	3.2	—	.3	4.6	.4
Total	97.2	32.1	90.1	183.6	183.8	55.1	158.5	166.1
Total trade with non-Bloc world	493.7	381.8	632.9	806.3	533.5	423.5	599.4	780.0
Trade with underdeveloped countries as % of trade with non-Bloc world	20%	8%	15%	23%	35%	13%	26%	21%

TABLE G *(Continued)*

NOTES:

(—) $50,000 or less, including zero.
n.a. Not available.
n.r. Not reported in source.
a January-November.
b January-September.
c January-August.
d Refers to Indochina in 1948 and 1953.
e Soviet exports to Syria and Lebanon together amounted to $0.2 million in 1948.

SOURCES:

1948-1955: U. S. Mutual Defense Assistance Control Act Administrator, *The Strategic Trade Control System 1948-1956* (Washington: GPO, 1957), pp. 92-107; and *Survey of East-West Trade in 1955* (Washington: GPO, 1956), pp. 80-93.

1956: U. S. Department of Commerce, "Exports and Imports of Free World Countries to Soviet Bloc, January-December 1956," Value series (Washington: Author, 1957), mimeographed.

TABLE H

European Soviet Bloc Trade (Excluding U.S.S.R.) with Underdeveloped Countries, 1948, 1953, 1955, 1956
(millions of U. S. dollars)

Trading Partners	Bloc Exports				Bloc Imports			
	1948	*1953*	*1955*	*1956*	*1948*	*1953*	*1955*	*1956*
Egypt	16.9	23.8	28.3	42.9	21.7	25.9	61.4	99.0
Ghana (Gold Coast)	2.8	2.1	5.0	4.4[a]	2.8	—	—	—[a]
Iran	3.6	5.3	5.5	9.0	—	2.3	3.6	3.4
Iraq	4.7	3.0	3.6	6.3	—	1.3	.1	n.a.
Israel	5.9	2.4	5.3	3.3	n.a.	.9	1.7	3.1
Lebanon	2.9[e]	3.3	5.3	4.4[b]	.1[e]	.6	1.0	.3[b]
Morocco	1.2	6.0	3.7	4.6	1.5	1.9	7.7	4.5
Nigeria	3.6	3.9	8.0	10.1	.3	.8	.7	1.3
Sudan	.5	3.2	3.4	6.7	1.5	—	2.9	3.6
Syria	3.0[e]	3.5	5.1	11.3	.2[e]	—	1.4	8.5
Turkey	22.9	29.5	83.0	54.2	18.4	26.9	63.5	53.4
Yugoslavia	109.1	—	18.6	34.6	108.5	—	17.6	31.3
Burma	.5	.7	1.7	7.7[c]	—	—	20.4	8.4[c]
Ceylon	.3	1.6	1.5	1.4	.3	.6	.3	.3
India	5.8	3.5	9.1	21.0	11.4	6.5	3.3	10.2
Indonesia	4.0	4.8	30.2	14.0[a]	1.4	4.5	27.7	11.9
Malaya	6.0	5.9	4.1	5.2	8.3	13.6	11.5	22.9

TABLE H (Continued)

Trading Partners	Bloc Exports 1948	1953	1955	1956	Bloc Imports 1948	1953	1955	1956
Pakistan	1.0	3.7	2.9	1.0	5.8	5.1	5.3	4.5
Vietnam[d]	.1	n.r.	n.r.	.1	—	n.r.	n.r.	n.a.
Argentina	17.4	15.3	71.4	28.5	47.5	13.1	54.2	18.6
Brazil	11.9	9.9	38.1	46.1	20.3	10.4	41.3	38.8
Cuba	.5	.8	1.3	2.6	.1	.1	1.4	3.1
Uruguay	1.6	.8	2.4	7.4	2.9	.9	5.9	7.4
Total	226.2	133.0	337.5	326.7	253.0	117.5	332.9	334.5
Total trade with non-Bloc world	1,026.0	807.9	1,281.5	1,459.6	900.7	677.9	1,158.5	1,312.7
Trade with under-developed countries as a % of trade with non-Bloc world	22%	16%	26%	22%	28%	17%	29%	25%

NOTES:

(—) $50,000 or less, including zero.
n.a. Not available.
n.r. Not reported in source.
a January-November.
b January-September.
c January-August.
d Refers to Indochina in 1948 and 1953.
e Bloc exports and imports to Syria and Lebanon together amounted to $5.9 million and $0.3 million in 1948.

SOURCES:

See sources, Table G, p. 217.

TABLE I

Chinese Trade with Underdeveloped Countries, 1953, 1955, 1956
(millions of U. S. dollars)

	Chinese Exports			*Chinese Imports*		
Trading Partners	*1953*	*1955*	*1956*	*1953*	*1955*	*1956*
Egypt	.7	.9	11.1	10.4	24.5	24.2
Ghana (Gold Coast)	—	.1	.1[a]	—	—	—[a]
Iran	1.9	—	n.r.	—	—	n.r.
Iraq	n.r.	1.5	—	n.r.	.1	n.a.
Israel	—	—	—	—	—	—
Lebanon	.2	.2	n.r.	.1	—	n.r.
Morocco	7.2	19.0	19.8	—	—	—
Nigeria	—	.7	1.3	n.r.	—	—
Sudan	—	.1	.3	.1	.8	2.5
Syria	1.1	.2	.5	—	.2	1.5
Turkey	—	—	n.r.	—	—	—
Yugoslavia	—	—	3.5	—	—	4.4
Burma	1.5	2.3	12.7[b]	1.4	17.5	12.8[b]
Ceylon	43.9	16.8	28.1	50.9	25.5	38.3
India	3.5	8.1	20.1	7.3	19.1	13.0
Indonesia	2.1	9.9	29.6[a]	—	6.2	11.7
Malaya	34.4	37.8	43.1	1.9	4.2	7.8
Pakistan	3.0	.4	.5	7.3	31.7	15.9
Vietnam[c]	6.0	9.2	4.1	n.r.	n.r.	n.a.
Argentina	—	n.r.	n.r.	—	1.0	.8[d]
Brazil	n.r.	n.r.	—	.9	4.6	.7
Cuba	—	—	—	—	.4	—
Uruguay	n.r.	—	—	—	—	.1
Total	105.5	107.2	175.8	80.3	135.8	133.7
Total trade with non-Bloc world	432.7	494.4	621.3	287.4	316.6	433.0
Trade with under-developed countries as % of trade with non-Bloc world	24%	22%	28%	28%	43%	31%

NOTES:
(—) $50,000 or less, including zero.
n.a. Not available.
n.r. Not reported in source.
a January-November.
b January-August.
c 1953 data refer to Indochina.
d January-June.

TABLE I *(Continued)*

SOURCES:

1953-1955: U. S. Mutual Defense Assistance Control Act Administrator, *The Strategic Trade Control System 1948-1956* (Washington: GPO, 1957), pp. 92-107; and *Survey of East-West Trade in 1955* (Washington: GPO, 1956), pp. 80-93.

1956: U. S. Department of Commerce, "Exports and Imports of Free World Countries to Soviet Bloc, January-December 1956," Value series (Washington: Author, 1957), mimeographed.

TABLE J

Trade of Underdeveloped Countries with Soviet Bloc, in Millions of U. S. Dollars, and as Percentage of Total Exports and Imports, 1956

	Millions of U. S. Dollars						Percentage of Total			
	Exports To			*Imports From*			*Exports To*		*Imports From*	
	World	*Soviet Bloc*	*U.S.S.R.*	*World*	*Soviet Bloc*	*U.S.S.R.*	*Soviet Bloc*	*U.S.S.R.*	*Soviet Bloc*	*U.S.S.R.*
	(A)	(B)	(C)	(D)	(E)	(F)	(G)	(H)	(I)	(J)
Egypt	405	139.2	16.0	534	76.7	22.7	34.4	4.0	14.4	4.3
Ghana[a] (Gold Coast)	221	4.7	4.7	225	4.5	—	2.1	2.1	2.0	—
Iran	109	18.3	14.9	266	26.5	17.5	16.7	13.7	10.0	6.6
Iraq	n.a.	n.a.	n.a.	319	6.3	—	n.a.	n.a.	2.0	—
Israel	104	4.7	1.6	364	3.7	0.4	4.6	1.5	1.0	0.1
Lebanon[b]	32	0.8	0.5	185	5.5	1.1	2.5	1.6	3.0	0.6
Morocco	339	4.5	0.2	444	24.5	0.1	1.4	—	5.5	—
Nigeria	377	1.3	—	427	11.3	—	0.3	—	2.7	—
Sudan	192	6.1	—	130	7.4	0.4	3.2	—	5.7	0.3
Syria	145	11.3	1.1	320	12.7	0.9	7.8	0.8	4.0	0.3
Turkey	305	60.0	6.6	408	59.4	5.2	19.7	2.2	14.6	1.3
Yugoslavia	321	77.4	41.6	472	108.5	70.4	24.1	13.0	23.0	14.9

TABLE J (*Continued*)

	Exports To			*Imports From*			*Exports To*		*Imports From*	
	World	*Soviet Bloc*	*U.S.S.R.*	*World*	*Soviet Bloc*	*U.S.S.R.*	*Soviet Bloc*	*U.S.S.R.*	*Soviet Bloc*	*U.S.S.R.*
Burma[c]	168	31.2	10.1	124	23.2	2.8	18.6	6.0	18.7	2.3
Ceylon	364	38.5	n.r.	342	29.7	0.2	10.6	n.r.	8.7	—
India	1,253	49.4	26.2	1,714	72.3	31.3	3.9	2.1	4.2	1.8
Indonesia[d]	882	23.6	—	770	43.9	0.3	2.7	—	5.7	—
Malaya	1,361	42.2	11.5	1,357	48.4	0.1	3.1	0.8	3.6	—
Pakistan	340	20.4	—	354	1.9	0.3	6.0	—	0.5	0.1
Argentina	912	35.9	16.5	1,123	55.2	26.7	3.9	1.8	4.9	2.4
Brazil	1,482	39.5	—	1,234	46.1	—	2.7	—	3.7	—
Cuba	666	17.3	14.2	649	2.6	—	2.6	2.1	0.4	—
Uruguay	211	8.0	0.4	206	10.6	3.2	3.8	0.2	5.2	1.6
Totals		634.3	166.1		680.9	183.6				

NOTES:

(—) Less than 0.1 per cent, or less than $50,000, including zero.
n.a. Not available.
n.r. Not reported in source.

a January-November.
b January-September.
c January-August.
d Imports, January-November.

SOURCES:

U. S. Department of Commerce, "Exports and Imports of Free World Countries to Soviet Bloc, January-December 1956," Value series (Washington: Author, 1957), mimeographed.

BIBLIOGRAPHY OF SOURCES CITED

1. *Official publications*

General Agreement on Tariffs and Trade. *International Trade 1956.* Geneva: Author, 1957. 278 p.

International Bank for Reconstruction and Development. *Annual Reports.* Washington: Author, various years.

International Monetary Fund. *International Financial News Survey.*

United Nations. Department of Economic Affairs. *Relative Prices of Exports and Imports of Underdeveloped Countries.* New York: Author, 1949. 156 p.

———. Economic Commission for Asia and the Far East. *Economic Survey of Asia and the Far East in 1956.* Bangkok: Author, 1957. 233 p.

———. Economic Commission for Europe. *Economic Bulletin for Europe,* v. 9 (May 1957).

———. ———. *Economic Survey of Europe in 1955.* Geneva: Author, 1956. 247 p.

———. ———. *Economic Survey of Europe in 1957.* Geneva. Author, 1958. 291 p.

———. Statistical Office. *Demographic Yearbook 1956.* New York: Author, 1956. 742 p.

———. ———. *Statistical Yearbook 1956.* New York: Author, 1956. 646 p.

U. S. Bureau of the Census. *Statistical Abstract of the United States, 1956.* Washington: GPO, 1956. 1049 p.

U. S. Bureau of Foreign Commerce. "Exports and Imports of Free World Countries to the Soviet Bloc, January-December 1956." Value series. Washington: Author, 1957. (Mimeographed.)

U. S. Congress. Joint Economic Committee. *Soviet Economic Growth: A Comparison with the United States,* by the Legislative Reference Service of the Library of Congress. 85th Cong., 1st sess. Washington: GPO, 1957. 149 p.

U. S. Department of Commerce. *Business Statistics: 1957 Biennial Edition.* A Supplement to the *Survey of Current Business.* Washington: GPO, 1957. 344 p.

———. *Foreign Grants and Credits by the United States Government.* Quarterly reports. Washington: Author, various years.

U. S. Department of State. *The Sino-Soviet Economic Offensive in the Less Developed Countries.* Washington: GPO, 1958. 111 p.

U. S. International Cooperation Administration. *Operations Reports.* Washington: Author, various years.

U. S. Mutual Defense Assistance Control Act Administrator. *The Strategic Trade Control System 1948-1956.* Ninth Report to Congress on Operations under the Mutual Defense Assistance Control Act of 1951. Washington: GPO, 1957. 115 p.

———. *Survey of East-West Trade in 1955.* Eighth Report to Congress on Operations under the Mutual Defense Assistance Control Act of 1951. Washington: GPO, 1956. 98 p.

U. S. Senate. Special Committee to Study the Foreign Aid Program. *Foreign Aid Program.* 85th Cong., 1st sess., Senate Doc. no 52. Washington: GPO, 1957.

American Enterprise Association, Inc. *American Private Enterprise, Foreign Economic Development, and the Aid Programs.* Study no. 7, pp. 539–618.

Armstrong, Hamilton Fish. *Lebanon, Jordan, and Iraq.* Survey no. 2, pp 1223–1256.

Council for Economic and Industry Research, Inc. *Foreign Assistance Activities of the Communist Bloc and Their Implications for the United States.* Study no. 8, pp. 619-766.

Stuart Rice Associates, Inc. *Foreign Aid Activities of Other Free Nations.* Study no. 11, pp. 1057–1161.

———. Subcommittee on Technical Assistance Programs. *Soviet Technical Assistance.* 84th Cong., 2d sess., Staff Study no. 7. Washington: GPO, 1956. 62 p.

II. *Books and pamphlets*

Allen, Robert Loring. *Middle Eastern Economic Relations with the Soviet Union, Eastern Europe, and Mainland China.* Charlottesville: University of Virginia Press, 1958. 127 p.

Berliner, Joseph S. *Factory and Manager in the U.S.S.R.* Cambridge: Harvard University Press, 1957. 386 p.

Browder, Robert Paul. *The Origins of Soviet-American Diplomacy.* Princeton: Princeton University Press, 1953. 256 p.

Clark, M. Gardner. *The Economics of Soviet Steel.* Cambridge: Harvard University Press, 1956. 400 p.

Gerschenkron, Alexander. *Economic Relations with the U.S.S.R.* New York: Committee on International Economic Policy, 1945. 73 p.

Heymann, Hans, Jr. *Future Prospects for Soviet Economic Aid.* P–1269. Santa Monica: Rand Corporation, 1958. 17 p.

Kaplan, Norman M., and William L. White. *A Comparison of 1950 Wholesale Prices in Soviet and American Industry.* RM-1443. Santa Monica: Rand Corporation, 1955. 352 p.

Kindleberger, Charles P. *Economic Development.* New York: McGraw-Hill, 1958. 325 p.

———. *The Terms of Trade: A European Case Study.* New York: Technology Press and Wiley, 1956. 382 p.

Moorsteen, Richard. *Prices of Prime Movers, U.S.S.R., 1927/28–1949.* RM–1225. Santa Monica: Rand Corporation, 1954. 164 p.

———. *Prices of Railroad Rolling Stock, U.S.S.R., 1927/28–1949.* RM–1258. Santa Monica: Rand Corporation, 1954. 66 p.

Sosnovy, Timothy. *The Housing Problem in the Soviet Union.* New York: Research Program on the U.S.S.R., 1954. 300 p.

III. *Articles*

Allen, Robert Loring. "United Nations Technical Assistance: Soviet and East European Participation," *International Organization,* v. 11, no. 4 (Autumn 1957), pp. 615-634.

American Enterprise Association, Inc. See U. S. Senate, *Foreign Aid Program.*

Armstrong, Hamilton Fish. See U. S. Senate, *Foreign Aid Program.*

Bergson, Abram, Roman Bernaut and Lynn Turgeon. "Prices of Basic Industrial Products in the U.S.S.R., 1928–1950," *Journal of Political Economy,* v. 64 (August 1956), pp. 303–328.

Blackman, James H. "Transportation," in Abram Bergson, ed., *Soviet Economic Growth.* Evanston, Ill.: Row, 1953. Pp. 126–161.

Clark, M. Gardner. "Soviet Iron and Steel Industry: Recent Developments and Prospects," *Annals of the American Academy of Political and Social Science,* v. 303 (January 1956), pp. 50–61.

———. "Comments," in Abram Bergson, ed., *Soviet Economic Growth*. Evanston, Ill.: Row, 1953. Pp. 179-183.

Collado, Emilio G., and Jack F. Bennett. "Private Investment and Economic Development," *Foreign Affairs*, v. 35, no. 4 (July 1957), pp. 631–645.

Council for Economic and Industry Research, Inc. See U. S. Senate, *Foreign Aid Program*.

Eckstein, Alexander. "Moscow-Peking Axis: The Economic Pattern," in Howard L. Boorman and others, *Moscow-Peking Axis*. New York: Council on Foreign Relations, 1957. Pp. 54–111.

Hodgman, Donald R. "Soviet Foreign Economic and Technical Assistance," in *Recent Soviet Trends*. Proceedings of the conference held at the University of Texas, October 11-12, 1956, pp. 79–97.

Hoeffding, Oleg. "Recent Trends in Soviet Foreign Trade," *Annals of the American Academy of Political and Social Science*, v. 303 (January 1956), pp 75–88.

Hudson, G. F. "Moscow and Peiping: Seeds of Conflict," *Problems of Communism*, v. 5 (November-December 1956), pp. 17–23.

———. "Soviet Policy in Asia," *Soviet Survey*, no. 16/17 (June-July 1957), pp. 1–6.

Hunter, Holland. "Comments," in Abram Bergson, ed., *Soviet Economic Growth*. Evanston, Ill.: Row, 1953. Pp. 157–161.

Kaplan, Norman M. "Capital Formation and Allocation," in Abram Bergson, ed., *Soviet Economic Growth*. Evanston, Ill.: Row, 1953. Pp. 37–87.

Laqueur, Walter Z. "Soviet Prospects in the Middle East," *Problems of Communism*, v. 6 (July-August 1957), pp. 20-26.

Pizer, Samuel, and Frederick Cutler. "Record Growth of Foreign Investments," *Survey of Current Business* (U. S. Department of Commerce), v. 37 (August 1957), pp. 22–30.

———. "The Role of U. S. Investments in the Latin American Economy," *Survey of Current Business* (U. S. Department of Commerce), v. 37 (January 1957), pp. 6–15.

Rodin, Nicholas W. "Comments," in Abram Bergson, ed., *Soviet Economic Growth*. Evanston, Ill.: Row, 1953. Pp. 183–185.

Rubinstein, Alvin Z. "Soviet Policy toward Underdeveloped Areas in the Economic and Social Council," *International Organization*, v. 9, no. 2 (May 1955), pp. 232–243.

Shimkin, Demitri B. "Comments," in Abram Bergson, ed., *Soviet Economic Growth.* Evanston, Ill.: Row, 1953. Pp. 183–185.

Stuart Rice Associates, Inc. See U. S. Senate, *Foreign Aid Program.*

Turgeon, Lynn. "Cost-Price Relationships in Basic Industries during the Soviet Planning Era," *Soviet Studies* (October 1957).

Volin, Lazar. "Soviet Agricultural Policy after Stalin: Results and Prospects," *Journal of Farm Economics*, v. 38 (May 1956), pp. 274–286.

IV. *Soviet sources*

Azov, V., and D. Fokin, "Razvitie vneshnei torgovli SSSR v 1956 godu" (Development of Soviet Foreign Trade in 1956), *Vneshniaia torgovlia*, no. 11 (1957), pp. 35–43.

Fituni, L. "Ob ekonomicheskoi pomoshchi slaborazvitym stranam" (Economic Aid to Underdeveloped Countries), *Voprosy ekonomiki*, no. 11 (1953), pp. 80–95.

Stalin, Joseph. *Economic Problems of Socialism in the U.S.S.R.* New York: International Publishers, 1952. 71 p.

Tsentral'noe statisticheskoe upravlenie. *Narodnoe khoziaistvo SSSR: statisticheskii sbornik* (The U.S.S.R. National Economy: A Statistical Handbook). Moscow: State Statistical Press, 1956. 262 p.

———. *Promyshlennost' SSSR: statisticheskii sbornik* (U.S.S.R. Industry: A Statistical Handbook). Moscow: State Statistical Press, 1957. 447 p.

Vasil'eva, V. "Ekonomicheskoe razvitie kolonii v gody vtoroi mirovoi voiny" (Colonial Economic Development during World War II), *Mirovoe khoziaistvo i mirovaia politika*, no. 5 (1947), pp. 51–64.

Zolotarev, V. "Torgovye sviazi Sovetskogo Soiuza s sotsialisticheskimi stranami" (U.S.S.R. Trade Relations with Socialist Countries), *Vneshniaia torgovlia*, no. 11 (1957), pp. 44–52.

* * *

References are also made to the following Soviet newspapers and periodicals: *Kommunist*, *New Times*, *Pravda*, *Vneshniaia torgovlia*, *Voprosy ekonomiki.*

INDEX

The index is to be used in conjunction with the subheads shown in the Table of Contents and with the list of tables. It does not cover the Appendices, Bibliography, or, with a few exceptions, the tables. Except for China and the U.S.S.R., Soviet Bloc countries are not separately indexed. Commodities, industries, etc. are not separately indexed.